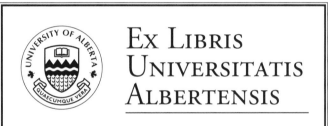

THE

Charles Ives

Tunebook

THE
Charles Ives
Tunebook

Second Edition

Clayton W. Henderson

INDIANA UNIVERSITY PRESS
Bloomington & Indianapolis

This book is a publication of

Indiana University Press
601 North Morton Street
Bloomington, IN 47404-3797 USA

http://iupress.indiana.edu

Telephone orders	800-842-6796
Fax orders	812-855-7931
Orders by e-mail	iuporder@indiana.edu

First edition published by Harmonie Park Press
© 1990, 2008 by Clayton W. Henderson
All rights reserved

The paper used in this publication meets the minimum requirements of American National Standard for Information Sciences—Permanence of Paper for Printed Library Materials, ANSI Z39.48-1984.
Manufactured in the United States of America

Library of Congress Cataloging-in-Publication Data

Henderson, Clayton W., date
The Charles Ives tunebook / Clayton W. Henderson.—2nd ed.
p. cm.
Includes bibliographical references and indexes.
ISBN 978-0-253-35090-9 (cloth: alk. paper)   1. Ives, Charles, 1874–1954—Thematic catalogs
2. Ives, Charles, 1874–1954—Sources.   I. Title.
ML134.I9A2   2008
780.92—dc22   2007042681

1   2   3   4   5   13   12   11   10   09   08

Frontis: Ives outside his summer home in West Redding, Connecticut, ca. 1946. Photo by Halley Erskine.
Courtesy the Charles Ives Papers in the Irving S. Gilmore Music Library of Yale University.

To Elizabeth

The humblest composer will not find true humility in aiming low—he must never be timid or afraid of trying to express that which he feels is far above his power to express, any more than he should be afraid of breaking away, when necessary, from easy first sounds. . . .

CHARLES IVES, *Essays Before a Sonata*

CONTENTS

PREFACE

By the time of his death in 1954, Charles Ives and his music had gradually become known to a wider public than had been the case in the previous four decades.[1] Some, beyond his immediate circle of family, friends, and professional colleagues, were aware that he had won the Pulitzer Prize for music in 1947 for his *Symphony No. 3,* a work he had begun to compose more than forty years earlier. Some, more attuned to the world of business than to things musical, would have known Ives as the creative partner in the insurance firm of Ives and Myrick. Others might have connected Ives's name with the *"Concord" Sonata,* whose music and performance by John Kirkpatrick critic Lawrence Gilman had praised mightily less than a brief decade and a half earlier.[2]

Since his death,[3] however, recordings, performances, critical studies of his music, and the fruits of research, oral history, and symposia have enabled us to view the composer and his music in a broader historical and musical context than was possible earlier.[4] Charles Ives has become an iconic figure in the history of music in America, one whose name and music do, indeed, have "widespread recognition" and whose influence has been felt in the musical world and beyond.[5]

There is, in the best of Ives's music, an "Ivesian" sound—the "ecstasy of angelic choiring," in Henry Cowell's wonderful turn of phrase.[6] That sound, the techniques to achieve it, and the architecture to embrace it have become models to which his spiritual descendants have turned. To give but one recent example: writing about John Adams's memorial to the victims of the attack on the World Trade Center of September 11, 2001, David Schiff compares Adams's *On the Transmigration of Souls* to an Ives piece whose inspiration had a similar genesis—tragedy brought about through treachery. On the seventh of May 1915, the news of the sinking of the *Lusitania* dominated the thoughts of Ives and others as they waited for the evening elevated trains at the Hanover Square Station in New York City.[7] As they waited, weary bodies and minds made heavier by the news, and fearful of what was to come, a hand-organ or hurdy-gurdy player broke the customary noise of the station as he began to play the old hymn tune *In the Sweet Bye and Bye.* As the wheezy sound spread through the station, people began to sing along, not "in fun, but as a natural outlet for what their feelings had been going through all day long,"[8] in the sure and certain hope—"In the sweet bye and bye we shall meet on that beautiful shore"—of being with those who had perished on that day. Ives recalled that the simple hymn tune faded away as a crowd of people got on one of the departing trains, but that the effect of that experience still showed. "Almost nobody talked—the people acted as though they might be coming out of a church service. In going uptown, occasionally little groups would start singing or humming the tune."[9]

Moved by what he had heard and seen in what Schiff describes as an act of "communal mourning," Ives soon began work on *From Hanover Square North, at the End of a Tragic Day, the Voice of the People Again Arose.* By the fall of 1915, less than six months after the tragedy, he had finished the first version of what would become the last movement of his *Orchestral Set No. 2.* To evoke that May 7th evening, Ives layers sounds and musical experiences in which borrowings from *In the Sweet Bye and Bye,* Stephen Foster's *Massa's in the Cold Ground* and *My Old Kentucky Home,* the hymn *Ewing* (whose words evoke that milk-and-honey-blessed land of "Jerusalem the golden"), and an allusion to an Anglican chant version of the *Te Deum* ("We praise thee, O God; we acknowledge thee to be the Lord") mingle with his own music. These "imaginary utopian venues," again in the words of Schiff, served as inspiration for Adams.

Present at the moment the people broke into song, Ives captured the "choiring" response of the milling commuters. His composition is not *about* the *Lusitania* or its victims. Rather, it is about a reaction of a group of commuters to the deliberate sinking of the ship and the inevitable consequence of that incident.

Unlike Ives, who had heard first-hand the reaction of a group of people, John Adams was not present at the destruction of the World Trade Center. He had to reconstruct the sonic world of that horrific day—a world in which the urgent sounds—street noises, the wailings of emergency vehicles, people singing and speaking and crying—all have a part to play in his *Transmigration.* Some of the unanswerable questions of that day are manifested in the musically and philosophically enigmatic music of Ives's *The Unanswered Question,* from which Adams borrows.

Ives's people are anonymous, saved from the physical pain that those who died on the *Lusitania* suffered. On the other hand, Adams's people are the survivors of the actual attack *and* are from among those killed during those hours of infamy. The tolling of the names of some of the dead creates a musical tapestry in which those names become personal, while simultaneously becoming an aural memorial, one incapable of being corrupted. "Like Ives, but in an entirely new way, Adams extends our sense of music—there is music in the sound bites and the street noises, music in our own state of sensory overload."[10]

Adams's borrowing from Ives is an act of homage to a revered mentor. No other sonic world but Ives's would have served Adams as well. For many, Ives's music had become the model—musically, architecturally, and programmatically—for the expression of the elegiac, of memorial, or solemn occasion. *From Hanover Square North, at the End of a Tragic Day, the Voice of the People Again Arose; Decoration Day; The "St. Gaudens" in Boston Common (Col. Shaw and his Colored Regiment);* and *An Elegy to Our Forefathers* are but four examples of larger orchestral works of this kind of music. One can find it in his chamber music and songs as well.

The borrowing of music from others figures prominently in Ives's music throughout his entire creative life—from his song *Slow March* of possibly the summer of 1887 in which he cited Handel's *Saul,* to the adaptation he made in 1942 of the song *They Are There!* where allusions to a dozen or so different patriotic tunes serve to underscore the deeds of "our soldier boys" "fighting for the People's New Free World" where there is "Liberty for all."

Borrowing from others, as in Adams's appropriation of Ives, is something one finds throughout the centuries. The recycling of the musical past is one of the chief features in Ives's music that has attracted particular notice and comment.[11]

Early on, the Renaissance parody, or imitation, Mass and the quodlibet are examples that readily come to mind. From Ives's own lifetime, one can point to musical borrowings in the works of Mahler, Debussy, Rachmaninov, Vaughan Williams, Bartók, and Stravinsky, to name only a few composers. With Ives, however, borrowed music is a far more pervasive element than it is with any other composer in the history of music. Appearing as it does in more than two hundred of his compositions, it became part of his musical "signature."[12]

Even though the borrowed tunes are older than their new settings, they are often familiar to the listener and performer at the time the composer re-uses them. With the passing of time, however, the original sources gradually become unfamiliar to new generations of listeners and have to be rediscovered by the specialist. The recognition of some of Ives's sources has been dulled in the comparatively short span of years since he wrote his music.[13] Since some of his musical models are not as familiar today as they were during the composer's youth and creative life, it is important to identify them now before they, and more of them, are forgotten and their rediscovery is left to musicologists working some centuries distant from us. The purpose of *The Charles Ives Tunebook* is to preserve in one source book those tunes from which Ives borrowed.

In the form of hymns, military and patriotic music, college and popular songs, instrumental music, and "classical" models, borrowed music formed a large repository of pre-existent material to which Ives frequently turned—his own anthology of nearly two hundred fifty sources from the eighteenth century through the early twentieth century. In addition to the use of borrowed music as building blocks for the construction of many of his compositions, the nostalgic element in Ives cannot be underestimated in any attempts to fathom his music, for he "found meaning and beauty through nostalgia."[14] In his *Memos*, the *Essays Before a Sonata*, manuscripts, and the program notes he appended to some of his scores, Ives spoke eloquently about the atmospheric, evocative, and nostalgic intent of his music. He brings to life the "barn dance at the Centre" in *Washington's Birthday* through numerous fiddler's tunes; the "picture in sounds of the sounds of nature and of happenings that men would hear some thirty or so years ago . . . when sitting on a bench . . . on a hot summer night" is interpreted in *Central Park in the Dark* through citations of *Hello! Ma Baby; Ben Bolt;* and *Violets*. The composer mentions *Adeste Fideles, Taps,* and David Reeves's "inspiring" *Second Regiment Connecticut National Guard March* in the commentary to *Decoration Day*. Through these citations and similar ones, Ives recalls thoughts and events of one Memorial Day observance. The second movement of *Sonata No. 1 for Violin and Piano* suggests "a mood when *The Old Oaken Bucket* and *Tramp, Tramp, Tramp, the Boys are Marching* would come over the hills, trying to relive the sadness of the old Civil War Days."[15]

Even when Ives did not provide us with explicit program notes, he used borrowed music to create and reinforce atmosphere. A plantation song and Civil War melodies summon the spirits of both Colonel Robert Gould Shaw and his Negro soldiers to hover over the gentle first movement of *Three Places in New England*. Shaw, the white, twenty-six-year-old leader of a troop of black soldiers, was killed with sixty-two of his men in their assault on Fort Wagner, South Carolina, on the eighteenth of July 1863. In 1882, a group of Bostonians began to plan a monument to Shaw and his men and two years later, they commissioned Augustus St. Gaudens, one of the most prominent nineteenth-century sculptors, to create a work that would commemorate Shaw and his men. The long-awaited result was the moving bas-relief sculpture, dedicated in the Boston Common across from the State House on Memorial (Decoration) Day, 1897. More than a decade later, Ives composed *The "St. Gaudens" in Boston Common (Col. Shaw and his Colored Regiment),* music whose magnificence is equal to the visual majesty in St. Gaudens's work. There is no doubt that Ives was moved by what he saw in St. Gaudens's piece, for there is an aura of ineffable sadness to the music. The inevitability of the fate of Shaw and his men seems to be foreshadowed in the gently plod-ding, inexorable ostinato figure that Ives borrows from Stephen Foster's *Old Black Joe*. The insistence of the melody to the words "I'm coming, I'm coming" not only provides unity for the movement, but, when thought of with its text, adds another layer of interpretation to the words that a Negro sings in Foster's song. Ives added a poem, one of the finest he ever wrote, to his poignant musical rendering of Shaw and his men. It begins:

> Moving,—Marching—Faces of Souls! Marked with generations of pain, Part-freers of a Destiny, Slowly, restlessly—swaying us on with you Towards other Freedom. . . .

Ives also believed that some music, when combined with extraordinary experiences, endowed those moments with near-mystical properties:

> In the early morning of a Memorial Day, a boy is awakened by martial music—a village band is marching down the street—and as the strains of Reeves's majestic *Seventh Reg-iment March* [*sic*] come nearer and nearer—he seems of a sudden translated—a mo-ment of vivid power comes, a consciousness of material nobility—an exultant some-thing gleaming with the possibilities of this life—an assurance that nothing is impossible, and that the whole world lies at his feet. But, as the band turns the corner, at the soldiers' monument, and the march steps of the Grand Army become fainter and fainter, the boy's vision slowly vanishes—his "world" becomes less and less probable—but the experience ever lies within him in its reality. Later in life, the same boy hears the Sabbath morning bell ringing out from the white steeple at the "Center," and as it draws him to it, through the autumn fields of sumach and asters, a Gospel hymn of simple devotion comes out to him—"There's a wideness in God's mercy"—an instant suggestion of that Memorial Day morning comes—but the moment is of deeper import—there is no personal exultation—no intimate world vision—no magnified per-sonal hope—and in their place a profound sense of spiritual truth—a sin within reach of forgiveness. And as the hymn voices die away, there lies at his feet—not the world, but the figure of the Saviour—he sees an unfathomable courage—an immortality for the lowest—the vastness in humility, the kindness of the human heart, man's noblest strength—and he knows that God is nothing—nothing—but love![16]

Of his experiences surrounding those Memorial or Decoration Day experiences, Ives also wrote,

> In the early morning the garden and woods about the village are the meeting places of those who, with tender memories and devoted hands, gather the flowers for the day's memorial. During the forenoon, as the people join each other on the green, there is felt at times a fervency and intensity—a shadow, perhaps, of the fanatical harshness—re-flecting old abolitionist days. It is a day, Thoreau suggests, when there is a pervading consciousness of "Nature's kinship with the lower order—man." After the Town Hall is filled with the Spring's harvest of lilacs, daisies, and peonies, the parade is slowly formed on Main Street. . . . The march to Wooster Cemetery is a thing a boy never for-gets. The roll of muffled drums and *Adeste Fideles* answer for the dirge. A little girl on the fencepost waves to her father and wonders if he looked like that at Gettysburg.
>
> After the last grave is decorated, *Taps* sounds out through the pines and hicko-ries, while a last hymn is sung. Then the ranks are formed again and "we all march back to town" to a Yankee stimulant—Reeves' inspiring *Second Regiment Quickstep*—though, to many a soldier, the sombre thoughts of the day underlie the tunes of the

band. The march stops—and in the silence the shadow of the early morning flower-song rises over the Town, and the sunset behind West Mountain breathes its benedictions upon the Day.[17]

Ives underscores those "sombre thoughts of the day" with motives from *Bethany* and *Taps* which provide a foundation for the extensive quotation of David W. Reeves's *Second Regiment Connecticut National Guard March;* the stream-of-consciousness effect is unmistakable.[18] The ineffable beauty of the opening—the flower-song that permeates much of the movement, perhaps a gentle citation from the *Dies irae*—returns one last time, sounded in the English horn; Ives then draws the music to a close—the "benedictions upon the Day"—with the first three notes of *Taps*, harmonized by a plagal "Amen" cadence. Ives's abilities to evoke a time and place remembered are truly astonishing.

Through his program notes and choice of appropriate borrowed music that would focus on his ideas, Ives attempted to guide the listener to an interpretation of the music that would coincide with his own intentions:

> If [*Washington's Birthday*] is played separately, without outlining the program, it may give (and it has given) the wrong idea of what it is and what it was made for. These three holiday movements (perhaps less in *Thanksgiving,* which has some religious significance) are attempts to make pictures in music of common events in the lives of common people (that is, of fine people), mostly of the rural communities. That's all there is to it. . . . They could be played as abstract music (giving no titles [or] program), and then they would be just like other "abstract" things in art—one of two things: a covering up, or ignorance of (or but a vague feeling of) the human something at its source—or just an emasculated piece of nice embroidery! So if *Washington's Birthday* were put on a program with no program-[notes], the D.A.R. would think it pretended to have something to do with Washington, or his birthday, or "These United States"—or a speech by Senator Blowout![19]

Ives also used borrowed music as a vehicle for his philosophical thoughts. This is suggested in the lengthy description of *Symphony No. 4,* where his citations are intended to convey "the searching questions of What? And Why? which the spirit of man asks of life [and the] diverse answers in which existence replies."[20] The Beethoven motto, used with great insistence in the *"Concord" Sonata,* had a similar extra-musical philosophical-spiritual significance for Ives: "We would . . . strive to bring it [the opening four notes of Beethoven's *Fifth Symphony*] towards the spiritual message of Emerson's revelations—even to the 'common heart' of Concord—the Soul of humanity knocking at the door of the Divine mysteries, radiant in the faith that it *will* be opened—and that the human will become Divine!"[21]

Ives's transcendentalist views held that the music of the common man also contained the true substance of life, a unity underlying all diversity, a simplicity behind the complexities of existence. In using homely tunes, Ives attempted to represent this substance, this unity and simplicity, albeit clothed in complicated accompanying sound fabrics.

The various roles that borrowings play are not at all mutually exclusive. Evocation, populist, and philosophical thought, the transcendent power of simple musical utterance, and structural purpose are inextricably woven together in Ives's thought and music.

Secular music is cited in religious works, and hymns and spiritual songs appear in temporal compositions. This mélange of borrowings—often in juxtaposition and in concurrent statements—bumping into and mixed in with Ives's original music—this diversity—creates a part of Ives's style.[22]

> Ives made no real distinction, in his music or his philosophy, between the sacred and the secular. The fervor of a barn dance and the fervor of a camp meeting were for him merely different forms of the outpouring of man's inner spirit. . . . The most heterogeneous elements of life were ultimately bound together in an invisible, transcendental order. The lowest and most insignificant event had its divine meaning.[23]

Lest one think that Ives always clothes his borrowings with some sort of lofty, profound purpose, one need only listen to the second movement of the *Trio for Violin, Violoncello, and Piano* to hear Charles Ives, the musical prankster. Titled TSIAJ[24] Medley on the Fence [or] on the Campus! the movement is an unfolding collage of at least two dozen citations, each cascading against the other, domino toppling domino, one tune tipping another, in turn tipping another—instrumental tunes sharing space with college songs, popular songs, and patriotic tunes—a joke in one big outrageous stream-of-consciousness musical pun.

For his borrowings, Ives was drawn especially to music composed in the verse-and-refrain/chorus structure. Many hymns, popular songs, and patriotic tunes use this design and make up almost three quarters of the pieces of existing music to which Ives turned. When Ives borrowed from music that bore this structure, he nearly always used melodies from the refrain, or chorus, where the most easily recognized and remembered segment of the tune lay.

While many of his sources have words, Ives was little influenced by them in terms of his borrowings. He does, however, mention specific stanzas of text in connection with the citation of *Duke Street* in *Thanksgiving and Forefathers' Day* and *There'll Be No Dark Valley* in his *Sonata No. 3 for Violin and Piano*. Words of a minstrel tune are printed beneath the appearance of its melody in the horn part of *In the Night*. There, however, the player is only supposed to think of the text while he plays. This is reminiscent of the practice of George Ives, who, according to Charles

> could play, on his horn, a Franz Schubert or Steve Foster song better than many singers could sing it—he often taught songs and parts to singers or choirs etc. by playing. But he always insisted that the words should be known and thought of, while playing.[25]

And who

> once gave a concert in Danbury on the basset horn, playing songs of Schubert and Franz. He had the words printed on a sheet and passed them through the audience, who were expected to read the words and sing silently with him.[26]

The musical style of the material which Ives cited is in no way remarkable, regardless of the type of source. Melodic lines are essentially conjunct; the harmonies—unimportant in terms of Ives's borrowing needs—are, for the most part, diatonic, although chromaticism is found increasingly in the music that dates from the latter part of the nineteenth century. Such chromaticism is in the nature of diminished-seventh chords and secondary dominants, and is almost never used to underscore the sentiments of the original texts. Major tonality prevails: only two tunes—*Windsor* and *When Johnny Comes Marching Home*—are in minor; the verses of *Tammany* and of *Streets of Cairo* are in the minor mode but their respective choruses change to the relative major key and remain there.

The rhythms of the sources are generally bland, with only *Hello! Ma Baby* and *Alexander* illustrating some of the rhythmic shifts typical of ragtime music of the late nineteenth and early twentieth centuries.

Taken as a single body, Ives's sources are nearly always marked by a general melodic, harmonic, and rhythmic simplicity and straightforward quality that makes them perfect foils for the often complex musical settings he invents for them.

Most of the hymns and patriotic songs from which he borrowed date from around 1830 to 1890. Most of them are from George Ives's generation. The son's use of these melodies is only one instance of Charles paying homage to George. Another manifestation of this reverence is in the son's repeated attempts to recapture, through music, either events of his father's life such as the Civil War, or the camp meeting, barn dance, and marching band experiences in which they both shared.[27] He accomplished these nostalgic reviews largely with borrowings from the very music that formed much of George Ives's own musical world. Thus, the son pays two-fold homage to his father: in the subject matter of the new music, and in supporting those subjects by using borrowed music that the father would have known well. Charles reinvents, relives George's life to the extent that it becomes *his* life as well. "The whole remembered world of his childhood," in John Kirkpatrick's phrase, could apply to either the son or to the father.[28]

Whether as a structural component or as a melodic line pregnant with extra-musical meaning—or both—Ives invests his borrowed music with meanings above and beyond its original intentions. The fact that humorous musical punning can exist with musical borrowing that undergirds a spiritual message is certainly a sign of the diversity that underlies the unity in Ives's creative impulses.

In *Quotation and Originality,* Ralph Waldo Emerson, a man whom Ives took as his ideal, remarked:

> A great man quotes bravely, and will not draw on his invention when his memory serves him with a word as good. What he quotes, he fills with his own voice and humor.[29]

Ives did, indeed, quote "bravely," and transformed the quotations "with his own voice and humor." The ultimate test of Ives's music, however, will be neither in the extra-musical value of the music from which he borrows, nor in how creatively he uses such materials. The recognition of his borrowed tunes will not be a factor in assessing the merits of his own music for people listening to Ives a century from now—let's give them a true test by having them identify even a small number of borrowings in *The Fourth of July.* What *will* matter is how well his compositions transcend any limitations of the borrowed music—how well they can stand on their own. To the extent that his scores—borrowed music or not—achieve that independence, Emerson's words will prove to have been remarkably prophetic for his disciple:

> however received, these elements [of quotation] pass into the substance of his constitution, will be assimilated, and tend always to form, not a partisan, but a possessor of truth.[30]

Growing up in Connecticut, near Ives country, I first became aware of Ives in a few newspaper and magazine accounts that dwelt more on the unusual sides of this

Connecticut Yankee, this maverick composer, than they did on his music.[31] Only later, as a teenager, did I first hear a little of his music. To my delight, I recognized occasional hymns that surfaced in Ives's music—hymns that I had played as a young substitute organist during summers at the Montowese Baptist Church, close by my home. From time to time, I recognized a popular song or two from my experiences as a piano player (pianist would be too dignified a title) in clubs, and bars, at dances, and for other social events.

As I came to know more about Ives, I became aware of other similarities that existed between the composer's life and my own: as a youngster, I had attended the Danbury Fair a number of years, even winning a blue ribbon for a childish cartoon I had entered in a contest there; I, too, had "spelled" piano players from time to time.[32] I had worked at Sylvester Poli's Bijou Theatre in New Haven (albeit as an usher rather than as a piano player), where Ives, as a Yale student, had "spelled" George Felsburg.[33] The somber march to the cemetery to place flowers on the graves of the war dead on Decoration Day were part of my own experiences as a boy growing up in a small Connecticut town. In my mind, the Montowese and North Haven cemeteries—the Wooster Cemetery of my existence—will be forever associated with this act of homage.[34] I had sung in the choir of men and boys at Trinity Church on the Green—the Episcopal church next to Center Church, where Ives was organist from 1894 to 1898.

All these things led to a continuing interest in Ives and his music, and although other projects captured my interest and time, Charles Ives seemed always to be close at hand. When I first began my serious study of Ives four decades ago, it was because of my attraction to the detective work of ferreting out the borrowed music. I thought I had finished with that fascination in 1990 when *The Charles Ives Tunebook* first appeared. I was wrong.

Returning to Ives has been like visiting an old friend I had not seen in some time: on one hand, I saw and heard things—in this case, music—I had not heard before, or missed before because I was now more aware of the composer and his music than I had been forty years ago. On the other hand, old memories welled up, made all the more powerful—and, at times, bittersweet—by their reappearance. Savoring them again became important. More especially for me, the visit reaffirmed what I had already known about Charles Ives: he has the genius to move one ineffably with his finest music and to conjure up, at least for this Connecticut Yankee, that "whole remembered world of [my own] childhood" in that small Connecticut town.

ACKNOWLEDGMENTS

The response to the first edition of *The Charles Ives Tunebook* was most gratifying. Many helped in the development of that edition. First and foremost was John Kirkpatrick. Any student of Ives soon realizes and appreciates the enormity of Kirkpatrick's contributions to Ives scholarship. His *Catalogue,*[1] studies, and editions of Ives are testaments to his painstaking scholarship, his meticulous organization, his love and admiration for Ives and his music. He was generous in sharing information, lists, analyses, his study, and his table in his New Haven home for discussions about that remarkable man, Charles Ives.

Two anecdotes: working with Kirkpatrick in his Orange Street home in New Haven one morning, I could not help but be impressed with the meticulous organization of his study—everything in its place amid what, to some, might seem like the chaos of photocopies, volumes of books, music, and other trappings of this performer-scholar's life. After a couple of hours of work—I recall that one of the topics was the lineage of Ives's song *Charlie Rutlage*—we stopped for a simple, but nourishing meal and conversation, joined by John's wife, Hope. Then it was time for us to walk to Yale, to what was known at the time as the "Ives Room." As we walked, I tried to carry on a conversation with Kirkpatrick. To give the impression that we walked *together* is misleading, for I soon trailed behind him, somewhat chagrined that I couldn't keep up with this man who was some thirty years my senior. His energy level always seemed to be amazingly high.

Never to be forgotten is a New Year's day when Kirkpatrick allowed me to work alone in the "Ives Room" when the university was closed. Once he had retrieved the compositions I needed for my work, and reminding me to close the main door tightly when I left for the day, he departed, leaving me alone in the building. There I was, handling, not copies of Ives's compositions, but his original manuscripts! Later that afternoon, I answered the telephone, whose insistent ringing was annoying. It was John Kirkpatrick, calling long distance, and asking me if I knew the identity of a tune he was about to sing into the telephone. It was one that Ives borrowed for his own uses. That entire day remains a special one for me.

In the decade and a half since the publication of *The Charles Ives Tunebook,* the work of many scholars has added significantly to our understanding of Ives and his music. John Kirkpatrick's seminal work in Ives continues today in the tireless efforts of James B. Sinclair. His meticulous and magisterial *A Descriptive Catalogue of the Music of Charles Ives* is a fitting successor to the *Catalogue* that Kirkpatrick began only a month after the composer's death.[2]

J. Peter Burkholder's contributions to Ives scholarship are well known. His essays, articles, and books offer perceptive observations and analyses of the composer and his music. He has offered me many suggestions that I have incorporated in this edition of the *Tunebook.* His *All Made of Tunes: Charles Ives and the Uses of Musical Borrowing* has remained at my side throughout all my own work in revising the *Tunebook.*[3] I have agreed with many of Burkholder's "takes" on the identity of some tunes I missed or could not identify in the first edition of the *Tunebook*. I remain less persuaded with some of his other identifications; whatever my decision was, however, Burkholder's fresh eyes (and those of a few others) opened my own to new ways of looking at Ives and his music. Late in the revision process when I could not get a copy of *The Celestial Railroad* through the Ives Estate to review for borrowings, Peter generously gave me a copy of Thomas Brodhead's unpublished edition of the piece. I thank him for his continuing support and encouragement.

Richard Boursy, Archivist for the Irving S. Gilmore Music Library at Yale University, and Suzanne Eggleston Lovejoy, Assistant Music Librarian for Public Services at Yale, met my every question and request with patience and unfailing courtesy.

J. Bunker Clark originally suggested this project and its title some three decades or more ago. Friend, editor, and supporter, Bunker was a necessary thorn, albeit a gentle one, in my side from time to time, urging me to complete this revision. I regret that he did not live to see the final product. I like to think that he would have been pleased with the result.

The Center for Academic Innovation at Saint Mary's College, through its Faculty Development Grant program, gave support to this project. Patrick White, then the Director of the Center, encouraged my efforts at every turn. I thank my colleague, Laurel Thomas, for the support and the enthusiasm with which she tackled the job of putting together an evening of Ives's songs and selections from his writings. Her students who sang the songs and this author, who read from Ives's writings, gained much from observing the ways in which the composer's words and some of his songs interacted with one another. More important was the sheer pleasure we had in hearing and doing live performances of Ives. My conversations with Gayle Sherwood, Ives scholar, and speaker at our Ives evening, were helpful in determining some of the course this book has taken.

The author gratefully acknowledges the generous assistance from the Lloyd Hibberd Publication Endowment Fund of the American Musicological Society.

Location can provide an author with a special ingredient that fires the imagination and the creative juices. For a number of summers, mine has been in Door County, Wisconsin, where Bob and Mary Lou Bizzaro were always gracious hosts. I thank them and remember, with great affection, Bob, who passed away in 2004.

The support and encouragement of Jane Behnken, my editor at Indiana University Press, have been what any author would wish to have. Her good cheer helped me especially during those moments when I wondered if I would ever finish this revision. Bethany Kissell, at the time Assistant Music Editor at Indiana University Press, helped me through the mysteries of technology when it came to translating my music examples into formats the publisher could readily understand. I thank Miki Bird, Managing Editor, for her thorough review of the manuscript, for her suggestions, and for catching errors that would have proved embarrassing. The book is all the better for her review.

The love and support of my family have been inestimable. They have been most patient with me, especially when I've been with them, but have not really "been there," an authorial disease which afflicts many writers. My son Ethan read portions of the manuscript, which are improved because of his suggestions and his eagle eyes. He spent hours locating many of the sources for the new borrowings that I and others have ferreted out since the first version of *The Charles Ives Tunebook* appeared. I am especially grateful to him for his help and will long remember our conversations about Ives—conversations carried on over coffee, walking, telephonically, and electronically.

My wife, Elizabeth, to whom this book is dedicated, has always supported my projects, giving me understanding, good humor, and gentle prodding. No author could wish for more. For the past decade and more, when I had turned my attention to other areas, she probably thought I had finished my work with Charles Ives. As the reader can see, this has not been the case. Ives has reentered the Henderson household almost as another member of our family. John Kirkpatrick once wrote that Ives "bestows the privilege of a great unfolding, demanding a steady growth toward the horizon of the unknown."[4] I hope that, in some small measure, this edition of *The Charles Ives Tunebook* reflects that kind of growth.

Granger, Indiana
Summer 2006

THE

Charles Ives

Tunebook

INTRODUCTION

The original edition of *The Charles Ives Tunebook*, the Kirkpatrick *Catalogue*, Burkholder's *All Made of Tunes*, Sinclair's *A Descriptive Catalogue of the Music of Charles Ives*, and the suggestions of others are the sources for the identification of borrowed music for this edition of the *Tunebook*. Other borrowings may be found, but I suspect that they will not significantly alter the picture we now have of Ives and his music.

Sometimes it is difficult to distinguish between and among certain sources from which Ives borrows, because their melodic contours are similar. The beginnings of *Missionary Chant* and the opening notes of Beethoven's *Symphony No. 5* are a case in point: the melodies of both drop a minor third after a repetition of opening notes. The only initial difference between these two sources is that *Missionary Chant* has four iterations of the opening pitch before the descending third, while the Beethoven has three before it, too, drops a third.

from Beethoven, *Symphony No. 5*, first movement

from *Missionary Chant*

Among other pairs are *Azmon* and *Shining Shore, Happy Day* and *Bringing in the Sheaves, Happy Day* and *There'll Be No Dark Valley,* and *Work Song* and *Old, Old Story.*

from *Azmon*

from *Shining Shore*

from *Happy Day*

from *Bringing in the Sheaves*

In the few cases where identification of the tune could have been a problem, Ives usually told what his model was, or clearly delineated in his citation, if only for a moment, his choice between paired sources or from among a variety of possibilities.

Context can also be brought to bear in identifying the correct tune. Beginning in measure 65 in the concluding movement of *Symphony No. 4,* the oboe cites a tune that could be *Eli Yale* ("As freshmen first, we come to Yale"). Although there exist numerous examples where Ives quoted from disparate sources in a single work, the citation of *Eli Yale* here would have been inappropriate, given the other borrowed music—hymn tunes—in the movement and in relation to what the movement is about: a "finale of transcendental spiritual content" as an "apotheosis of the preceding content [i.e., movements,] in terms that have something to do with the reality of existence and its religious experience."[1] It is not *Eli Yale* that Ives borrowed here, but a phrase from the hymn *There Is a Happy Land* ("where saints in glory stand").

Because of the similarities between sources, even Ives was probably confused at least once about a tune that he said he used. In the description he wrote for the first movement of *Fourth Violin Sonata,* he recalled:

> The children, especially the boys, liked to get up and join in the marching kind of hymns. And as these meetings were "out-door," the "march" sometimes became a real one. One day Lowell Mason's—"Work for the Night is Coming" [*Work Song*] got the boys going.[2]

It was not the Mason hymn that he used in this sonata, however, but William Doane's *Old, Old Story.* With the sole exception of their respective starting pitch, the first seven notes, rhythm, and harmony of both *Work Song* and *Old, Old Story* are identical. That Ives consistently borrowed the first seven notes of the latter hymn here clearly shows that he was using *Old, Old Story* and not the Mason tune he remembered from the "out-door" camp meetings.

from *Work Song*

from *Old, Old Story*

Occasionally words will help to identify Ives's source. His song *Remembrance* begins with a melodic pattern that is nearly the same as the opening notes of two hymns—*David* and *Hexham*—and of the popular nineteenth-century song *Kathleen Mavourneen*. "A sound of a distant horn, O'er shadowed lake is borne, my father's song," the words Ives wrote for his song, are reminiscent of Kathleen Mavourneen's lover's remarks, "The horn of the hunter is heard on the hill." The music that accompanies those words, however, is not what we hear at the beginning of Ives's song. There, the contour is from the very opening of *Kathleen Mavourneen*. Even though those notes are nearly identical to *David* and *Hexham*, it is most certainly the *Mavourneen* tune that Ives uses. The words of the hymns, in no way, reflect Ives's thoughts in this song, but there is an emotional pairing of the words of Kathleen's lover and Ives's poetry. In this instance, words help to identify one source from between, or among, a variety of possibilities. Having said that, however, one, or both of the hymns may have triggered Ives's memory of *Mavourneen*, which, in turn, may have led his mind to those words of Mavourneen's lover. And, having said that, the process may have been reversed or consisted of a combination of these things.

from *Kathleen Mavourneen*

from *David*

from *Hexham*

Sometimes there are melodic cells whose contours hint at a possible borrowing. Following Peter Burkholder's suggestion and taking a page from Sinclair's *Descriptive Catalogue*, I have added the category of "Possible Borrowings" to this edition of *The Charles Ives Tunebook*. I have left it to the reader to decide for her/himself if Ives did, indeed, borrow from that particular tune in the work cited.

I have retained the section given over to tunes that may well be borrowed, but some of which have not yet been identified—at least to my satisfaction. This section was originally titled "Unknown Tunes," certainly an incorrect title, for the tunes must be known by someone—if, indeed, they are borrowings. I have changed the title to "Newly Identified and Unidentified Tunes" to accurately reflect the contents of this chapter.

Three kinds of borrowings that do not quite fit into other categories should be mentioned. They are not dealt with beyond this brief mention.

In the first instance, Ives often borrowed from himself. In this respect, he was following a long line of composers who recycled their own music. Self-borrowing becomes a way of recasting earlier music in new contexts. Examples of this occur most frequently with the composer's incomplete *Country Band March*. Composed in the last half of 1906, the music resurfaces almost whole around 1914 as *Putnam's Camp, Redding, Connecticut;* in about 1911 as part of the *Hawthorne* movement of the *"Concord" Sonata,* and between 1911 and 1916 in the second movement of *Symphony No. 4*. Ives also uses bits of it in *The Celestial Railroad* and in the opening measures of *He Is There!* in both vocal and choral versions. The manner in which Ives used his own material differs significantly from the way he employed borrowed music of others. In turning to the latter, Ives often divided his borrowed material into small segments, using them as building blocks, accumulating more and more notes of his source until the entire tune, or most of it, appears at the end of the work. In borrowing from his own music, however, Ives more frequently used the entire source immediately without going through the building-block process. The reader interested in these borrowings should consult the "Derivation" and/or "Borrowing" categories in Sinclair's *Descriptive Catalogue.*

Secondly, Ives alludes to the B-A-C-H motive briefly in a number of works. It is difficult to determine whether these appearances are happenstance or the result of a deliberate working-out by the composer. Because the motives are mostly isolated, rather than worked over as other borrowings are, it seems that they are more the result of chromaticism than they are conscious actions by Ives.[3]

Finally, reworking someone else's composition is a time-honored method by which a young composer can learn principles of instrumentation and orchestration and style. Before he entered Yale in 1894, Ives had already tried his hand at this in the *Polonaise* of 1887. There, the sextet from the second act of Donizetti's *Lucia di Lammermoor* is Ives's model. As one might expect, this *Polonaise,* an incomplete work of only eighteen measures and a cadenza, clearly betrays the hand of its youthful composer. Even the melody, probably to be played by two cornets, is entirely derivative. There is nothing in this *Polonaise* to hint of what is to come.

Part of Ives's education in composition involved working with models from the world of "classical" music. Music by Beethoven, Schubert, Mendelssohn, Schumann, Robert Franz, and Peter Cornelius, among others, served Ives in this way. In those scores he could see how others had dealt with the myriad things that go into a composer's arsenal of technique, among them dynamics, key relationships, phrasing, instrumentation, melodic contours, structure, and style.

One of the original purposes of the *Tunebook* was to cite the first appearance of a borrowed melody in an Ives composition. Because the first citation is sometimes tenuous or ambiguous, some readers suggested that a revised *Tunebook* could be more helpful if it distinguished between such a borrowing and a subsequent unequivocal statement of that borrowed tune. While this suggestion has merit, I have chosen to retain the original purpose of the book. The fine line that sometimes exists between a hint and a less ambiguous statement of a borrowed tune is a distinction that I found too subjective and one, if carried out consistently, might clutter the book unnecessarily.

Since manuscripts exist for Ives's incomplete works I have included such works in this *Tunebook*. In some cases, persons other than the composer have "realized" or "completed" these compositions for publication. In most cases, however, I have chosen to deal with these works as they exist in Ives's manuscript form—what *he* put down on paper. I have not accounted for lost works—more than ninety in number—indicated in Sinclair by the lowercase prefix letter "x."

Each piece of borrowed music has been classified according to its traditional use and/or origin and placed into one of six categories: hymns, military or patriotic music, popular songs, college songs, popular instrumental tunes (mostly "fiddle" tunes), and "classical" music.[4]

The following information is given for each example: discrete entry number;[5] title and subtitle or alternate title(s); initial words (where known and/or appropriate); source of the example presented here; author (where appropriate); composer; date of composition or copyright. The dating of most sources was not difficult, since much of this music was copied from original dated editions, or the information was otherwise available in various anthologies (i.e., hymnals and collections of popular music).[6]

Since Ives was primarily interested in the melody of his source, that is the only music element usually given in the *Tunebook*. Complete melodies are presented—except for those marches, "classical" music, and some popular models where it was both unnecessary and impractical to give more than those sections that are pertinent to Ives's citations. Preludes, interludes, and postludes have been treated in a similar fashion.

There is almost never a correlation between the words of a borrowed source and that source's appearance in an Ives score. I have presented most models with a text for the first stanza unless Ives expressed a preference for words from another stanza. I have not been able to determine the precise words that Ives may have known or favored for some of the hymns where more than one text was commonly associated with the same melody. These tunes are presented, therefore, without text, but with an explanation to that effect.

In the first edition of this *Tunebook*, Ives's music was identified according to the system used by John Kirkpatrick (with Paul C. Echols) in the work-list for *The New Grove Dictionary of American Music*.[7] For this edition the numbering of each of Ives's compositions follows the one that Sinclair developed for *A Descriptive Catalogue of the Music of Charles Ives*. Readers who wish to compare the Kirkpatrick numbering with that of Sinclair may do so by consulting Sinclair's Concordance 1: "Kirkpatrick's *Temporary Catalogue* Numbers to Sinclair Numbers."

A summary version of Sinclair's numbering system follows.

I. Works for Orchestra (001–051)

    A. Symphonies (001–006)

    B. Sets (007–020)

        i. Orchestral Sets (007–009)

        ii. Sets for Chamber Orchestra (010–020)

    C. Overtures (021–027)

    D. Marches (028–033)

    E. Other Works (034–051)

II. Works for Band (052–056)

III. Works for Chamber Ensemble (057–086)

    A. String Quartets (057–058)

    B. Violin Sonatas (059–063)

    C. Other Works (064–086)

IV. Works for Piano (087–129)

    A. Sonatas (087–089)

    B. Studies (090–108)

    C. Marches (109–115)

    D. Other Works (116–125)

    E. Duets (126–129)

V. Works for Organ (130–142)

VI. Works for Choral Ensemble (143–202)

    A. Sacred Works (143–178)

        i. Multi-Movement Works (143–145)

        ii. Psalms (146–155)

        iii. Other Works for Choral Ensemble (156–178)

    B. Secular Works (179–202)

        i. Choruses with Instrumental Ensemble (179–190)

        ii. Partsongs (191–202)

VII. Works for the Stage (203–204)

    A. Projected Operas [Only lost or projected works]

    B. Fraternity Shows (203–204)

All dates of composition are taken from Sinclair's *Descriptive Catalogue* and do not take into account the claim of questionable dating practices proposed by Maynard Solomon.[8]

Incomplete works for which manuscripts exist are often in sketch form, and frequently lack measure and/or specific instrumental designations. The location of the borrowings in these is identified by the number of the microfilm print and staff on which the borrowed music appears.[9] For instance, *In the Sweet Bye and Bye* in 009 ii 29 n3002, staff 2 is tune number 29 (*In the Sweet Bye and Bye*), quoted in the second movement of *Orchestral Set No. 3* for the first time in microfilm number n3002, on staff 2. I have not indicated an instrument when such a designation is unclear or missing.

I have not followed any particular rule of thumb to determine the first appearance of a borrowing. The majority of first soundings are unmistakable. The initial citation of a tune in a given composition, together with the instrument sounding it, are indicated in the parenthesis following the Sinclair number and the entry number of the borrowed tune. Thus, in 004 iii 3 (116—trombone), tune number 3—*Antioch*—is heard in the third movement of *Symphony No. 4* for the first time, played by the trombones in measure 116.[10] When a borrowing is heard simultaneously in different instrumental parts, I have indicated only the predominating instrument.

I have made every effort to provide the models as Ives probably knew them. This was not a difficult task except for some hymns and "fiddle" tunes. My review of the books left in the Ives home after his death gave me no idea what hymnals he and his family definitely used.[11] My educated guesses as to probable sources are based on hymnals Ives probably used as a church organist in Danbury and New Haven. In copying the examples, I have retained all of the idiosyncrasies of their publication, including unusual barring, word divisions, and spelling that appear in my sources. Because most of the "fiddle" tunes were not first written out as in "art" music, evolving instead from improvisational practices, definitive printed models probably do not exist. I have given these tunes in a version that Ives certainly would have recognized, even though the printed copy might well be a pale reflection of the actual performance sound that he heard. This book is a reference tool and is not intended as a performance edition. Any reader wishing to perform these tunes in their entirety should consult the music sources, a complete list of which is given in the bibliography.

Finally, there is a danger in assuming that one has "found" Ives because one has ferreted out borrowings from every nook and cranny of his music. What one has found—the tunes that "come from somewhere near the soul"—is the "substance" of Ives's concept of substance and manner.[12] In his best works, Ives creates a seamless mix of borrowing and originality to produce music of ineffable beauty—that second level of "substance," if you will. Part of the enigma of Ives's music—part of that ineffable sound, I think—is when originality and borrowing become one in an expressive end. Often it is difficult to tell when borrowing ends and originality begins, or what is Ives and what is an appropriation.

Ives's musical language, as that of Bela Bartók and Ralph Vaughan Williams, to name but two composers, involves, in part, the assimilation of the seeming disparate languages of the vernacular, the cultivated, and the original, each inextricably connected and interwoven with the other. *The Charles Ives Tunebook,* I hope, will provide one of the steps in the comprehension of that musical language.

Part 1

[1]

Hymns

Ives borrowed more frequently from hymns than he did from any other type of music. They give us an inventory of many of the tunes familiar to him from his experiences as a child

> at the outdoor Camp Meeting services in Redding, [Connecticut, where] all the farmers, their families, and field hands, for miles around, would come afoot or in their farm wagons. [He remembered] how the great waves of sound used to come through the trees—when things like *Beulah Land, Woodworth, Nearer My God To Thee, The Shining Shore, Nettleton, In the Sweet Bye and Bye* and the like were sung by thousands of "let out" souls. . . . There was power and exaltation in these great conclaves of sound from humanity.[1]

Recalled in his music are many of the hymns he played as an organist from 1889 to 1902.[2] In addition to his organ preludes, postludes, and interludes based on hymns, Ives derived significant portions of movements of many larger pieces from this kind of music.[3]

Hymn tunes have provided a point of departure for organists' variations and improvisations for centuries, and Ives continued this tradition, often writing down the fruits of his improvisations. Some of his results, however, went beyond the scope of typical late nineteenth- and early twentieth-century improvisatory practices. As early as 1892, he began to tamper with the genteel and bland harmonies that one finds in the majority of nineteenth-century hymns, reharmonizing some of them with his unique pungent musical language. In doing so he often created a sound that had to have caused his congregation considerable consternation. The following example that Ives says he played at Center Church in New Haven in December of 1895 certainly goes far in altering Lowell Mason's original simple harmonies of *Bethany* ("Nearer, my God, to Thee").

As if to rationalize what he did, he wrote:

> When a man has played at church services for ten or fifteen years steadily, he gets slightly used to the three fundamental triads, in the hymns and anthems as well as in the plain chants. In . . . [*In the Night,* based in part on a hymn-anthem composed for the Central Presbyterian Church in New York in 1901,] I tried to find three chords that might be used in a similar or parallel sense to the usual tonic, dominant, and sub-dominant—a combination of chords that would not be undignified, that would have some musical sense and relation, and about which melodies or counterpoints could be used as a natural outcome from these combinations. In this movement, D-flat was taken as the main chord (or the tonic) and B-flat (in this case a tone above the dominant A-flat) was used as the dominant, and the chord of E major (a tone below the subdomi-nant G-flat) was used for the subdominant. These chords have a note in common with the tonic, and B-flat used as the dominant seems to have a stronger resolving value than the subdominant, E major. Then the tune, *Abide With Me,* as a kind of cantus firmus, was sung by the male voices, with a [higher] counterpoint as a second melody played on one of the lighter manual [stops,] and in this case in B-flat (the dominant chord). And a piano in the Sunday-school room played another distinct counterpoint, but, as I re-member, this attempt in the church service was not successful—it went better in an organ recital—in fact, Dr. Merle Smith turned around and glowered at the choir.[4]

One can be certain that Wilton Merle-Smith, the pastor to whom Ives refers, was not alone in his reaction to such experimentation. How many in the congregations Ives served were bewildered by his music but just suffered his experiments in silence isn't known, but at least he professed sensitivity to this. He asked himself,

> is one justified in doing something which, to him, is quite in keeping with his under-standing and feelings—but [not] to the congregation, who [may be] unused to the id-iom, or rather some of the sound combinations and so naturally might misunderstand and be disturbed?[5]

Continuing, he wrote:

> to a body of people who come together to worship—how far has a man a right to do what he wants, if he knows that by so doing he is interfering with the state of mind of the listeners, who have to listen regardless, and are helpless not to?

So, as I look back, I seemed to have worked with more natural freedom, when I knew the music was not going to be inflicted on others.[6]

Despite these sentiments, however, Ives continued to subject his "captured" audience to his hymn experiments—even as a substitute organist after 1902.[7]

Ives held hymns—the unpretentious, unsophisticated religious music of the common man—in high regard. He found

> in them—some of them—a vigor, a depth of feeling, a natural-soil rhythm, a sincerity— emphatic but inartistic—which, in spite of a vociferous sentimentality, carries him nearer the "Christ of the people" than does the *Te Deum* of the greatest cathedral. These tunes have . . . a truer ring than many of those groove-made, even-measured, monotonous, non-rhythmed, indoor-smelling, priest-taught, academic, English or neo-English hymns (and anthems)—well-written, well-harmonized things, well-voice led, well-counterpointed, well corrected and well O.K'd, by well corrected Mus. Bac. R. F. O. G.'s.[8]

Is there a contradiction here between what Ives said and what he did in actual practice? Why, if he really believed that some of those hymns could carry one "nearer the 'Christ of the people,'" did he alter his sources so radically? In borrowing from hymns, rare are those instances in which Ives quoted even a phrase of the original harmony and rhythm intact. Instead, he almost always changed the harmony to bring it in line with his own musical thought. He held somewhat ambiguous feelings about the rhythm of his borrowed hymns, altering it just about as often as he accepted it without change. The melodic line was, however, a different matter. Here lay the "depth of feeling," that "sincerity," that true "ring" of his source. One can nearly always pick out the melody that Ives borrowed. His reverence for the melody of his source, always there, rarely altered beyond a few insignificant notes, reminds one of the sanctity accorded Gregorian chant in a Mass or motet by composers of the late medieval and early Renaissance periods. The "tune" is nearly always there intact.[9] This analogy soon breaks down because Ives's melodic citations are mere snippets when compared to the unfolding of lengthy sections of chant in a Mass or motet. Too, the liturgical appropriateness of a chant to a Mass or motet is lacking in Ives's scores. Nevertheless, the melody of his source was a near-sacred thing to him, and he rarely tampered with it to the degree that he altered the other musical elements.

Most of the major figures associated with nineteenth-century hymnody provided Ives with inspiration. William Bradbury, William Howard Doane, Thomas Hastings, Robert Lowry, George Minor, Ira Sankey, George Webb, and Isaac B. Woodbury are represented, but it is Lowell Mason from whom Ives borrowed most often. Fifteen different tunes that Mason either composed or arranged find their way into between sixty and seventy-one separate movements or works by Ives.

The hymns from the post-Mason period, with their slightly more daring harmonic patterns (usually involving only a little, simple chromaticism) and livelier rhythms, include *The Beautiful River, Beulah Land, Bringing in the Sheaves, Where Is My Wand'ring Boy?, Throw Out the Life-Line,* and *There'll Be No Dark Valley.* With the single exception of *Windsor,* all the hymns are in the major mode. *Windsor,* underscored by the minor key and with its dark and solemn majesty, stands in sharp relief from the other hymns.

The list of authors is not as impressive, but Isaac Watts from the eighteenth century and Frances Jane (Fanny) Crosby, the blind poetess and most prolific writer of hymn texts in the nineteenth, are represented.

I have chosen the versions of most of the tunes that appear here from a variety of hymnals dating from two years before Ives's birth to his twentieth year, 1872 to 1894. Represented are hymnals for use in the different churches in which Ives served as organist. A comparison of twentieth-century editions of these tunes with their nineteenth-century counterparts reveals that the augmented note values in the latter (chiefly half notes instead of quarters), some irregular barring, and unusual word divisions constitute the only differences between them.

A few tunes defied my efforts to locate them in hymnals of the latter third of the nineteenth century. I have resorted to twentieth-century versions for these, believing that they also are probably not substantially different from their appearance a century or so ago.

1
ADESTE FIDELES

(Portuguese Hymn)

("O come, all ye faithful")

SOURCE: *Hymns of the Faith,* no. 55

Latin, 18th century
Translation by Frederick Oakeley, 1852

JOHN FRANCIS WADE, ca. 1750

O come, all ye faith - ful, joy - ful and tri - um - phant, O

come ye, O come—— ye to Beth - le - hem!

Come and be - hold Him, born the King of an - gels! O

come, let us a - dore Him, O come let us a - dore Him, O

come, let us a - dore Him,—— Christ—— the Lord!

005 ii (1—violin I)	*Decoration Day* [from] *A Symphony: New England Holidays*
027 (50—trumpet)	*Robert Browning Overture*
064 (f0712, m. 1—1—piano)	*Decoration Day* for Violin and Piano
131 (2)	*"Adeste Fideles"* in an Organ Prelude

2

ALL SAINTS NEW

("The Son of God goes forth to war")

SOURCE: *The New Hymnal*, no. 852

Reginald Heber, 1812

HENRY S. CUTLER, 1872

The Son of God goes forth to war, A king - ly crown to

gain; His blood - red ban - ner streams a - far: Who

fol - lows in his train? Who best can drink his

cup of woe, Tri - um - phant o - ver pain; Who

pa - tient bears his cross be - low, He fol - lows in his train.

277 (21—voice) *In Flanders Fields*

3

ANTIOCH

("Joy to the World")

SOURCE: *The Baptist Praise Book,* no. 281

From Psalm 98
Isaac Watts, 1719

LOWELL MASON, 1839
(after George Frideric Handel)

Joy to the world! the Lord is come; Let earth re - ceive her King;

Let ev - ery heart___ pre - pare Him room, ___ And

heaven and na - ture sing, And heaven and na - ture sing, And

heaven and heaven ___ and na - ture sing.

002 v (69—horn I)	Allegro molto vivace [from] *Symphony No. 2*
004 iii (116—trombone)	*Fugue* [from] *Symphony No. 4*
004 iv (50—bassoon)	Largo [from] *Symphony No. 4*
105 (11)	*Study No. 21: Some Southpaw Pitching*
Possible borrowing:	
235 (12—voice) (or) *Olivet* 46	*Disclosure*

3-a

ARLINGTON

("We walk by faith, and not by sight")

SOURCE: *The New Hymnal,* no. 270

Henry Alford, 1844   THOMAS A. ARNE, 1762

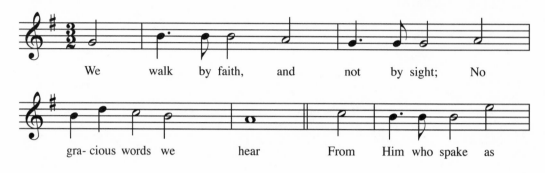

We walk by faith, and not by sight; No gra- cious words we hear From Him who spake as

man ne'er spake, But we be - lieve Him near.

005 iv (50—viola I)   *Thanksgiving and Forefathers' Day* [from]
                                            A Symphony: New England Holidays

4

AUTUMN

("For the grandeur of Thy nature"—2nd stanza)

SOURCE: *New Laudes Domini,* no. 470

Robert Robinson   arr. from FRANÇOIS-HIPPOLYTE BARTHÉLÉMON, 1785
(2nd stanza preferred by Ives)

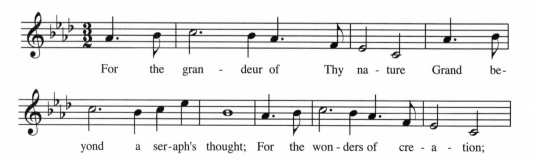

For the gran - deur of Thy na - ture Grand be- yond a ser-aph's thought; For the won - ders of cre - a - tion;

Works with skill and kind - ness wrought; For Thy prov - i-dence that

gov - erns Thro' Thine em - pire's wide do - main___ Wings an

an - gel, guides a spar - row, Bless - ed be Thy gen - tle reign

5

AZMON

("O for a thousand tongues")

SOURCE: *The Church Book,* no. 315

John Wesley, 1780

CARL GOTTHELF GLASER, 1828
arr. by LOWELL MASON, ca. 1839

O for a thou - sand tongues to sing My

great Re - deem - er's praise; The glo - ries of my

God   and   King,   the___   tri-umphs of   His   grace!

004 iv (53—horn)	Largo [from] *Symphony No. 4*
003 i (6—violin I)	*Old Folks Gatherin'* [from] *Symphony No. 3*
003 iii (13—violin I)	*Communion* [from] *Symphony No. 3*
005 iv (169—oboe I)	*Thanksgiving and Forefathers' Day* [from] *A Symphony: New England Holidays*
009 i (n1058, staff 2): appears in preliminary sketches but not in Porter's performance score	[Andante moderato] [from] *Orchestral Set No. 3*
009 ii (p. 16: n3002, section 2, staff 1, violin II)	*An Afternoon or During Camp Meetin' Week— One Secular Afternoon (In Bethel)* [from] *Orchestral Set No. 3* [incomplete]
009 iii (p. 28: n3057, staff 4)	[no tempo heading] [from] *Orchestral Set No. 3* [incomplete]
069 (f5563, staff 3)	*Fugue in Four Keys on "The Shining Shore"* [incomplete]
222 (5—piano)	*The Camp Meeting*
331 (8—voice)	*Religion*

Possible borrowing:

012 i (f2743, 6—solo English horn)	*Adagio sostenuto: At Sea* [from] *Set No. 3*
016 i (f6156, m. 6—voice)	*At Sea* [from] *Set No. 7: Water Colors*
213 (6—voice)	*At Sea*

6

THE BEAUTIFUL RIVER

("Shall we gather at the river")

SOURCE: *The Baptist Praise Book,* no. 1045

Robert Lowry

ROBERT LOWRY, 1864

Shall we gath-er at the riv-er,   Where bright   an-gel feet have

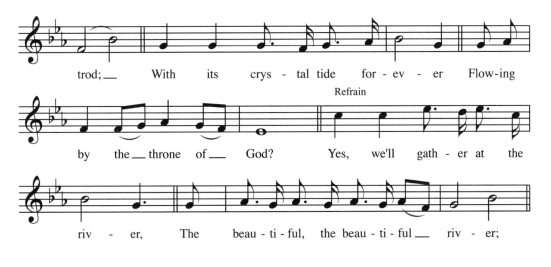

trod; __ With its crys - tal tide for - ev - er Flow-ing

Refrain

by the __ throne of __ God? Yes, we'll gath - er at the

riv - er, The beau - ti - ful, the beau - ti - ful __ riv - er;

Ga - ther with the saints __ at the riv - er

That flows by the throne of __ God.

003rej. iv (f0657)	Rejected 4th movement of *Symphony No. 3*
004 ii (48—solo piano)	Allegretto [from] *Symphony No. 4*
009 i (52—flute and trumpet)	[Andante moderato] [from] *Orchestral Set No. 3* [incomplete]
062 ii (53—violin)	Allegro [from] *Sonata No. 3 for Violin and Piano*
063 iii (1—piano)	Allegro [from] *Sonata No. 4 for Violin and Piano: Children's Day at the Camp Meeting*
084 iii (1—violin)	*Adagio cantabile: The Innate* [from] *A Set of Three Short Pieces*
214 (5—voice)	*At the River*
284 (1—piano)	*The Innate*

7

BETHANY

("Nearer, my God, to Thee")

SOURCE: *Hymns of Worship and Service*, no. 251

Sarah Flower Adams, 1841   LOWELL MASON, 1859

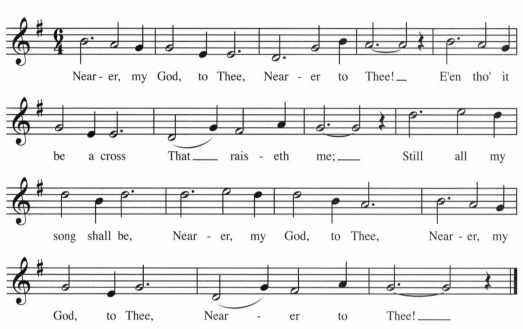

004 i (2—2 violins)	*Prelude* (Maestoso) [from] *Symphony No. 4*
004 iv (6—5 violins)	Largo [from] *Symphony No. 4*
005 ii (75—violins 1a)	*Decoration Day* [from] *A Symphony: New England Holidays*
006 Section A (f1831, 7 staves from top of page)	*Universe Symphony*
006 Section C (f1845, staff 1)	*Universe Symphony*
009 i (72—clarinet)	[Andante moderato] [from] *Orchestral Set No. 3* [incomplete]
009 iii (f1804, staff 3)	Third movement [from] *Orchestral Set No. 3*
015 iv (f6153, staff 3, last notes of voice)	*Evening* [from] *Set No. 6: From the Side Hill*
016 i (f6156, m. 5—voice)	*At Sea* [from] *Set No. 7: Water Colors*
018 i (f2749, m. 13—English horn)	*Andante con moto: The Last Reader* [from] *Set No. 9 of Three Pieces*
021 (f2488, m. 3)	*Alcott Overture* [mostly lost]
037 (f2211, brace 2)	*The General Slocum* [incomplete]
058 iii (49—violin)	*The Call of the Mountains* (Adagio-Andante-Adagio) [from] *String Quartet No. 2*

064 (f0716, m. 75—piano)	*Decoration Day* for Violin and Piano
094 (f5491, m. 1)	*Study No. 6: Andante*
137 ii (f5068)	*Interlude for Bethany*
236 (35—voice)	*Down East*
244 (16—voice)	*Evening*
286 (6—voice)	*The Last Reader*
331 (10—piano)	*Religion*

Possible borrowing:

012 i (f2777, staff 1, m. 1) (or) *Nettleton* 42	*Adagio sostenuto: At Sea* [from] *Set No. 3*
012 ii (f2777, staff 1, m. 1) (or) *Nettleton* 42	*Luck and Work* [from] *Set No. 3*
213 (2—voice)	*At Sea*

8

BEULAH LAND

("I've reached the land of corn and wine")

SOURCE: *Gospel Hymn and Tune Book,* no. 334

Edgar P. Stites   JOHN R. SWENEY

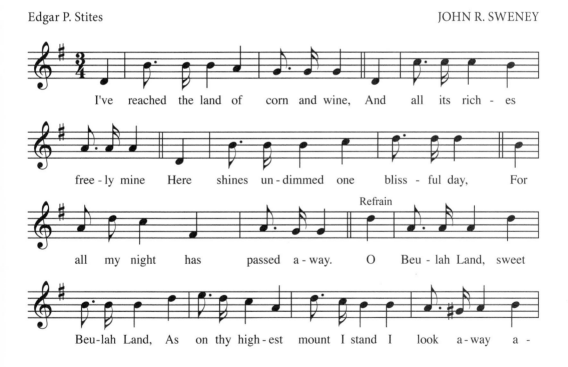

cross the sea, Where man-sions are pre-pared for me, And view the shin-ing

glo-ry-shore, My Heav'n, my home for-ev-er-more!

001 i (12—flute)	Allegro [from] *Symphony No. 1*
002 iii (11—violin I)	Adagio cantabile [from] *Symphony No. 2*
004 ii (1—bass)	Allegretto [from] *Symphony No. 4*
057 ii (8—violin I)	*Prelude* [from] *String Quartet No. 1: From the Salvation Army*
057 iii (39—violin I)	*Offertory* [from] *String Quartet No. 1: From the Salvation Army*
062 i (114—violin I)	*Adagio* [from] *Sonata No. 3 for Violin and Piano*
116 (f4860, staff 1)	*The Celestial Railroad*

9

BLESSED ASSURANCE

("Blessed assurance, Jesus is mine!")

Frances Jane Crosby   PHOEBE P. (Mrs. Joseph F.) KNAPP, 1873

Bles-sed as-sur-ance, Je-sus is mine!____ Oh, what a

fore-taste of glo-ry di-vine!____ Heir of sal-va-tion, pur-chase of

God,____ Born of His Spi-rit, wash'd in His blood.____

This is my sto - ry, this is my song, ___ Prais-ing my

Sav - iour all the day long; ___ This is my sto - ry, this is my

song, ___ Prais - ing my sav - iour all the day long. ___

Possible borrowing:

003 ii (70—violin I)　　　　　　　　　*Children's Day* [from] *Symphony No. 3: The Camp Meeting*

10

BRINGING IN THE SHEAVES

("Sowing in the morning")

SOURCE: *Sacred Songs No. 1,* no. 209

Knowles Shaw　　　　　　　　　　　　　　　GEORGE A. MINOR

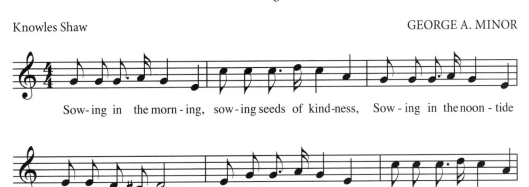

Sow- ing in the morn - ing, sow-ing seeds of kind-ness, Sow - ing in the noon - tide

and the dew - y eve; Wait-ing for the har - vest and the time of reap-ing,

We shall come re-joic - ing, bring-ing in the sheaves.

Refrain

Bring-ing in the sheaves, bring-ing in the sheaves, We shall come re-joic-ing,

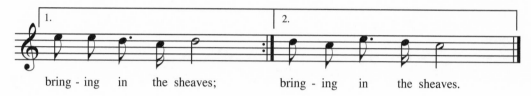

1.

bring - ing in the sheaves;

2.

bring - ing in the sheaves.

002 ii (42—violin)	Allegro [from] *Symphony No. 2*
008 ii (38—violin I)	*The Rockstrewn Hills Join in the People's Outdoor Meeting* [from] *Orchestral Set No. 2*
020 ii (41—piano)	*In the Inn* [from] *Set for Theatre Orchestra*
043 i (20—clarinet)	*Ragtime Dance No. 1* [from] *Four Ragtime Dances*
043 ii (5—violin)	*Ragtime Dance No. 2* [from] *Four Ragtime Dances*
043 iii (15—clarinet)	*Ragtime Dance No. 3* [from] *Four Ragtime Dances*
043 iv (13—violin)	*Ragtime Dance No. 4* [from] *Four Ragtime Dances*
[This might be *Happy Day* 27]	
046 (f2428, score 2, m. 1)	*Skit for Danbury Fair* [incomplete]
057 ii (18—cello)	*Prelude* [from] *String Quartet No. 1: From the Salvation Army*
060 i (65—violin)	Andante-Allegro vivace [from] *Sonata No. 1 for Violin and Piano*
083 (2—cello)	*Scherzo for String Quartet*
084 ii (2—cello)	*Scherzo: Holding Your Own!* [from] *A Set of Three Short Pieces*
087 iia (4)	Allegro moderato-Andante [from] *Sonata No. 1 for Piano*
087 iib (100)	Allegro-Meno mosso con moto [from] *Sonata No. 1 for Piano*
087 ivb (8)	Allegro-Presto-Slow [from] *Sonata No. 1 for Piano*
127 (f4968, staff 1, m. 2)	*Drum Corps or Scuffle*
[This might be *Happy Day* 27]	

10-a

BROWN

("The golden gates are lifted up, The doors are open'd wide")

SOURCE: *Hymns of Worship and Service,* no. 151

("Approach, my soul, the mercy seat, Where Jesus answers prayer")

SOURCE: *The Otterbein Hymnal,* no. 240

C. P. Alexander, 1852, 1858
John Newton, 1779

WILLIAM B. BRADBURY, 1840

Ap - proach, my soul, the mer - cy - seat Where Je - sus an - swers

prayer; There hum - bly fall be - fore his feet, For none can per - ish there.

Possible borrowing:

004 iii (89—flute)

Fugue [from] *Symphony No. 4*

11

CHERITH

(preferred text unknown)

SOURCE: *Laudes Domini,* no. 989

arr. from LUDWIG SPOHR

011 iii (1—cornet)   *Andante: The Last Reader* [from] *Set No. 2*
018 i (1—cornet)   *Andante con moto: The Last Reader* [from] *Set No. 9 of Three Pieces*
286 (1—voice)   *The Last Reader*

12
CHRISTMAS

(Siroe)

("Awake, my soul, stretch ev'ry nerve")

SOURCE: *The Baptist Praise Book,* no. 288

Philip Doddridge, 1755   GEORGE FRIDERIC HANDEL, 1728
                                                    arr. in 1815

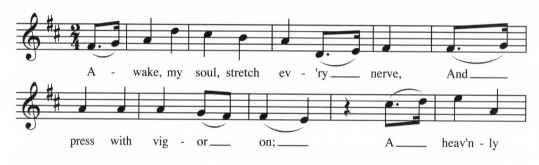

004 iii (14—violin II)   *Fugue* [from] *Symphony No. 4*
027 (371—horn)   *Robert Browning Overture*
057 i (12—viola)   *Chorale* [from] *String Quartet No. 1: From the Salvation Army*

12-a

CHURCH TRIUMPHANT

("Again the Lord's own day is here")

SOURCE: *Hymns Ancient and Modern New Standard*, no. 20

ascribed to Thomas a Kempis
Translation by J. M. Neale

J. W. ELLIOTT

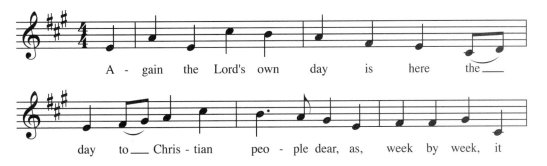

A - gain the Lord's own day is here the ___

day to __ Chris - tian peo - ple dear, as, week by week, it

bids them tell how Je - sus rose from death and hell.

Possible borrowing:

    004 iii (89—clarinet)

Fugue [from] *Symphony No. 4*

12-b

CLEANSING STREAM

(Refrain: "The cleansing stream I see! I see!")

Phoebe Palmer

PHOEBE P. (MRS. JOSEPH) KNAPP, ca. 1871

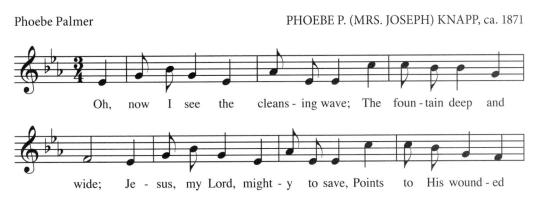

Oh, now I see the cleans - ing wave; The foun - tain deep and

wide; Je - sus, my Lord, might - y to save, Points to His wound - ed

side.   The   cleans-ing stream I   see!   I   see!   I

plunge, and, oh   it   cleans - eth me!   Oh,   praise the Lord!   It

cleans - eth me!   It   cleans - eth me - yes, cleans - eth me!

Possible borrowing:

002 iii (16—flute)   Adagio cantabile [from] *Symphony No. 2*

12-c

CONSOLATION

Come Ye Disconsolate

("Come, ye disconsolate")

<small>SOURCE:</small> *The New Hymnal,* no. 388

Thomas Moore, 1816   arr. from SAMUEL WEBBE, 1792

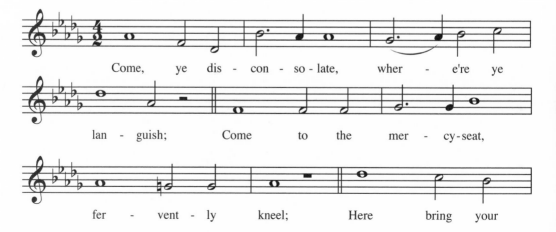

Come,   ye   dis - con - so - late,   wher - e're   ye

lan - guish;   Come   to   the   mer - cy-seat,

fer - vent - ly   kneel;   Here   bring   your

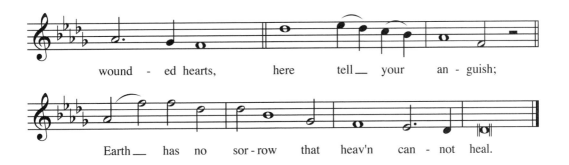

wound - ed hearts, here tell__ your an - guish;

Earth__ has no sor - row that heav'n can - not heal.

Possible borrowing:

012 i (f2743, m. 8—English horn)	*Adagio sostenuto: At Sea* [from] *Set No. 3*
016 i (f6156, m. 2—voice)	*At Sea* [from] *Set No. 7: Water Colors*
213 (2—voice)	*At Sea*

13

CORONATION

("All hail the power of Jesus' name")

SOURCE: *The Baptist Praise Book,* no. 446

Edward Perronet, 1780   OLIVER HOLDEN, 1793

All hail the power of Je - sus' name! Let an - gels pros - trate

fall; Bring forth the roy - al di - a - dem, And

crown him Lord of __ all; Bring forth the roy - al

di - a - dem, And crown Him Lord__ of all.

004 iii (21—flute)	*Fugue* [from] *Symphony No. 4*
057 i (16—violins)	*Chorale* [from] *String Quartet No. 1: From the Salvation Army*
057 iv (1—violin)	*Postlude* [from] *String Quartet No. 1: From the Salvation Army*

13-a

CRUSADER'S HYMN

(St. Elizabeth)

("Fairest Lord Jesus")

SOURCE: *The Methodist Hymnal,* no. 118

Silesian Melody
pub. Leipzig, 1842

| 004 i (25—flute) | *Prelude* [from] *Symphony No. 4* |
| 168 (f5837, m. 1—soprano) | *Hymn,* Op. 2, No. 1 [incomplete] |

Possible borrowing:

088 i (page 3, staff 3)   *Emerson* [from] *Sonata No. 2 for Piano: Concord, Mass., 1840–60*

13-b

DAVID

(Thatcher)

(Thacher)

=possibly former Unknown Tune 219

see also *Hexham* 28-a and *Kathleen Mavourneen* 112

("Come, Holy Spirit come, with energy divine")

SOURCE: *The Methodist Hymnal,* no. 182

Benjamin Beddome   arr. from GEORGE FRIDERIC HANDEL

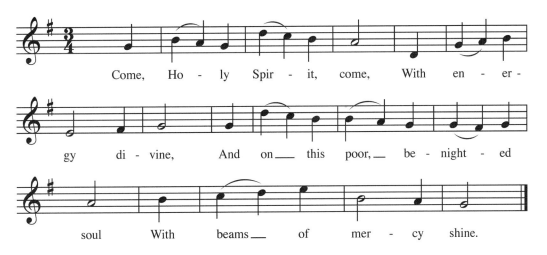

Come, Ho - ly Spir - it, come, With en - er - gy di - vine, And on this poor, be - night - ed soul With beams of mer - cy shine.

016 iii (1—horn)   *The Pond* [from] *Set No. 7: Water Colors*

    [This may be *Kathleen Mavourneen* 112 or *Hexham* 28-a]

Possible borrowing:

    040 (3—voice)   *The Pond*

    084 i (21—solo cello)   Largo cantabile: *Hymn* [from] *A Set of Three Short Pieces*

    [This may be *Kathleen Mavourneen* or *Hexham*]

    267 (15—voice)   *Hymn*

    332 (1—voice)   *Remembrance*

14

DEEP RIVER

("Deep river, my home is over Jordan")

SOURCE: *The New Blue Book of Favorite Songs,* p. 251

1st known appearance in print: 1875

Deep Riv - er, my home is o - ver Jor - dan____ Deep____ Riv - er, Lord, I

1. **2.** *Fine*

want to cross o - ver in - to camp-ground. camp-ground. Oh,

don't you want to go____ to that gos - pel

feast,____ That prom - is'd land____ where

all____ is peace?__ Oh, don't you want to go to that

D.C. al Fine

prom - is'd land__ where all____ is peace?

007 i (56—horn)

Possible borrowing:
378 (2—voice)

The "St. Gaudens" in Boston Common (Col. Shaw and his Colored Regiment) [from] *Orchestral Set No. 1: Three Places in New England*

Tom Sails Away

14-a

DIES IRAE

=possibly former Unknown Tune 220

("Dies irae, dies illa, Solvet saeclum in favilla"/

"Day of wrath, o day of mourning")

SOURCE: *Liber Usualis,* p. 1810, ff.

THOMAS OF CELANO

Di- es ir - ae di - es il - la   Sol - vet ___ sae - cu-lum in   fa - vil - la

009 i (p. 13: q3000, section E of sketch; staff 14; distant piano; celesta); does not appear in Porter's performance score — [Andante moderato] [from] *Orchestral Set No. 3*

Possible borrowing:

005 ii (5—English horn) — *Decoration Day* [from] *A Symphony: New England Holidays*

064 (f0712, 4—violin) — *Decoration Day* for Violin and Piano

15

DORRNANCE

(Talmar)

(Chester)

(preferred text unknown)

SOURCE: *Hymns of Worship and Service,* no. 122

ISAAC BAKER WOODBURY, 1845

004 iv (11—violin I) Largo [from] *Symphony No. 4*

007 iii (3—cello) *The Housatonic at Stockbridge* [from] *Orchestral Set No. 1: Three Places in New England*

009 i (13—piano) [Andante moderato] [from] *Orchestral Set No. 3*

009 iii (p. 35 n3008-a, staff 6) [no tempo heading] [from] *Orchestral Set No. 3* [incomplete]

266 (8—voice) *The Housatonic at Stockbridge*

16

DUKE STREET

("O God, beneath Thy guiding hand")

SOURCE: *The Service of Song,* no. 898

Leonard Bacon, 1833

JOHN HATTON
appeared anon. first in 1793

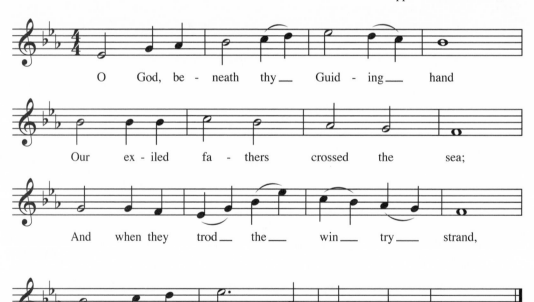

O God, be - neath thy ___ Guid - ing ___ hand

Our ex - iled fa - thers crossed the sea;

And when they trod ___ the ___ win ___ try ___ strand,

With prayer and psalm they wor - shipped thee.

005 iv (51—horns III and IV) *Thanksgiving and Forefathers' Day* [from] *A Symphony: New England Holidays*

17

ERIE

(CONVERSE)

("What a friend we have in Jesus")

SOURCE: *The Baptist Hymnal,* no. 406

Joseph Scriven, ca. 1855   CHARLES CROZAT CONVERSE, 1868

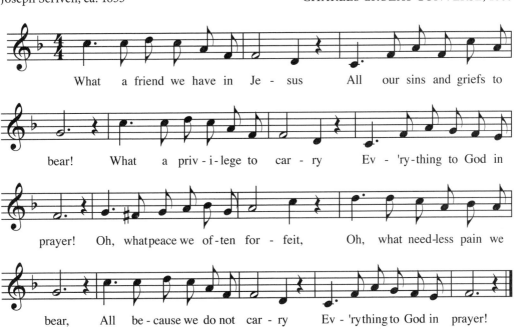

What a friend we have in Je - sus   All   our sins and griefs to

bear!   What   a priv - i - lege to   car - ry   Ev - 'ry-thing to God in

prayer!   Oh, whatpeace we of - ten for - feit,   Oh,   what need-less pain we

bear,   All   be - cause we do not car - ry   Ev - 'rything to God in   prayer!

003 i (3—violin I)	*Old Folks Gatherin'* [from] *Symphony No. 3: The Camp Meeting*
015 iii (f6180, staff 4, last portion—voice)	*Afterglow* [from] *Set No. 6: From the Side Hill*
087 iii (2)	Largo-Allegro-Largo [from] *Sonata No. 1 for Piano*
207 (133—voice)	*Afterglow*

Possible borrowing:

006 (Section A: f1832, staff 1)	*Universe Symphony*
015 iii (f6180, staff 4, last portion: voice]	*Afterglow* [from] *Set No. 6: From the Side Hill*

18

EVEN ME

("Lord, I hear of showers of blessing")

SOURCE: *The Church Book,* no. 253

Elizabeth Codner

WILLIAM BATCHELDER BRADBURY, 1872

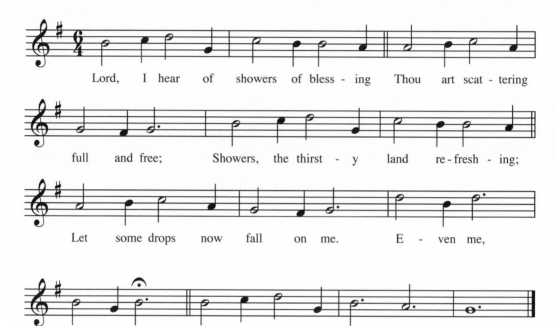

Lord, I hear of showers of bless - ing Thou art scat - tering
full and free; Showers, the thirst - y land re - fresh - ing;
Let some drops now fall on me. E - ven me,
E - ven me, Let some drops now fall on me.

009 iii (p. 33: n3058, staff 9, trumpet)

[no tempo heading] [from] *Orchestral Set No. 3* [incomplete]

103 (f4803, bottom staff, m. 1)

Study in major and minor intensities [from] *Study No. 19* [incomplete]

19

EVENTIDE

("Abide with me: fast falls the eventide")

SOURCE: *The Service of Song,* no. 973

Henry Francis Lyte, 1847   WILLIAM H. MONK, 1861

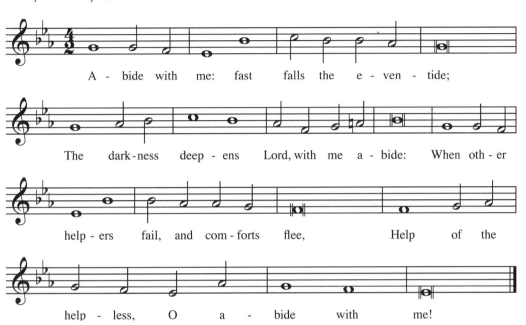

A - bide with me: fast falls the e - ven - tide;

The dark-ness deep - ens Lord, with me a - bide: When oth - er

help - ers fail, and com - forts flee, Help of the

help - less, O a - bide with me!

020 iii (11—solo cello)   *In the Night* [from] *Set for Theatre Orchestra*
080 (3—trombone)   *Prelude on "Eventide"*
593 (f2610)   Unidentified fragment: one line on 3 staves
                                              on title page of song *Mists* (II) 301

20

EWING

("Jerusalem, the golden")

SOURCE: *The Baptist Praise Book,* no. 1202

Bernard of Cluny, 12th century
Translation by John M. Neale, 1751

ALEXANDER EWING, 1853

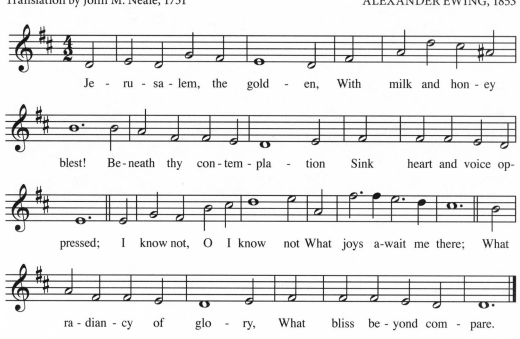

Je - ru - sa - lem, the gold - en, With milk and hon - ey blest! Be - neath thy con - tem - pla - tion Sink heart and voice op- pressed; I know not, O I know not What joys a-wait me there; What ra - dian - cy of glo - ry, What bliss be - yond com - pare.

052 (1—cornet)

Fantasia on *"Jerusalem the Golden"*

21

EXPOSTULATION

("Oh, turn ye, oh, turn ye")

SOURCE: *The Baptist Praise Book,* no. 628

Josiah Hopkins

JOSIAH HOPKINS, 1830

Oh, turn ye, oh, turn ye, for why will ye die? When

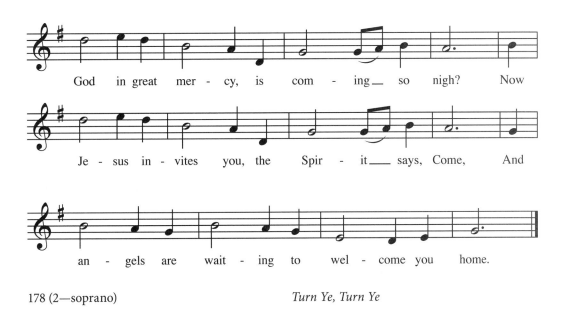

God in great mer - cy, is com - ing__ so nigh? Now

Je - sus in - vites you, the Spir - it__ says, Come, And

an - gels are wait - ing to wel - come you home.

178 (2—soprano)   *Turn Ye, Turn Ye*

22
FEDERAL STREET
(preferred text unknown)

source: *Hymns of Faith*, no. 86

HENRY KEMBLE OLIVER, 1832

005 iv (4—flute)

Thanksgiving and Forefathers' Day [from] *A Symphony: New England Holidays*

23

FOUNTAIN

Cleansing Fountain

("There is a fountain filled with blood")

SOURCE: *The Baptist Praise Book,* no. 473

William Cowper

early 19th-century melody
arr. by LOWELL MASON

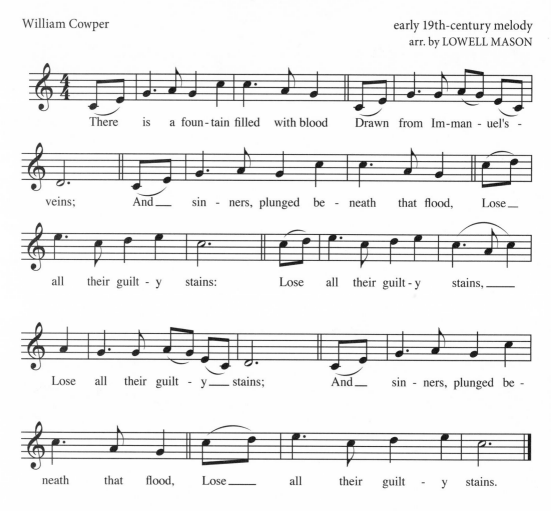

003 ii (2—violin I)	*Children's Day* [from] *Symphony No. 3: The Camp Meeting*
013 iii (f8148, last 3 measures)	*Matthew Arnold* [from] *Set No. 4: Three Poets and Human Nature*
023 (f2335, score 2, m. 6)	*Matthew Arnold Overture*
086 ii (187—piano)	Presto ("TSIAJ" or Medley on the Fence [or] on the Campus!) [from] *Trio for Violin, Violoncello, and Piano*
181 (4—voice)	*General William Booth Enters into Heaven*
255 (4—voice)	*General William Booth Enters into Heaven*
388 (43—piano)	*West London*

23-a

GIVE ME JESUS

("In the morning when I rise")

SOURCE: *With One Voice*, no. 777

NEGRO SPIRITUAL, before 1850

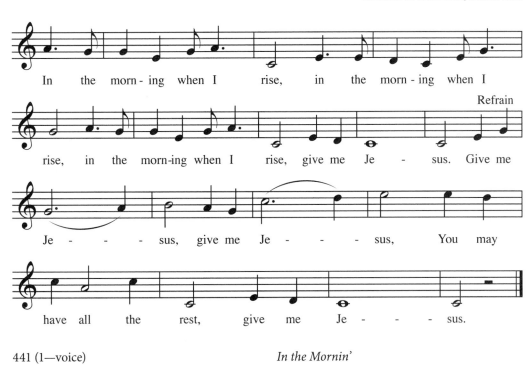

In the morn-ing when I rise, in the morn-ing when I rise, in the morn-ing when I rise, give me Je - sus. Give me Je - - - sus, give me Je - - - sus, You may have all the rest, give me Je - - - sus.

441 (1—voice)	*In the Mornin'*

24

GOD BE WITH YOU

("God be with you till we meet again")

SOURCE: *Worship and Service Hymnal,* no. 154

Jeremiah E. Rankin   WILLIAM G. TOMER, 1882

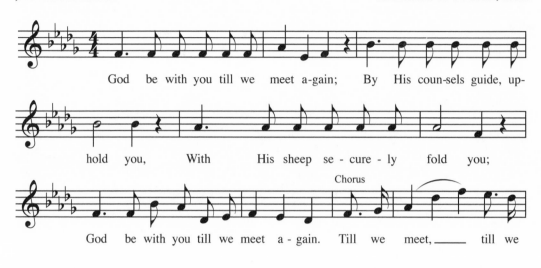

God be with you till we meet a-gain; By His coun-sels guide, up-

hold you, With His sheep se - cure - ly fold you;

Chorus

God be with you till we meet a - gain. Till we meet,____ till we

meet,__ till we meet at Je - sus'__ feet; Till we

meet,____ till we meet, God be withyou till we meet a - gain.

004 ii (1—bassoon)	Allegretto [from] *Symphony No. 4*
059 i (f3236, m. 11—violin)	Allegretto moderato [from] *Pre-First Sonata for Violin and Piano*
116 (f4869, staff 6)	*The Celestial Railroad*

25

GREENWOOD

(preferred text unknown)

SOURCE: *The Baptist Praise Book,* no. 165

JOSEPH EMERSON SWEETSER, 1849

009 ii (p. 19, n3004, staff 13)

An Afternoon or During Camp Meetin' Week—
One Secular Afternoon (In Bethel) [from]
Orchestral Set No. 3 [incomplete]

26

HAMBURG

("When I survey the wondrous cross")

SOURCE: *New Laudes Domini,* no. 404

Isaac Watts, pub. 1707

from a Gregorian chant
arr. by Lowell Mason, pub. 1825

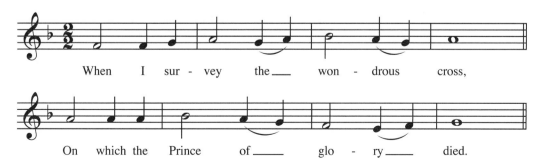

When I sur - vey the__ won - drous cross,

On which the Prince of__ glo - ry__ died.

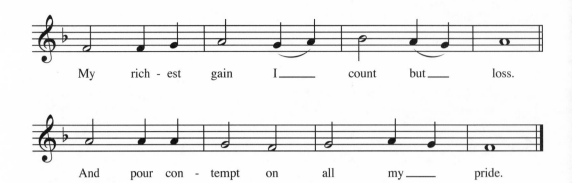

My rich - est gain I____ count but____ loss.

And pour con - tempt on all my____ pride.

002 ii (137—trombone I)   Allegro [from] *Symphony No. 2*

27

HAPPY DAY

("O happy day that fixed my choice")

SOURCE: *The Baptist Praise Book,* no. 715

Philip Doddridge, 1740   1855

O hap- py day that fixed my choice On Thee, my sav - iour and my God.

Well may this glow - ing heart re - joice, And tell its rap - tures all a -

Refrain

broad. Hap - py day, hap - py day, When Je - sus

washed my sins a - way! He taught me how to watch and

pray, And live re - joic - ing ev - 'ry day Hap - py

day,   hap - py   day,   When Je - sus washed   my sins a - way!

007 ii (8—bassoon)	*Putnam's Camp, Redding, Connecticut* [from] *Orchestral Set No. 1: Three Places in New England*
008 ii (28—piano)	*The Rockstrewn Hills Join in the People's Outdoor Meeting* [from] *Orchestral Set No. 2*
020 ii (73—piano)	*In the Inn (Potpourri)* [from] *Set for Theatre Orchestra*
042 (f2481, score 1, m. 1)	*[2nd Ragtime Dance]* [from] *Three Ragtime Dances* [mostly lost]
043 i (49—violin)	*Ragtime Dance No. 1* [from] *Four Ragtime Dance*
043 ii (5—violin)	*Ragtime Dance No. 2* [from] *Four Ragtime Dances*
043 iv (53—trombone)	*Ragtime Dance No. 4* [from] *Four Ragtime Dances*
046 (f2428, score 1)	*Skit for Danbury Fair* [incomplete]
061 (40—piano)	*"In the Barn"* [from] *Sonata No. 2 for Violin and Piano*
062 iii (8—piano)	*Adagio cantabile* [from] *Sonata No. 3 for Violin and Piano*
086 ii (125—violin)	*Presto ("TSIAJ" or Medley on the Fence* [or] *on the Campus!)* [from] *Trio for Violin, Violoncello, and Piano*
087 iia (1)	*Allegro moderato-Andante* [from] *Sonata No. 1 for Piano*
087 iib (132)	*Allegro-Meno mosso con moto; "In the Inn"* [from] *Sonata No. 1 for Piano*
087 ivb (45)	*Allegro-Presto-Slow* [from] *Sonata No. 1 for Piano*
087 v (131)	*Andante maestoso-Adago cantabile-Allegro-Andante* [from] *Sonata No. 1 for Piano*
122 iv (2)	*Scene-Episode* [from] *Set of Five Take-Offs*
127 (f4968, staff 2, m. 2)	*Drum Corps or Scuffle* [mostly lost]
128 ii (66—piano I)	*Allegro* [from] *Three Quarter-Tone Pieces*

28

HEBRON

(preferred text unknown)

SOURCE: *The Baptist Praise Book,* no. 355

LOWELL MASON

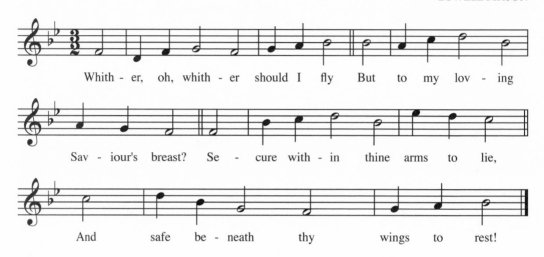

Whith - er, oh, whith - er should I fly But to my lov - ing

Sav - iour's breast? Se - cure with - in thine arms to lie,

And safe be - neath thy wings to rest!

009 i (f1789, section C, staff 10)

[Andante moderato] [from] *Orchestral Set No. 3* [does not appear in Porter's performance score]

28-a

HEXHAM

(Consolation)

=possibly former Unknown Tune 219

see also *David* 13-b and

Kathleen Mavourneen 112

("Still, still with Thee, when purple morning breaketh")

SOURCE: *The Methodist Hymnal,* no. 43

Harriet Beecher Stowe

adapted from MENDELSSOHN's *Consolation* [from] *Songs Without Words*, Op. 30, no. 3

Still, still with Thee, when pur - ple morn - ing break - eth,

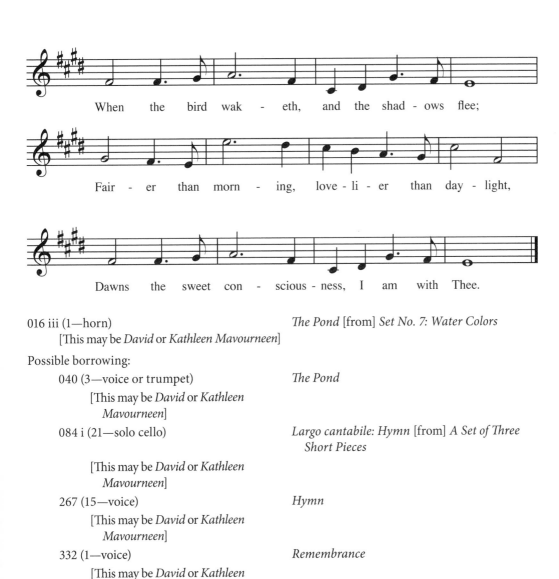

When the bird wak - eth, and the shad - ows flee;

Fair - er than morn - ing, love - li - er than day - light,

Dawns the sweet con - scious - ness, I am with Thee.

016 iii (1—horn)   *The Pond* [from] *Set No. 7: Water Colors*
    [This may be *David* or *Kathleen Mavourneen*]

Possible borrowing:

    040 (3—voice or trumpet)   *The Pond*
        [This may be *David* or *Kathleen Mavourneen*]

    084 i (21—solo cello)   *Largo cantabile: Hymn* [from] *A Set of Three Short Pieces*

        [This may be *David* or *Kathleen Mavourneen*]

    267 (15—voice)   *Hymn*
        [This may be *David* or *Kathleen Mavourneen*]

    332 (1—voice)   *Remembrance*
        [This may be *David* or *Kathleen Mavourneen*]

29

IN THE SWEET BYE AND BYE

("There's a land that is fairer than day")

SOURCE: *Gospel Hymn and Tune Book,* no. 437

Sanford Fillmore Bennett   JAMES PHILBRICK WEBSTER, pub. 1868

There's a land that is fair - er than day,   And by

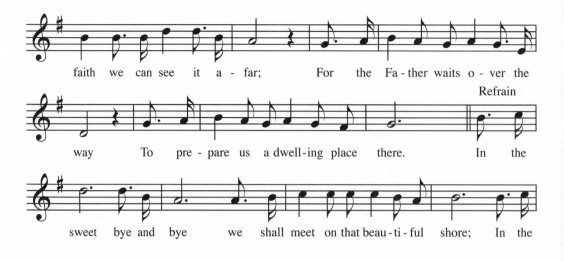

faith we can see it a - far; For the Fa - ther waits o - ver the way Refrain

To pre - pare us a dwell-ing place there. In the

sweet bye and bye we shall meet on that beau - ti - ful shore; In the

sweet bye and bye, We shall meet on that beau - ti - ful shore.

004 i (5—cello)	*Prelude* [from] *Symphony No. 4*
004 ii (38—violin I/the others)	Allegretto [from] *Symphony No. 4*
005 iv (172—flute)	*Thanksgiving and Forefathers' Day* [from] *A Symphony: New England Holidays*
008 iii (23—clarinet)	*From Hanover Square North, at the End of a Tragic Day, the Voice of the People Again Arose* [from] *Orchestral Set No. 2*
009 ii (p. 15: n3002, staff 2)	*An Afternoon or During Camp Meetin' Week— One Secular Afternoon (In Bethel)* [from] *Orchestral Set No. 3* [incomplete]
039 (f2490)	*Piece for Small Orchestra and Organ* [mostly lost]
086 ii (84—piano)	Presto ("TSIAJ" or Medley on the Fence [or] on the Campus!) [from] *Trio for Violin, Violoncello, and Piano*
282 (f6766, brace 2)	Incomplete song [II]
372 (15—voice)	*The Things Our Fathers Loved*
461 (f0901)	4 measures in 2/4 meter
Possible borrowing:	
116 (f4844, Staff 1)	*The Celestial Railroad*

30

JESUS LOVES ME

(China)

(Renar)

("Jesus loves me, this I know")

SOURCE: *Worship and Service Hymnal,* no. 490

Anna B. Warner, 1859

WILLIAM BATCHELDER BRADBURY, 1862

Je - sus loves me! this I know, For the Bi - ble tells me so;

Lit - tle ones to Him be-long; They are weak, but He is strong.

Refrain

Yes, Je - sus loves me, Yes, Je - sus loves me,

Yes, Je - sus loves me, The Bi - ble tells me so.

008 i (21—trumpet)	*An Elegy to Our Forefathers* [from] *Orchestral Set No. 2*
063 ii (1—piano)	Largo-Allegro (conslugarocko)-Andante con spirito-Adagio cantabile-Largo cantabile [from] *Sonata No. 4 for Violin and Piano: Children's Day at the Camp Meeting*
Possible borrowing:	
007 i (2—bass)	*The "St. Gaudens" in Boston Common (Col. Shaw and his Colored Regiment)* [from] *Orchestral Set No. 1: Three Places in New England*
see also *Old Black Joe* 128	
286 (20—voice)	*The Last Reader*
see also *Watchman* 61	

31

LABAN

("My Soul, be on thy guard")

SOURCE: *The Baptist Praise Book,* no. 959

George Heath, 1806   LOWELL MASON, 1830

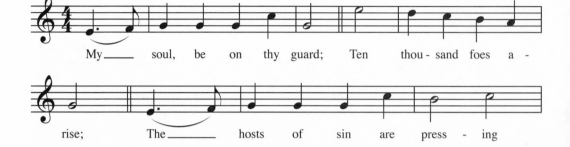

My___ soul, be on thy guard; Ten thou - sand foes a -

rise; The___ hosts of sin are press - ing

hard To draw thee from the skies.

005 iv (29—violin)   *Thanksgiving and Forefathers' Day* [from]
A Symphony: New England Holidays

32

LAMBETH

("People of the living God")

SOURCE: *The Church Hymnary,* no. 777

James Montgomery

Peo - ple of___ the liv - ing God, I have sought the

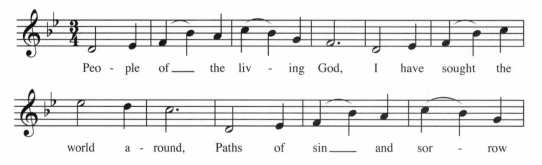

world a - round, Paths of sin___ and sor - row

trod,   Peace   and   com - fort   no - where found.

Possible borrowing:

005 ii (20—violin I)   *Decoration Day* [from] *A Symphony: New England Holidays*

33

LEBANON

("I was a wand'ring sheep")

SOURCE: *The Baptist Praise Book,* no. 723

Horatius Bonar, 1844   JOHN ZUNDEL, 1855

I was a wan - d'ring sheep, — I did not love — the fold; — I did not love my Shep - herd's voice, I would not be con - trolled. — I was a way - ward child, — I did not love — my home; — I did not love my Fa - ther's voice; I loved a - far to roam. —

| 087 i (12) | Adagio con moto-Andante con moto-Allegro risoluto-Adagio cantabile [from] *Sonata No. 1 for Piano* |
| 087 v (5) | Andante maestoso-Adagio cantabile-Allegro-Andante [from] *Sonata No. 1 for Piano* |

Possible borrowing:

| 426 (1—piano); or *Bingo* 148 | *Burlesque Harmonization in C* |

33-a

LISCHER

(preferred text unknown)

SOURCE: *The Methodist Hymnal*, no. 67

FRIEDRICH JOHANN CHRISTIAN SCHNEIDER
arr. by LOWELL MASON, 1841

Possible borrowing:

| 004 iii (89—flute) | *Fugue* [from] *Symphony No. 4* |

34

MANOAH

(preferred text unknown)

SOURCE: *The Baptist Praise Book,* no. 77

probably a composite adapted by
HENRY W. GREATOREX, from E. H. MÉHUL'S
Joseph (1807) and FRANZ JOSEPH HAYDN'S
The Seasons (1801); appears in 1851

011 iii (8—cornet)	*Andante: The Last Reader* [from] *Set No. 2*
018 i (8—cornet)	*Andante con moto: The Last Reader* [from] *Set No. 9 of Three Pieces*
286 (7—voice)	*The Last Reader*

35

MARTYN

("Jesus, lover of my soul")

SOURCE: *The Baptist Praise Book,* no. 685

Charles Wesley, 1740   SIMEON B. MARSH, 1834

Je- sus, lov- er of my soul, Let me to Thy bos - om fly, ___

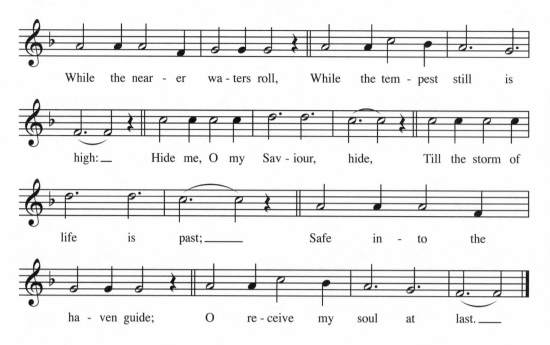

While the near-er wa-ters roll, While the tem-pest still is high:___ Hide me, O my Sav-iour, hide, Till the storm of life is past;_____ Safe in-to the ha-ven guide; O re-ceive my soul at last.___

004 ii (6—solo piano)	Allegretto [from] *Symphony No. 4*
004 iv (24—clarinet)	Largo [from] *Symphony No. 4*
088 ii (p. 33, score 1)	*Hawthorne* [from] *Sonata No. 2 for Piano: Concord, Mass., 1840–60*
088 iii (p. 53, score 3)	*The Alcotts* [from] *Sonata No. 2 for Piano: Concord, Mass., 1840–60*
116 (f4858, staff 25, right hand)	*The Celestial Railroad*
123 i (f4908, staff 1, m. 2, right hand)	Slowly [from] *Four Transcriptions from "Emerson"*
123 ii (f4910, staff 3, right hand)	Moderato [from] *Four Transcriptions from "Emerson"*
123 iv (f4919, staff 2, right hand)	Allegro agitato-Broadly [from] *Four Transcriptions from "Emerson"*

Possible borrowing:

088 i (p. 19, score 3, right hand)	*Emerson* [from] *Sonata No. 2 for Piano: Concord, Mass., 1840–60*
088 iv (p. 6, staff 1)	*Thoreau* [from] *Sonata No. 2 for Piano: Concord, Mass., 1840–60*

36

MATERNA

("O mother dear, Jerusalem")

SOURCE: *The New Hymnal,* 510

Earliest form of text is in
British Library, Ms. Add. 15225,
based on passages from 15th-century *Meditationes*

SAMUEL A. WARD, 1882

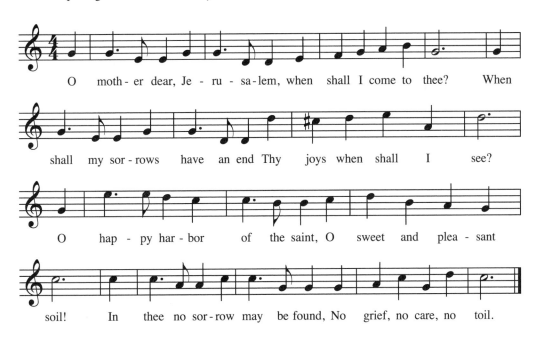

O moth-er dear, Je-ru-sa-lem, when shall I come to thee? When
shall my sor-rows have an end Thy joys when shall I see?
O hap-py har-bor of the saint, O sweet and plea-sant
soil! In thee no sor-row may be found, No grief, no care, no toil.

002 iii (14—violin I)

009 i (p. 9: q2998; section C of sketch; staff 15)
does not appear in Porter's performance
score

009 ii (p. 16: n3002; section 2, staff 1; violin II)

Adagio cantabile [from] *Symphony No. 2*

[Andante moderato] [from] *Orchestral
Set No. 3*

*An Afternoon or During Camp Meetin' Week—
One Secular Afternoon (In Bethel)* [from]
Orchestral Set No. 3

36-a

MERCY

(See also 180)

("Softly now the light of day")

SOURCE: *The Methodist Hymnal,* no. 53

George W. Doane

LOUIS MOREAU GOTTSCHALK
arr. by Edwin Pond Parker

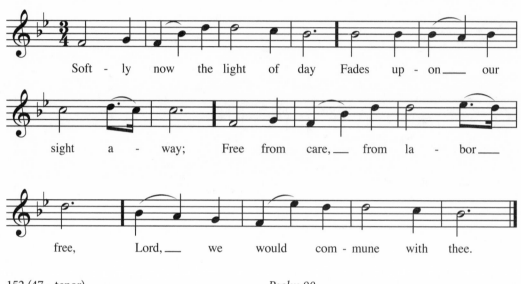

Soft - ly now the light of day Fades up - on____ our sight a - way; Free from care,____ from la - bor____ free, Lord,____ we would com - mune with thee.

152 (47—tenor)

Psalm 90

37

MISSIONARY CHANT

("Ye Christian heralds, go, proclaim")

SOURCE: *The Baptist Praise Book,* no. 1202

Bourne Hall Draper, 1803

CHARLES ZEUNER, pub. 1832

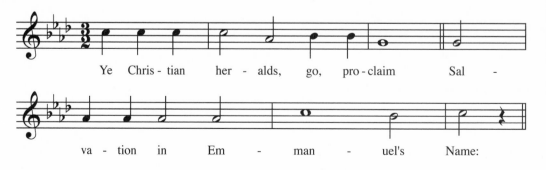

Ye Chris - tian her - alds, go, pro - claim Sal - va - tion in Em - man - uel's Name:

To dis - tant climes the tid - ings bear,

and plant the Rose of Shar - on there.

002 iii (45—horns I and II)	Adagio cantabile [from] *Symphony No. 2*
002 v (228—trumpet II)	Allegro molto vivace [from] *Symphony No. 2*
004 iv (36—flute)	Largo [from] *Symphony No. 4*
007 iii (6—horn)	*The Housatonic at Stockbridge* [from] *Orchestral Set No. 1: Three Places in New England*
016 i (f6156, m. 8—voice)	*At Sea* [from] *Set No. 7: Water Colors*
021 (f2488)	*Alcott Overture* [mostly lost]
022 (f2214, brace 3)	*Emerson Overture for Piano and Orchestra* [incomplete]
088 iii (p. 53, staff 1)	*The Alcotts* [from] *Sonata No. 2 for Piano: Concord, Mass., 1840–60*
266 (6—voice)	*The Housatonic at Stockbridge*

Possible borrowing:

012 i (f2743, m. 8—English horn)	*Adagio sostenuto: At Sea* [from] *Set No. 3*
022 (f2214, brace 3)	Emerson Overture for Piano and Orchestra [incomplete]
213 (8—voice)	*At Sea*

38

MISSIONARY HYMN

("From Greenland's icy mountains")

SOURCE: *The Baptist Praise Book*, no. 1233

Reginald Heber, 1819   LOWELL MASON, ca. 1825

From green - land's i - cy moun - tains, From In - dia's cor - al

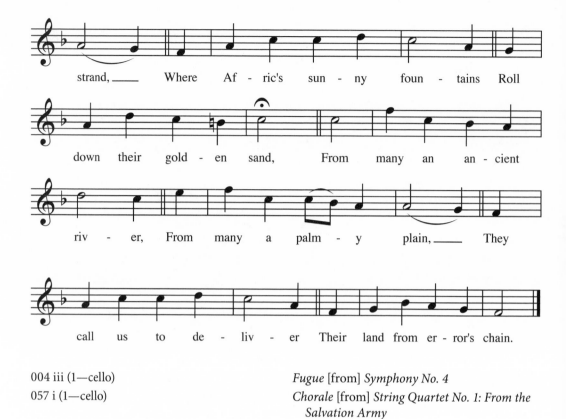

strand, ___ Where Af - ric's sun - ny foun - tains Roll down their gold - en sand, From many an an - cient riv - er, From many a palm - y plain, ___ They call us to de - liv - er Their land from er - ror's chain.

004 iii (1—cello)   *Fugue* [from] *Symphony No. 4*
057 i (1—cello)   *Chorale* [from] *String Quartet No. 1: From the Salvation Army*

39

MORE LOVE TO THEE

("More love to thee, O Christ")

SOURCE: *The Coronation Hymnal,* no. 150

Elizabeth P. Prentice   WILLIAM HOWARD DOANE, 1870

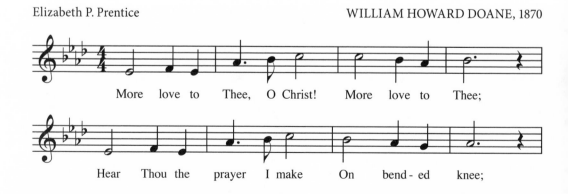

More love to Thee, O Christ! More love to Thee;

Hear Thou the prayer I make On bend - ed knee;

This is my earn-est plea, More love, O Christ, to Thee,

More love to Thee! More love to Thee!

084 i (4—violin I) *Largo cantabile: Hymn* [from] *A Set of Three Short Pieces*

267 (6—piano) *Hymn*

40

NAOMI

("Now from the altar of my heart")

SOURCE: *The Baptist Praise Book,* no. 390

John Mason, 1683

arr. from JOHANN G. NAEGELI
by LOWELL MASON, pub. 1836

Now from the al-tar__ of__ my heart Let in-cense flames a-rise;

As-sist me, Lord, to__ of-fer up Mine eve-ning sac-ri-fice.

002 ii (145—trombone I) *Allegro* [from] *Symphony No. 2*
003 ii (2—horn) *Children's Day* [from] *Symphony No. 3: The Camp Meeting*

41

NEED

("I need thee ev'ry hour")

SOURCE: *The Coronation Hymnal,* no. 377

Annie S. Hawks, 1872
refrain by Robert Lowry, 1872   ROBERT LOWRY, 1872

I need thee ev - 'ry hour, Most gra - cious

Lord; No ten - der voice like Thine can

Refrain

peace af - ford. I need Thee, O I

need Thee; Ev - 'ry hour I need Thee! O

bless me now, my sav - iour, I come to Thee.

062 i (4—violin)   Adagio [from] *Sonata No. 3 for Violin and Piano*

062 iii (1—piano)   Adagio cantabile [from] *Sonata No. 3 for Violin and Piano*

Possible borrowing:
    089 (37)   *Three-Page Sonata*

42

NETTLETON

(Hallelujah)

("Come, Thou Fount of ev'ry blessing")

SOURCE: *The Baptist Praise Book,* no. 349

Robert Robinson, 1758   attr. to ASAHEL NETTLETON, or JOHN WYETH, ca. 1812

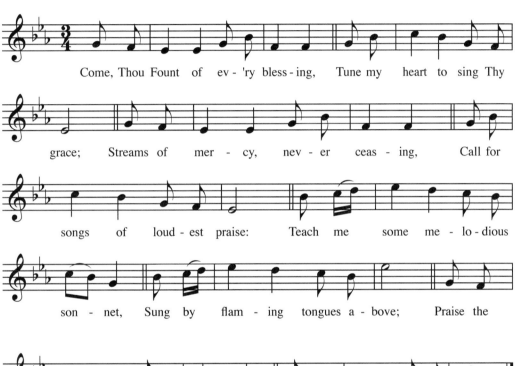

Come, Thou Fount of ev - 'ry bless - ing, Tune my heart to sing Thy grace; Streams of mer - cy, nev - er ceas - ing, Call for songs of loud - est praise: Teach me some me - lo - dious son - net, Sung by flam - ing tongues a - bove; Praise the

mount I'm fixed up - on it Mount of Thy re-deem-ing love.

002 i (10—violin I)	Andante moderato [from] *Symphony No. 2*
002 iii (49—horns I and II)	Adagio cantabile [from] *Symphony No. 2*
004 ii (13—violins I [2 only])	Allegretto [from] *Symphony No. 4*
004 iv (52—celesta)	Largo [from] *Symphony No. 4*
005 iv (35—flute)	*Thanksgiving and Forefathers' Day* [from] *A Symphony: New England Holidays*
008 i (23—zither)	*An Elegy to Our Forefathers* [from] *Orchestral Set No. 2*
009 i (33—celesta)	[Andante moderato] [from] *Orchestral Set No. 3*
009 iii (p. 28: n3057, staff 3)	[no tempo heading] [from] *Orchestral Set No. 3* [incomplete]

039 (f2490)	*Piece for Small Orchestra and Organ* [mostly lost]
057 iii (1—violin I)	*Offertory* [from] *String Quartet No. 1: From the Salvation Army*
058 iii (13—violins)	*The Call of the Mountains* [from] *String Quartet No. 2*
061 iii (1—violin)	*The Revival* [from] *Sonata No. 2 for Violin and Piano*
063 iv-a (f3278, staff 1, violin)	rejected *Adagio-Faster* [from] *Sonata No. 4 for Violin and Piano;* developed into 3rd movement of *Sonata No. 3 for Violin and Piano*
084 iii (3—piano)	*Adagio cantabile: The Innate* [from] *Three Short Pieces*
137 i (f5067, m. 1)	*Interludes for Hymns*
284 (27—voice)	*The Innate*
372 (7—voice)	*The Things Our Fathers Loved*

Possible borrowing:

12 i (f2777, staff 1, m. 1)	*Adagio sostenuto: At Sea* [from] *Set No. 3*
12 ii (f2777, staff 1, m. 1) or *Bethany* 7	*Luck and Work* [from] *Set No. 3*
19 ii (f2770, m. 5—Basset horn)	*Allegro-Andante: Luck and Work* [from] *Set No. 10 of Three Pieces*
293 (5—voice)	*Luck and Work*

43

OH, NOBODY KNOWS THE TROUBLE I'VE SEEN

("Oh, nobody knows the trouble I've seen")

SOURCE: *American Hymns Old and New,* p. 320

as early as 1865

Oh, no-bod-y knows the trou-ble I've seen, No-bod-y knows but Je-sus,

Fine

No-bod-y know the trou-ble I've seen, Glo-ry, Hal-le - lu - jah! Some-
Al -

times I'm up, some - times I'm down,   Oh,   yes,   Lord;   some - times I'm al - most
though you see me   goin' long so,   Oh,   yes,   Lord;   I   have my tri - als

D.C. al Fine

to   de   groun';   Oh,   yes,   Lord. _____
here be - low,   Oh,   yes,   Lord. _____

008 i (15—trumpet II)   *An Elegy to Our Forefathers* [from] *Orchestral Set No. 2*

44
OLD HUNDREDTH
(preferred text unknown)

SOURCE: *The Baptist Praise Book,* no. 52

attr. to LOUS BOURGEOIS, pub. 1551

009 i (2—bass)   [Andante moderato] [from] *Orchestral Set No. 3*
009 iii (p. 36: n3244, staff 6)   [no tempo heading] [from] *Orchestral Set No. 3*
                                     [incomplete]

45

OLD, OLD STORY

("Tell me the old, old story")

SOURCE: *The Baptist Hymnal,* no. 184

Catherine Hankey, 1865   WILLIAM HOWARD DOANE, 1866 or 1867

Tell me the old, old sto - ry of Un - seen things a -
bove, Of Je - sus and His glo - ry, Of
Je - sus and His love: Tell me the sto - ry
sim - ply As to a lit - tle child, For
I am weak and wea - ry, And help - less and de -

Refrain

filed. Tell me the old, old sto - ry.

Tell me the old, old sto - ry, Tell me the old, old sto - ry, of Je - sus and His love.

063 i (8—violin)

Allegro [from] *Sonata No. 4 for Violin and Piano: Children's Day at the Camp Meeting*

46

OLIVET

("My faith looks up to Thee")

SOURCE: *The Baptist Praise Book,* no. 1017

Ray Palmer, 1830

LOWELL MASON, pub. 1833

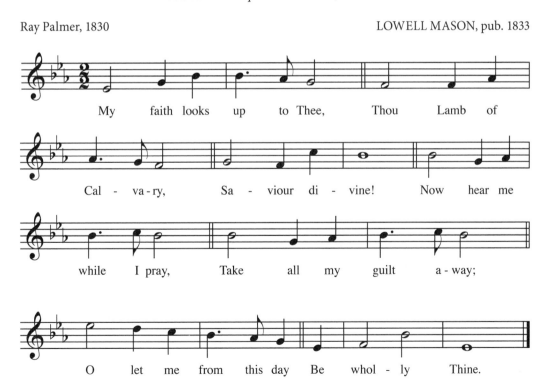

My faith looks up to Thee, Thou Lamb of Cal - va - ry, Sa - viour di - vine! Now hear me while I pray, Take all my guilt a - way; O let me from this day Be whol - ly Thine.

084 i (27—cello)   *Largo cantabile: Hymn* [from] *A Set of Three Short Pieces*

267 (21—voice)   *Hymn*

Possible borrowing:

    235 (12—voice) or *Antioch* 3   *Disclosure*

47

ONWARD, UPWARD

("Onward, upward! Christian soldier")

SOURCE: *Gospel Hymns Nos. 1–6*, no. 60

Frances Jane Crosby   IRA DAVID SANKEY

mands   thee,   Take   the   cross   and   win   the   crown.

181 (73—voice)   *General William Booth Enters into Heaven*

255 (72—voice)   *General William Booth Enters into Heaven*

48

PARAH

(preferred text unknown)

SOURCE: *The Church Book,* no. 22

LOWELL MASON

022 (f2214, brace 3)   *Emerson Overture for Piano and Orchestra*
                                                   [incomplete]

Possible borrowing:

    may be *Missionary Chant* 37 or
    Beethoven, *Symphony No. 5* i 173

49

PROPRIOR DEO

("More love to Thee, O Christ!")

SOURCE: *Laudes Domini,* no. 678

Elizabeth Prentiss, 1869   ARTHUR SEYMOUR SULLIVAN, pub. 1872

More   love   to   Thee,   O   Christ!   More   love   to   Thee!

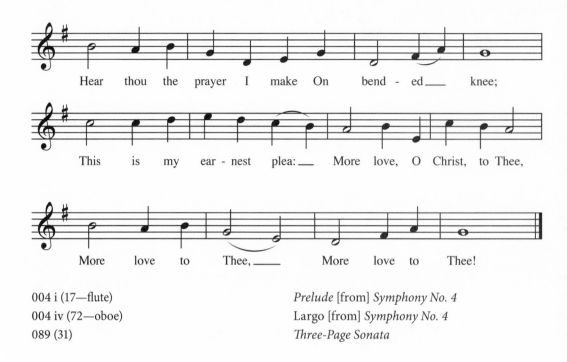

Hear thou the prayer I make On bend - ed knee;
This is my ear - nest plea: More love, O Christ, to Thee,
More love to Thee, More love to Thee!

004 i (17—flute)	*Prelude* [from] *Symphony No. 4*
004 iv (72—oboe)	*Largo* [from] *Symphony No. 4*
089 (31)	*Three-Page Sonata*

49-a

RATHBUN

("In the cross of Christ I glory")

SOURCE: *The Methodist Hymnal,* no. 143

John Bowring   ITHAMAR CONKEY, 1851

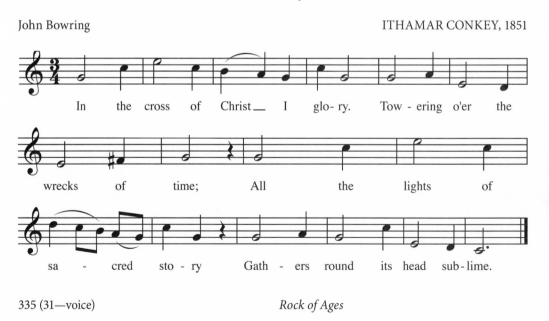

In the cross of Christ I glo- ry. Tow - ering o'er the
wrecks of time; All the lights of
sa - cred sto - ry Gath - ers round its head sub - lime.

335 (31—voice)   *Rock of Ages*

50

RETREAT

("From ev'ry stormy wind that blows")

SOURCE: *The Baptist Praise Book,* no. 27

Hugh Stowell

THOMAS HASTINGS, pub. 1842

From ev - 'ry storm - y wind that blows From ev - 'ry swell - ing tide of woes, There is a calm, a sure re-treat, 'Tis found be - neath the mer - cy seat.____

009 iii (p. 37: n3056, staff 6)

[no tempo heading] [from] *Orchestral Set No. 3*
[incomplete]

51

ST. HILDA

(St. Edith)

("O Jesus Thou Art Standing")

SOURCE: *Hymns of the Faith,* no. 245

William Walsham How, 1867

arr. by EDWARD HUSBAND, 1871
from JUSTIN H. KNECHT, 1799

O Je - sus Thou art stand-ing Out - side the fast - closed door, In low - ly____ pa - tience wait - ing To

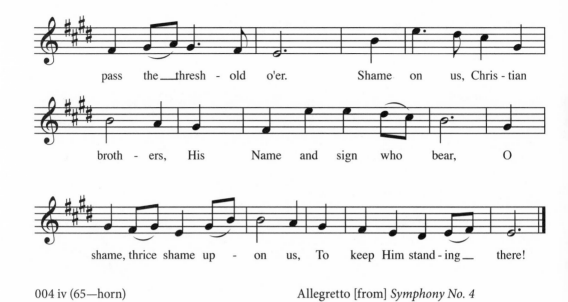

pass the thresh-old o'er. Shame on us, Chris-tian broth-ers, His Name and sign who bear, O shame, thrice shame up - on us, To keep Him stand-ing there!

004 iv (65—horn)   Allegretto [from] *Symphony No. 4*

52

ST. PETER

(preferred text unknown)

SOURCE: *The Church Book,* no. 237

ALEXANDER ROBERT REINAGLE, pub. ca. 1836

018 i (f2750, m. 17—English horn)	*Andante con moto: The Last Reader [from] Set No. 9 of Three Pieces*
273 (13—voice)	*Immortality*
286 (2—voice)	*The Last Reader*
379 (2—voice)	*Two Little Flowers*
Possible borrowing:	
011 iii (f2699, m. 17)	*Andante: The Last Reader [from] Set No. 2*

52-a

SEARCH ME, O LORD

Note: This may be by Ives or

it may be a borrowed tune by an unidentified composer.

[see Kirkpatrick in *American Grove*, p. 519]

This tune is placed here because of its

hymn-like qualities

446 (1—soprano)   *Search Me, O Lord*

53

SERENITY

(Ives quotes stanza from John Greenleaf Whittier's

Immortal Love, Forever Full, 1836)

SOURCE: *The Friends' Hymnal*, no. 328

Note: This source has words by L. Bacon: "Hail, tranquil hour of closing day!"

arr. from WILLIAM VINCENT WALLACE, 1855

015 ii (f6161, staff 2, m. 1—voice)   *The Rainbow* [from] *Set No. 6: From the Side Hill*
045 (12—English/basset horn)   *The Rainbow*
177 (f5593, m. 14—voice)   *Serenity* [mostly lost]
330 (13—voice)   *The Rainbow (So May It Be!)*
347 (2—voice)   *Serenity*

54

SHINING SHORE

("My days are gliding swiftly by")

SOURCE: *The Baptist Praise Book,* no. 1043

David Nelson, 1835   GEORGE FREDERICK ROOT, 1859

My days are glid - ing swift - ly by, And
I, a pil - grim stran - ger, Would not de - tain them,
as they fly, Those hours of toil and dan - ger; For
as we stand on Jor - dan's strand; Our
friends are pass - ing o - ver; And, just be - fore, the
shin - ing shore We may al - most dis - cov - er.

001 i (10—violin II)	Allegro [from] *Symphony No. 1*
005 iv (9—flute)	*Thanksgiving and Forefathers' Day* [from] *A Symphony: New England Holidays*
009 i (22—trombone)	[Andante moderato] [from] *Orchestral Set No. 3*
009 ii (p. 15: n3002, staff 5)	*An Afternoon or During Camp Meetin' Week— One Secular Afternoon (In Bethel)* [from] *Orchestral Set No. 3* [incomplete]

009 iii (p. 28: n3063, staff 2)	[no tempo heading] [from] *Orchestral Set No. 3* [incomplete]
057 ii (12—violin I)	*Prelude* [from] *String Quartet No. 1: From the Salvation Army*
057 iii (58—cello)	*Offertory* [from] *String Quartet No. 1: From the Salvation Army*
057 iv (147—violin II)	*Postlude* [from] *String Quartet No. 1: From the Salvation Army*
060 i (17—piano)	Andante-Allegro vivace [from] *Sonata for Violin and Piano No. 1*
069 (f3036, m. 1—cello)	*Fugue in 4 Keys on "The Shining Shore"* [incomplete]
282 (f6766)	*Incomplete song* [II]
318 (11—voice)	*On Judges' Walk*
331 (1—voice)	*Religion*
339 (12—voice)	*Rough Wind*

Possible borrowing:

397 (13—voice)	*The World's Highway*

Shining Shore also appears on manuscript pages 0888 and 0892 that are sketches for *Prelude for Thanksgiving Service* (lost; x701) and for *Postlude for Thanksgiving Service* (mostly lost 139)

55

SOMETHING FOR THEE

("Saviour, Thy dying love")

SOURCE: *Hymns of Worship and Service,* no. 255

Sylvanus Dryden Phelps, 1867   THEODORE EDSON PERKINS

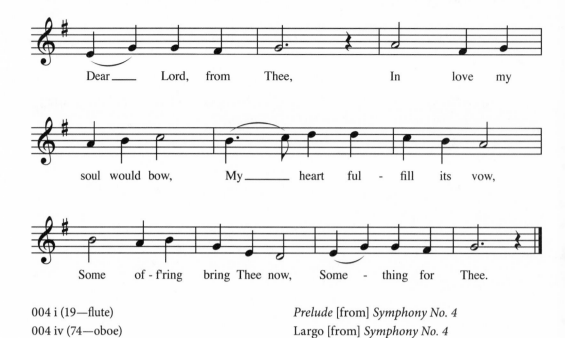

Dear___ Lord, from Thee, In love my soul would bow, My___ heart ful - fill its vow, Some of - f'ring bring Thee now, Some - thing for Thee.

004 i (19—flute) Prelude [from] *Symphony No. 4*
004 iv (74—oboe) Largo [from] *Symphony No. 4*

56

TAPPAN

(preferred text unknown)

SOURCE: *The Baptist Praise Book,* no. 156

GEORGE KINGSLEY, 1839

230 (8—voice) *The Collection*

56-a

TE DEUM

Note: The following example is taken from Ives's *From Hanover Square North, at the End of a Tragic Day, the Voice of the People Again Arose*, mm. 1–13

We __ praise Thee O God __ We ac-knowl-edge Thee to
be the Lord __ All the Earth doth wor - ship Thee __

008 iii (1—voice)

From Hanover Square North, at the End of a Tragic Day, the Voice of the People Again Arose [from] *Orchestra Set No. 2*

57

THERE IS A HAPPY LAND

("There is a happy land")

SOURCE: *The Baptist Praise Book,* no. 1057

Andrew Young

Hindoo air arr. by LOWELL MASON

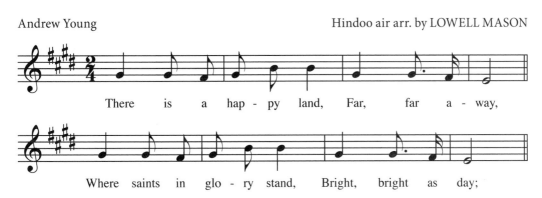

There is a hap - py land, Far, far a - way,
Where saints in glo - ry stand, Bright, bright as day;

Oh, how they sweet - ly sing, Wor - thy is our Sav - iour King,

Loud let his prais - es ring, Praise, praise for aye!

002 iii (15—violin II)	Adagio cantabile [from] *Symphony No. 2*
003 ii (50—flute)	*Children's Day* [from] *Symphony No. 3*
004 ii (115—flute)	Allegretto [from] *Symphony No. 4*
004 iv (65—oboe)	Largo [from] *Symphony No. 4*
087 v (143)	Andante maestoso-Adagio cantabile-Allegro-Andante [from] *Sonata No. 1 for Piano*

58

THERE'LL BE NO DARK VALLEY

(Ives refers to this hymn by its 2nd stanza, "There'll be no more
sorrow when Jesus comes," in *Memos*, p. 69, section 24, note 1)

SOURCE: *The Greatest Hymns*, no. 353

William Orcutt Cushing   IRA DAVID SANKEY, © 1896

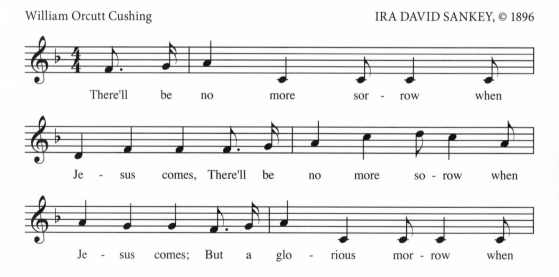

There'll be no more sor - row when

Je - sus comes, There'll be no more so - row when

Je - sus comes; But a glo - rious mor - row when

Je - sus comes To gath - er his loved ones home.

Refrain

To gath - er his loved ones home, To ___ gath - er his loved ones home; There'll be no dark val - ley when Je - sus comes To gath - er his loved ones home.

062 ii (15—violin)   Allegro [from] *Sonata No. 3 for Violin and Piano*

59

THROW OUT THE LIFE-LINE

("Throw out the Life-Line across the dark wave")

SOURCE: *Male Chorus No. 1,* no. 35

Edward S. Ufford   EDWARD S. UFFORD, pub. 1888

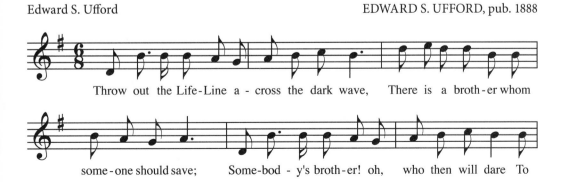

Throw out the Life-Line a - cross the dark wave, There is a broth - er whom some - one should save; Some - bod - y's broth - er! oh, who then will dare To

throw out the Life - Line, his per - il to share?

Throw out the Life - Line! Throw out the Life - Line! Some-one is drift - ing a -

way;___ Throw out the Life - Line! Throw out the Life - Line!

Some - one is sink - ing to - day___

004 ii (35—cello)   Allegretto [from] *Symphony No. 4*
037 (f2211, brace 2)   *The General Slocum* [incomplete]
116 (f4857, staff 1)   *The Celestial Railroad*
Possible borrowing:
   107 (53)   *Study No. 23: Allegro*

60

TOPLADY

("Rock of Ages, cleft for me")

SOURCE: *The Baptist Praise Book,* no. 692

Augustus Montague Toplady   THOMAS HASTINGS, pub. 1831

Rock of A - ges, cleft for me, Let me hide my-self in

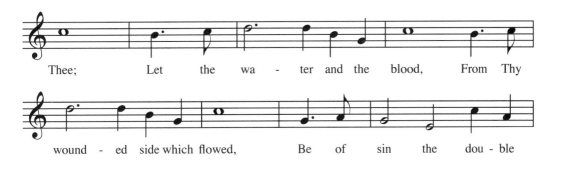

Thee; Let the wa - ter and the blood, From Thy
wound - ed side which flowed, Be of sin the dou - ble
cure, Save from wrath and make me pure.

086 iii (130—cello)

Presto ("TSIAJ" or Medley on the Fence [or]
on the Campus!) [from] *Trio for Violin,
Violoncello, and Piano*

60-a

VALENTIA

(preferred text unknown)

SOURCE: *Hymns and Songs for Social and Sabbath Worship*

TRAUGOTT MAXIMILIAN EBERWEIN
arr. by GEORGE KINGSLEY

005 iv (43—oboe I)

Thanksgiving and Forefathers' Day [from]
A Symphony: New England Holidays

61

WATCHMAN

("Watchman, tell us of the night")

SOURCE: *The New Hymnal,* no. 106

John Bowring, 1825   LOWELL MASON, 1830

Watch - man, tell   us   of   the night,   What   its   signs   of

prom - ise are.   Trav - 'ler, o'er   yon   moun - tain's height,

See   that glo - ry - beam - ing star.   Watch - man, does   its

beau - teous ray   Aught   of   joy   or   hope   fore - tell?

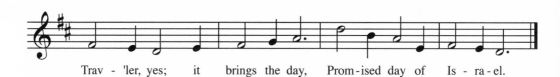

Trav - 'ler, yes;   it   brings the day,   Prom - ised day of   Is - ra - el.

004 i (17→voices)	*Prelude* [from] *Symphony No. 4*
060 iii (41—violin)	Allegro [from] *Sonata No. 1 for Violin and Piano*
386 (5—voice)	*Watchman*
Possible borrowing:	
286 (20—voice) (or possibly *Jesus Loves Me* 30)	*The Last Reader*

62

WEBB

("Stand up, stand up for Jesus")

SOURCE: *The Baptist Praise Book,* no. 965

George Duffield, Jr., 1858   GEORGE JAMES WEBB, 1837

Stand up, stand up for Je - sus, Ye sol - diers of the cross, Lift high His roy - al ban - ner, It must not suf - fer loss. From vic - t'ry un - to vic - t'ry His ar - my shall He lead;_____ Till

ev - 'ry foe is van - quished, And Christ is Lord in - deed.

057 iv (2—violin I)   *Postlude* [from] *String Quartet No. 1: From the Salvation Army*

63
WELCOME VOICE
("I hear Thy welcome voice")

SOURCE: *The Baptist Hymnal Book,* no. 303

Lewis Hartsough

LEWIS HARTSOUGH, 1872

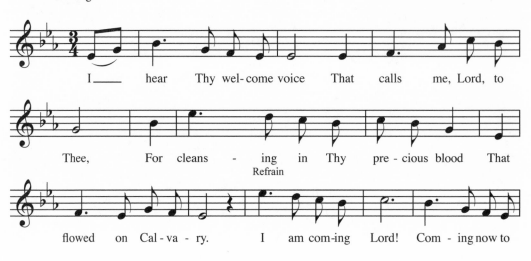

I___ hear Thy wel-come voice That calls me, Lord, to

Thee, For cleans - ing in Thy pre - cious blood That

Refrain

flowed on Cal - va - ry. I am com-ing Lord! Com - ing now to

Thee! Wash me, cleanse me in the blood That flowed on Cal-va - ry!

004 i (23—flute)	*Prelude* [from] *Symphony No. 4*
004 iii (111—clarinet)	*Fugue* [from] *Symphony No. 4*
008 ii (127—violin I)	*The Rockstrewn Hills Join in the People's Outdoor Meeting* [from] *Orchestral Set No. 2*
020 ii (125—violin)	*"In the Inn"* [from] *Set for Theatre Orchestra*
042 ii (f2481, staff 1, m. 3)	*[2nd Ragtime Dance]* [from] *Three Ragtime Dances* [mostly lost]
043 i (96—violin)	*Ragtime Dance No. 1* [from] *Four Ragtime Dances*
043 ii (63—violin)	*Ragtime Dance No. 2* [from] *Four Ragtime Dances*
043 iii (104—violin)	*Ragtime Dance No. 3* [from] *Four Ragtime Dances*
043 iv (104—flute)	*Ragtime Dance No. 4* [from] *Four Ragtime Dances*
087 iib (184)	Allegro-Meno mosso con moto; *"In the Inn"* [from] *Sonata No. 1 for Piano*
087 iva (98)	[no tempo heading] [from] *Sonata No. 1 for Piano*
087 ivb (149)	Allegro-Presto-Slow [from] *Sonata No. 1 for Piano*

64

WHERE IS MY WANDERING BOY?

("Where is my wand'ring boy tonight?")

SOURCE: *Male Chorus No. 1,* no. 73

Robert Lowry

ROBERT LOWRY, © 1877

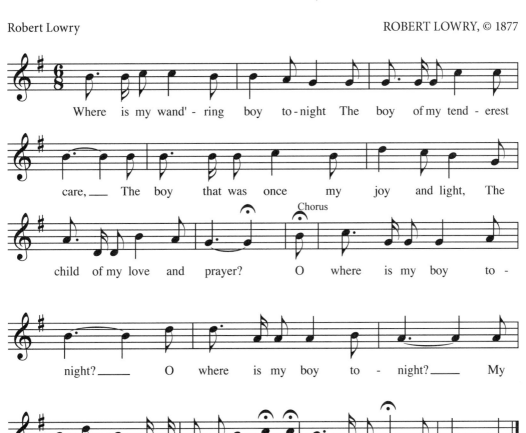

Where is my wand'- ring boy to-night The boy of my tend - erest

care, ___ The boy that was once my joy and light, The

child of my love and prayer? O where is my boy to -

night? ___ O where is my boy to - night? ___ My

heart o'er-flows, For I love him, he knows; O where is my boy to - night? ___

087 i

Adagio con moto-Andante con moto-Allegro-
risoluto-Adagio cantabile [from] *Sonata No.
1 for Piano*

65

WILD BELLS

("Ring out, wild bells, to the wild, wild sky")

SOURCE: *Hymns for the Living Age,* no. 107

Alfred Tennyson, 1850

HENRY LAHEE, ca. 1875

Ring out, wild bells, to the wild, wild sky, The fly - ing cloud the __ frost - y light; The year is dy - ing in the night; Ring out, wild bells and __ let him die.

065 (f2421, m. 1—high bells I)

From the Steeples and the Mountains

66

WINDSOR

(Eton)

(Dundee)

("That awful day will surely come")

SOURCE: *The Baptist Praise Book,* no. 661

Isaac Watts, 1707

first appears in WILLIAM DAMON'S (DAMAN) *Book of Musicke,* 1591

That aw - ful day will sure - ly come, Th'ap - point - ed hour makes haste,

When I must stand be - fore my judge, and pass the sol - emn test.

009 ii (p. 19: n3004, staff 9)

An Afternoon or During Camp Meetin' Week—
One Secular Afternoon (In Bethel) [from]
Orchestral Set No. 3 [incomplete]

67

WOODWORTH

("Just as I am, without one plea")

SOURCE: *The Baptist Praise Book,* no. 65b

Charlotte Elliott, 1836   WILLIAM BATCHELDER BRADBURY, pub. 1849

003 i (55—horns)   *Old Folks Gatherin'* [from] *Symphony No. 3:*
The Camp Meeting

003 iii (1—cello)   *Communion* [from] *Symphony No. 3: The Camp*
Meeting

009 i (28—woodwinds)   [Andante moderato] [from] *Orchestral Set No. 3*

009 iii (p. 28: n3057, staff 1, harp)   [no tempo heading] [from] *Orchestral Set No. 3*
[incomplete]

137 iv (f2352)   *Interlude for "Woodworth"* [from] *Interlude for*
Hymns

222 (11—voice)   *The Camp Meeting*

68

WORK SONG

(Diligence)

("Work, for the night is coming")

SOURCE: *The Baptist Praise Book,* no. 933

Annie L. Coghill

LOWELL MASON, 1864

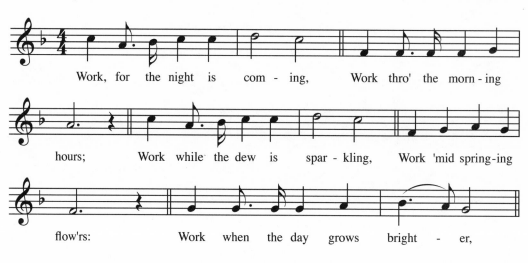

060 ii (82—violin)

Largo cantabile [from] *Sonata No. 1 for Violin and Piano*

060 iii (1—piano)

Allegro [from] *Sonata No. 1 for Violin and Piano*

[2]

Patriotic Songs and Military Music

Most of this music played an informal, but important, role in Ives's musical education. Many of these tunes were associated with the Civil War, a tragedy less than a generation removed from Ives's formative years. His father, George, who enlisted in the Union army in June 1863 at the age of seventeen, achieved a certain degree of celebrity as the young leader of the First Connecticut Volunteer Heavy Artillery First Brigade Band.[1] The tunes that his band played and that people sang to spur on the northern cause were among the most popular this nation has known, and they were still fresh in peoples' minds and ears when Charles was growing up.

Ives's use of patriotic music was not limited to the evocation of Civil War atmosphere. *Putnam's Camp, Redding, Connecticut* depicts "Once upon a '4th of July'."[2] A young boy (undoubtedly Ives himself) wanders away from a church picnic, lies down and begins to fall asleep; as he does, the "tunes of the band and the songs of the children grow fainter and fainter"[3] and are replaced by tunes from an earlier day, sounded by a fife and drum corps. Following a glimpse of Revolutionary War times, the boy awakens and his thoughts return to the present as he hears the tunes of his own day. In this work, Ives evokes his present and moves through the past to General Israel Putnam's quarters in the winter of 1778–89. He accomplishes his evocation of three different time levels—truly a *tour de force*—with citations from *Liberty Bell March* and *Semper Fideles* to reflect on his present of the 1880s and 1890s. He revisits Civil War days with borrowings from *Marching Through Georgia, The Battle Cry of Freedom, Massa's in de Cold Ground,* and *Happy Day;* and he summons up the late eighteenth and early nineteenth centuries with *Yankee Doodle, Hail! Columbia,* and *The British Grenadiers.*

Ives also extended his musical patriotism into the twentieth century, albeit not on as grand a scale as was his look to the past. In the songs *He Is There!, In Flanders Fields,* and *Tom Sails Away,* Ives commented on World War I. *He Is There!,* the most obvious of the three with its boisterous march rhythms, its unabashed enthusiasm for taking on the enemy, and its citations from *Yankee Doodle, Tenting on the Old Camp Ground,* and George M. Cohan's *Over There,* among others, strikes the contemporary listener with its wide-eyed naive and optimistic spirit. *In Flanders Fields* sounds a somewhat more tempered, although impassioned, tone with its words spoken by one of the soldiers who now lies buried in Flanders Fields. The citations of patriotic music are nearly always at the surface again; one cannot fail to be aware of most of them. On the other hand, *Tom Sails Away* is a gem of understatement for most of its length. Opening and closing with hushed recollections of "scenes from my childhood are with me"/ "are floating before my eyes" (to *Araby's Daughter* or *The Old Oaken Bucket*), the song builds to its climactic point when "In freedom's cause Tom sailed away for over there!" At that point, *Columbia, the Gem of the Ocean* is sounded on the piano and Cohan's *Over There* underpins the words in the vocal line. These songs are Ives's tributes to the gallant men who fought in the "Great War."

In 1942 Ives wrote new words to *He Is There!* of 1917 to fashion a patriotic song for World War II: *They Are There!*

Overture and March "1776" is one of Ives's works in which borrowed tunes charmingly transcend the limitations of their time of composition. While appropriate period music is included in the piece, intended for an opera about Benedict Arnold that Ives and his uncle Lyman Brewster had contemplated writing, Ives also used tunes from Civil War times.

In those compositions whose subject deals with the conflicts in which America has been involved, Ives touched on the two world wars of the twentieth century only briefly, in comparatively short works. On the other hand, he afforded the American Revolutionary War and especially the war between the states much more impressive and extensive treatments. His wish to evoke and to romanticize earlier periods in American history—more particularly that in which his father was involved—is obvious. Even though they were not of his own personal experience, those eras—through his father—figured prominently in his creative life.

An element one finds in nearly all of Ives's music in which borrowed patriotic tunes figure prominently is the "Street beat" or "Street cadence"—what Kirkpatrick refers to as "piano-drum writing."[4] These figures add to the rhythmic thrust of the music, effecting a mood appropriate to Ives's musical description. In *Decoration Day,* for example, the trumpeter sounds *Taps* and the notes of "Nearer, my God, to Thee" (*Bethany*)—"a last hymn"— are heard in the first violins "after the last grave is decorated." At the final note of *Taps,* the mood of the day and that of the music begin to change with the quiet announcement of a "Street beat" pattern in violas, cellos, and basses, joined two measures later by timpani. The "ranks are formed again" and within eight short measures, the "Street beat" has pushed the music forward from the mood of somber reflection to the outburst of thanksgiving in a glorious citation of Reeves's march, that "Yankee stimulant."

"Street beat" writing illustrated a practical side of Ives's musical education—something that went far beyond textbook learning. It reflected yet again the strong influence of father upon son. Charles recalled:

> When I was a boy, I played in my father's brass band, usually one of the drums. Except when counting rests, the practicing was done on a rubber-top cheese box or on the piano. The snare and bass drum parts were written on the same staff, and there were plenty of dittos. In practicing the drum parts on the piano (not on the drum—neighbours' requests), I remember getting tired of using the tonic and dominant and

subdominant triads, and Doh and Soh etc. in the bass. So [I] got to trying out sets of notes to go with or take-off the drums—for the snare drum, right-hand notes usually closer together—and for the bass drum, wider chords. They had little to do with the harmony of the piece, and were used only as sound-combinations as such. For the explosive notes or heavy accents in either drum, the fist or flat of the hand was sometimes used, usually longer groups in the right hand than left hand.[5]

What the young boy did under the guidance and the approval of George—"Father didn't object to all of this, if it was done with some musical sense. . . ."—he then revisits time and again in his adult work as a composer.[6]

With the exception of some of the tunes connected with the pre–Civil War period, most of the examples included here were selected from the original sheet music or from twentieth-century anthologies. Since music from *The Star Spangled Banner, America,* and *Hail! Columbia* underwent alterations between the times when they first appeared and Ives's own day, I have given them in the late nineteenth-century versions more familiar to Ives and to us than are their original renderings.

AMERICA

("My country, 'tis of thee")

SOURCE: *Twice 55 Plus Community Songs,* no. 1

Samuel Francis Smith, 1831

1st appearance of music:
Harmonia Anglicana (1744)
1st printing of Smith's words with this tune: 1832

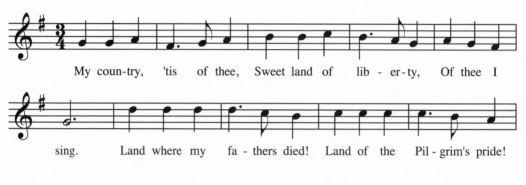

My coun-try, 'tis of thee, Sweet land of lib - er-ty, Of thee I

sing. Land where my fa - thers died! Land of the Pil - grim's pride!

From ev - 'ry — moun - tain - side, Let — free - dom ring!

002 iii (72—flute)	Adagio cantabile [from] *Symphony No. 2*
128 iii (6—piano I)	*Chorale* [from] *Three Quarter-Tone Pieces*
140 (1)	*Variations on "America"*
184 (32—trumpet)	*Lincoln, the Great Commoner*
187 (19—piano)	*Sneak Thief* [incomplete]
277 (14—voice)	*In Flanders Fields*
289 (voice—32)	*Lincoln, the Great Commoner*

70

ASSEMBLY

SOURCE: Sousa, *A Book of Instruction,* p. 67

1st known appearance: 1842

another version

005 iii (27—horn)

315 (44—obligato)

The Fourth of July [from] *A Symphony: New England Holidays*

Old Home Day

71

THE BATTLE CRY OF FREEDOM

("Yes, we'll rally round the flag, boys")

SOURCE: Root and Cady publication of 1862

George Frederick Root

GEORGE FREDERICK ROOT, 1861

Yes we'll ral-ly round the flag, boys, we'll ral-ly once a-gain,

Shout-ing the bat-tle-cry of Free-dom, We will ral-ly from the hill-side, we'll

Chorus

gath-er from the plain, Shout-ing the bat-tle-cry of Free-dom. The

Un-ion for-ev-er, Hur-rah boys, hur-rah! Down with the Trai-tor,

Up with the Star; While we ral-ly round the flag, boys, Ral-ly once a-gain,

Shout - ing the bat - tle - cry of Free - dom.

005 iii (27—cello)	*The Fourth of July* [from] *A Symphony: New England Holidays*
007 i (27—flute)	*The "St. Gaudens" in Boston Common (Col Shaw and his Colored Regiment)* [from] *Orchestral Set No. 1: Three Places in New England*
007 ii (32—trumpet)	*Putnam's Camp, Redding, Connecticut* [from] *Orchestral Set No. 1: Three Places in New England*
036 (55—cornet)	*"Country Band" March* [incomplete]
039 (f2490)	*Piece for Small Orchestra and Organ* [mostly lost]
059 i (f3240, m. 57—violin)	Allegretto moderato [from] Pre-First Sonata for Violin and Piano
061 ii (108—violin)	*In the Barn* [from] *Sonata No. 2 for Violin and Piano*
064 (f0715, m. 65—violin)	*Decoration Day* for Violin and Piano
116 (f4846, staff 4, bass clef)	*The Celestial Railroad*
128 ii (47—piano I)	Allegro [from] *Three Quarter-Tone Pieces*
182 (43—piccolo)	*He Is There!*
187 (22—trumpet)	*Sneak Thief* [incomplete]
188 (43—flute)	*They Are There! (A War Song March)*
262 (31—voice)	*He Is There!*
277 (6—piano)	*In Flanders Fields*
371 (38—voice)	*They Are There!*
372 (10—piano)	*The Things Our Fathers Loved*
593 (f2610)	Unidentified fragment: one line on 3 staves on title page of song *Mists* (II) 301

72

BATTLE HYMN OF THE REPUBLIC

(Glory, Hallelujah)

(John Brown's Body)

("Mine eyes have seen the glory of the coming of the Lord")

SOURCE: Oliver Ditson publication of 1862

Julia Ward Howe, 1861

attr. to WILLIAM STEFFE, 1862
taken from "Glory, Hallelujah," ca. 1856

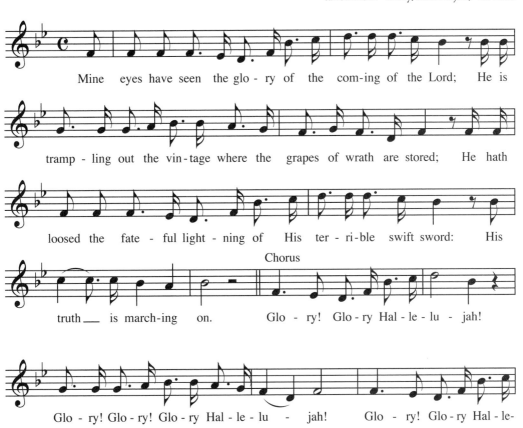

Mine eyes have seen the glo - ry of the com-ing of the Lord; He is

tramp - ling out the vin - tage where the grapes of wrath are stored; He hath

loosed the fate - ful light - ning of His ter - ri - ble swift sword: His

Chorus

truth __ is march-ing on. Glo - ry! Glo - ry Hal - le - lu - jah!

Glo - ry! Glo - ry! Glo - ry Hal - le - lu - jah! Glo - ry! Glo - ry Hal - le -

lu - jah! His truth is march - ing on.

005 ii (132—E-flat clarinet)   *Decoration Day* [from] *A Symphony: New England Holidays*

005 iii (49—violin)   *The Fourth of July* [from] *A Symphony: New England Holidays*

009 i (p. 11: q2999; section D of sketch; staff 6);
  does not appear in Porter's performance score   Andante moderato [from] *Orchestral Set No. 3*

009 ii (p. 15: n3002, staff 11,   *An Afternoon or During Camp Meetin' Week—*
  upside down; cornets)   *One Secular Afternoon (In Bethel)* [from]
                                                        Orchestral Set No. 3 [incomplete]

024 (42—clarinet)   *Overture and March "1776"*

104 (71)   *Study No. 20:* March (Slow Allegro or Fast
                                                        Andante)

182 (22—trombone)   *He Is There!*

184 (5—bassoon)   *Lincoln, the Great Commoner*

188 (22—trombone)   *They Are There! (A War Song March)*

289 (5—piano)   *Lincoln, the Great Commoner*

315 (20—voice)   *Old Home Day*

371 (22—voice)   *They Are There!*

Possible borrowing:

  064 (f0715, m. 60—piano)   *Decoration Day* for Violin and Piano

73

THE BRITISH GRENADIERS

("Some talk of Alexander, and some of Hercules"—traditional text)

("That seat of science, Athens, and earth's great mistress, Rome"—Dr. Warren's text)

1st reference to traditional words: 1706   1st printed ca. 1750 as *The British Granadiers*

In his *Memos*, p. 84, Ives mentions a new text by a "captain in one of Putnam's regiments" and says that the tune with this new text was first sung in 1779 "at a patriotic meeting in the Congregational Church in Redding Center." This "captain" was Dr. Joseph Warren, a Boston patriot who called his version "The New Massachusetts Liberty song," text first printed in 1770 in Edes and Gill's *North American Almanack and Massachusetts Register for the Year 1770*.

SOURCE: Charles Ives's *Memos*, 84

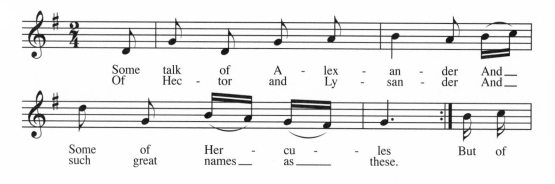

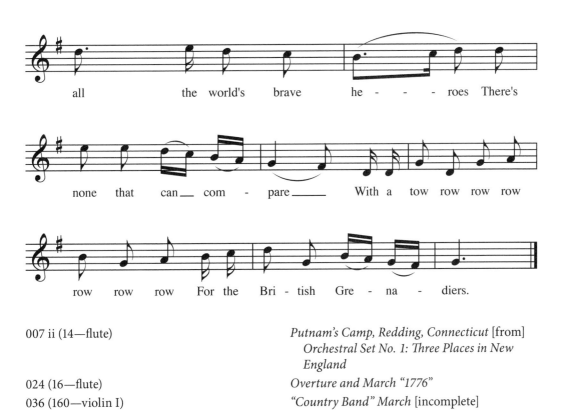

all   the world's   brave   he - - - roes There's

none   that   can__ com - pare_____ With a   tow row row row

row   row   row   For the   Bri - tish   Gre - na - diers.

007 ii (14—flute)	*Putnam's Camp, Redding, Connecticut* [from] *Orchestral Set No. 1: Three Places in New England*
024 (16—flute)	*Overture and March "1776"*
036 (160—violin I)	*"Country Band" March* [incomplete]

74

BUGLE CALL DERIVATIVES

Note: See Assembly 71; Reveille 83; and Taps 87 for this music

COLUMBIA, THE GEM OF THE OCEAN

(The Red, White, and Blue)

("O Columbia, the gem of the ocean")

SOURCE: *The Golden Book of Favorite Songs,* pp. 6–7

David T. Shaw
also credited to Thomas à Beckett

DAVID T. SHAW, 1843
also credited to Thomas à Beckett

Oh Co-lum-bia, the gem of the o-cean, The home of the brave and the free;___ The shrine of each pa-triot's de-vo-tion A world__ of-fers hom-age to thee. Thy man-dates make he-roes as-sem-ble, When Lib-er-ty's form stands in view; Thy ban-ners make tyr-an-ny trem-ble, When borne by the red, white, and blue! When

Chorus

borne by the red, white, and blue! When borne by the red, white, and

blue! Thy__ ban-ners make tyr - an-ny trem-ble, When

borne __ by the red, white, and blue!

76

DIXIE'S LAND

("I wish I was in de land ob cotton")

SOURCE: Firth and Pond publication of 1860

Daniel Decatur Emmett, 1859

DANIEL DECATUR EMMETT, 1859

I__ wish I was in de land ob cot-ton, Old times dar am

not for-got-ten, Look a-way! Look a-way! Look a-way! Dix-ie Land. In__

Dix-ie Land whar' I was born in, Ear-ly on one fros-ty morn-in', Look a-

Chorus

way! Look a-way! Look a-way! Dix-ie Land. Den I wish I was in

Dix-ie, Hoo-ray! Hoo-ray! In__ Dix-ie Land I'll take my stand To

lib and die in Dix-ie; A-way, A-way, A-way down south in Dix-ie, A-

way, A-way, A-way down south in Dix-ie.

005 iii (109—piccolo)	*The Fourth of July* [from] *A Symphony: New England Holidays*
039 (f2490)	*Piece for Small Orchestra and Organ* [mostly lost]
058 i (60—viola)	*Discussions* [from] *String Quartet No. 2*
086 ii (145—violin)	Presto ("TSIAJ" or Medley on the Fence [or] on the Campus!) [from] *Trio for Violin, Violoncello, and Piano*
182 (21—piccolo)	*He Is There!*
188 (21—flute)	*They Are There! (A War Song March)*
262 (21—obligato)	*He Is There!*
371 (21—obligato)	*They Are There!*
Possible borrowing:	
372 (1—voice)	*The Things Our Fathers Loved*

77

HAIL! COLUMBIA

(The President's March)

("Hail! Columbia happy Land!")

SOURCE: *Music for Patriots, Politicians, and Presidents*, pp. 144–45

Joseph Hopkinson, 1798

melody: "The President's March"
PHILIP PHILE, pub. 1793
music and text together, 1798

- joy'd the peace your va - lor won; let In - de-pen-dence be __ our __ boast,

ev - er mind-ful what it cost; ev - er grate - ful for the prize, let its Al-tar

Chorus

reach the Skies. Firm, u - ni - ted, let __ us __ be, ral - lying round our

Li - ber - ty, as a band of ___ Bro - thers join'd

peace ___ and ___ safe - ty we shall find.

004 ii (110—trumpets)	Allegretto [from] *Symphony No. 4*
005 iii (64—clarinet)	*The Fourth of July* [from] *A Symphony: New England Holidays*
007 ii (74—violin I)	*Putnam's Camp, Redding, Connecticut* [from] *Orchestral Set No. 1: Three Places in New England*
024 (5—oboe)	*Overture and March "1776"*
058 i (64—violin I)	*Discussions* [from] *String Quartet No. 2*
058 ii (87—violin I)	*Arguments* [from] *String Quartet No. 2*
184 (12—oboe)	*Lincoln, the Great Commoner*
289 (voice—12)	*Lincoln, the Great Commoner*
600 (f6923)	four measures, found on song, *The Housatonic at Stockbridge* (266) possibly for *Overture: Nationals*

78

LIBERTY BELL MARCH

SOURCE: John Church publication of 1893

JOHN PHILIP SOUSA, 1893

007 ii (27—piano)

Putnam's Camp, Redding, Connecticut [from]
Orchestral Set No. 1: Three Places in New
England

79

MARCHING THROUGH GEORGIA

("Bring the good old bugle, boys!")

SOURCE: Root and Cady publication of 1865

Henry Clay Work, 1865

HENRY CLAY WORK, © 1865

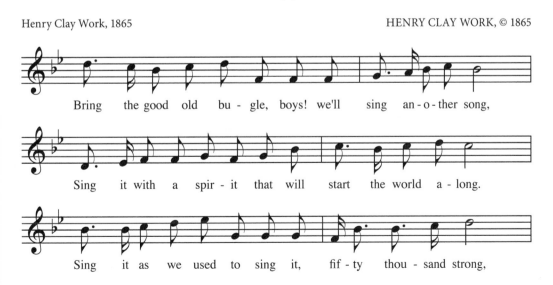

Bring the good old bu - gle, boys! we'll sing an - o - ther song,

Sing it with a spir - it that will start the world a - long.

Sing it as we used to sing it, fif - ty thou - sand strong,

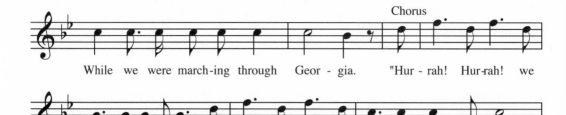

While we were march-ing through Geor - gia. "Hur - rah! Hur-rah! we

bring the Ju-bi-lee! Hur - rah! Hur-rah! the flag that makes you free!"

So we sang the cho - rus from At - lan - ta to the sea,

While we were march - ing through Geor - gia.

004 ii (39—bassoon)	Allegretto [from] *Symphony No. 4*
005 ii (37—flute)	*Decoration Day* [from] *A Symphony: New England Holidays*
005 iii (34—trumpet)	*The Fourth of July* [from] *A Symphony: New England Holidays*
007 i (38—violin I)	*The "St. Gaudens" in Boston Common (Col. Shaw and his Colored Regiment)* [from] *Orchestral Set No. 1: Three Places in New England*
007 ii (30—piano)	*Putnam's Camp, Redding, Connecticut* [from] *Orchestral Set No. 1: Three Places in New England*
010 v (26—clarinet)	*Calcium Light Night* [from] *Set No. 1 for Chamber Orchestra*
033 (81—horn)	*March: The Circus Band*
036 (50—flute)	*"Country Band" March* [incomplete]
038 (27—trumpet)	*The Gong on the Hook and Ladder or Firemen's Parade on Main Street*
058 i (62—violin II)	*Discussions* [from] *String Quartet No. 2*
058 ii (97—violin I)	*Arguments* [from] *String Quartet No. 2*
064 (f0714, m. 37—violin)	*Decoration Day* for Violin and Piano
070 (27—trumpet)	*The Gong on the Hook and Ladder or Firemen's Parade on Main Street*

086 ii (43—violin)	Presto ("TSIAJ" or Medley on the Fence [or] on the Campus!) [from] *Trio for Violin, Violoncello, and Piano*
116 (87)	*The Celestial Railroad*
125 (196)	*Waltz-Rondo*
182 (23—chorus)	*He Is There!*
187 (18—piano)	*Sneak Thief* [incomplete]
188 (23—flute)	*They Are There! (A War Song March)*
262 (11—voice)	*He Is There!*
371 (11—voice)	*They Are There!*

80

LA MARSEILLAISE

("Ye sons of France, awake to glory!")

SOURCE: *The Golden Book of Favorite Songs,* p. 100

Claude-Joseph Rouget de Lisle   CLAUDE-JOSEPH ROUGET DE LISLE, pub. 1792

Ye sons of France, a wake to Glo - ry! Hark! hark! what

myr - iads bid you rise! Your chil - dren, wives, and grand - sires

hoar - y, Be-hold their tears and hear their cries! Be-hold their

tears and — hear their cries! Shall hate - ful ty - rants, mis - chief

breed - ing, With hire-ling hosts, a ruf - fian band, Af-

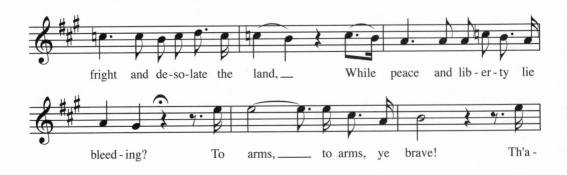

fright and de-so-late the land, — While peace and lib-er-ty lie

bleed-ing? To arms, —— to arms, ye brave! Th'a-

veng - ing sword un-sheathed! March on, march on!

all hearts re - solved on vic - to-ry or death.

81

MARYLAND, MY MARYLAND

(O Tannenbaum, O Tannenbaum!)

(Lauriger Horatius)

("The despot's heel is on thy shore")

SOURCE: Miller and Beacham publication of 1861

James Ryder Randall, 1861   1st publication of essential part of melody: 1799
words and music to "Maryland, My Maryland" © 1861

The des-pot's heel is on thy shore, Ma-ry-land, My Ma-ry-land! His

touch is at thy tem-ple door, Ma-ry-land, My Ma-ry-land! A-

venge the pa-tri-ot-ic gore That fleck'd the streets of Bal-ti-more, And

be the Bat-tle-Queen of yore, Ma-ry-land, My Ma-ry-land!

182 (29—piccolo)	*He Is There!*
188 (29—flute)	*They Are There! (A War Song March)*
262 (29—obligato)	*He Is There!*
371 (29—obligato)	*They Are There!*

82

OVER THERE

("Johnnie get your gun, get your gun")

SOURCE: Leo Feist publication of 1917

George Michael Cohan, 1917   GEORGE MICHAEL COHAN, 1917

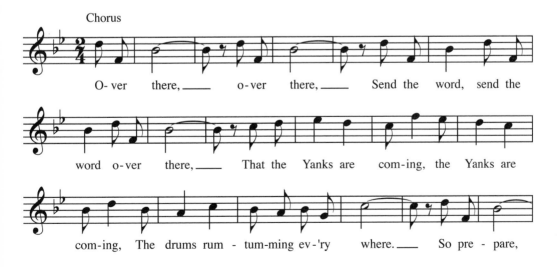

O-ver there, ____ o-ver there, ____ Send the word, send the

word o-ver there, ____ That the Yanks are com-ing, the Yanks are

com-ing, The drums rum-tum-ming ev-'ry where. ____ So pre-pare,

say a   pray'r, ___   Send the   word,   send the   word to be - ware,

___ We'll be   o - ver, we're com-ing   o - ver,   And we   won't come

back   till   it's   o - ver   o - ver   there.

005 ii (22—trumpet I)	*Decoration Day* [from] *A Symphony: New England Holidays*
180 (8—voices)	*An Election*
182 (28—piccolo)	*He Is There!*
188 (28—flute)	*They Are There! (A War Song March)*
262 (25—voice)	*He Is There!*
313 (8—voice)	*Nov. 2, 1920 (An Election)*
371 (25—voice)	*They Are There!*
378 (22—voice)	*Tom Sails Away*

83

REVEILLE

SOURCE: Sousa, *A Book of Instruction,* pp. 67–68

1st known printing: 1836

Fine

002 v (250—trumpet I)	Allegro molto vivace [from] *Symphony No. 2*
004 ii (132—trumpet III)	Allegretto [from] *Symphony No. 4*
005 iii (57—horn)	*The Fourth of July* [from] *A Symphony: New England Holidays*
007 i (54—horn)	*The "St. Gaudens" in Boston Common (Col. Shaw and his Colored Regiment)* [from] *Orchestral Set No. 1: Three Places in New England*
007 ii (18—bassoon)	*Putnam's Camp, Redding, Connecticut* [from] *Orchestral Set No. 1: Three Places in New England*
008 i (19—flute)	*An Elegy to Our Forefathers* [from] *Orchestral Set No. 2*
009 ii (p. 19: n3004, staff 3, fife)	*An Afternoon or During Camp Meetin' Week One Secular Afternoon (In Bethel)* [from] *Orchestral Set No. 3* [incomplete]
181 (70—voice)	*General William Booth Enters into Heaven*
182 (51—piccolo)	*He Is There!*
188 (51—flute)	*They Are There! (A War Song March)*
255 (70—voice)	*General William Booth Enters into Heaven*
262 (28—obligato)	*He Is There!*
277 (20—piano)	*In Flanders Fields*
282 (f6766, brace 2)	Incomplete song [II]
371 (28—obligato)	*They Are There!*

84

SECOND REGIMENT CONNECTICUT
NATIONAL GUARD MARCH

SOURCE: W. H. Cundy edition of 1880

DAVID WILLIS REEVES, © 1877

85

SEMPER FIDELES

SOURCE: Carl Fischer publication of 1888

JOHN PHILIP SOUSA, © 1888

007 ii (27—trombone)	*Putnam's Camp, Redding, Connecticut* [from] *Orchestral Set No. 1: Three Places in New England*
036 (53—clarinet)	*"Country Band" March* [incomplete]

86

THE STAR SPANGLED BANNER

(The Anacreontic Song)

(To Anacreon in Heaven)

("Oh say! Can you see, by the dawn's early light")

SOURCE: *The Golden Book of Favorite Songs,* pp. 4–5

Francis Scott Key, 1814

The Anacreontic Song
JOHN STAFFORD SMITH, 1775 or 1776
1st printing of Key text with music of *The Anacreontic Song:* 1814

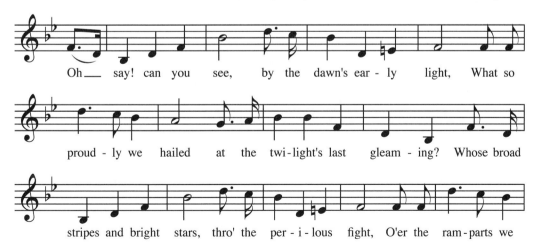

watch'd were so gal-lant-ly stream-ing? And the rock-ets' red

glare, the bombs burst-ing in air, Gave proof thro' the night that our

Chorus

flag was still there. Oh, say, does that Star-span-gled Ban-ner yet

wave O'er the land ___ of the free and the home of the brave?

STREET BEAT/STREET CADENCE

Note: The example given below is
only one of many *Street beat/Street cadence* passages in Ives's music

002 v (27—snare drum)	Allegro molto vivace [from] *Symphony No. 2*
004 ii (123—orchestra piano I)	Allegretto [from] *Symphony No. 4*
004 iv (1—battery unit)	Largo [from] *Symphony No. 4*
005 iii (66-a—drums; piano)	*The Fourth of July* [from] *A Symphony: New England Holidays*
007 ii (25—drums)	*Putnam's Camp, Redding, Connecticut* [from] *Orchestral Set No. 1: Three Places in New England*
009 i (19—strings) [this is not in the same pattern as typical "Street beat" borrowings; Ives indicates that all pizzicato strings here are "used as drums"]	[Andante moderato] [from] *Orchestral Set No. 3*
009 ii (p. 19: n3004, staff 4, snare drum)	*An Afternoon or During Camp Meetin' Week— One Secular Afternoon (In Bethel)* [from] *Orchestral Set No. 3* [incomplete]
024 (41—drum)	*Overture and March "1776"*
033 (41—drums)	*March: The Circus Band*
036 (45—drums)	*"Country Band" March* [incomplete]
064 (f0716, m. 81—piano)	*Decoration Day* for Violin and Piano
115 (f6411, m. 41)	*March for Piano: The Circus Band*
116 (f4862, staff 10—drum)	*The Celestial Railroad*
181 (1—piano)	*General William Booth Enters into Heaven*
229 (41—piano)	*The Circus Band*
255 (1—piano)	*General William Booth Enters into Heaven*
277 (28—piano)	*In Flanders Fields*
315 (23—piano)	*Old Home Day*

87

TAPS

(Extinguish Lights)

SOURCE: Sousa, *A Book of Instruction*, p. 14

attr. to Gen. DANIEL BUTTERFIELD, 1862

005 ii (74—trumpet)	*Decoration Day* [from] *A Symphony: New England Holidays*
016 iii (1—flute)	*The Pond* [from] *Set No. 7: Water Colors*
040 (10—flute)	*The Pond*
058 i (81—violin I)	*Discussions* [from] *String Quartet No. 2*
064 (f0716, m. 75)	*Decoration Day* for Violin and Piano
277 (14—piano)	*In Flanders Fields*
332 (8—piano)	*Remembrance*
333 (19—voice)	*Requiem*
378 (10—voice)	*Tom Sails Away*

Possible borrowing:

065 (f2421, m. 6—trumpets/trombones)	*From the Steeples and the Mountains*

88

TENTING ON THE OLD CAMP GROUND

("We're tenting tonight on the old Camp ground")

SOURCE: Oliver Ditson publication of 1864

Walter Kittridge, 1864   WALTER KITTRIDGE, 1864

We're   tent - ing to-night   on   the   old   Camp   ground,

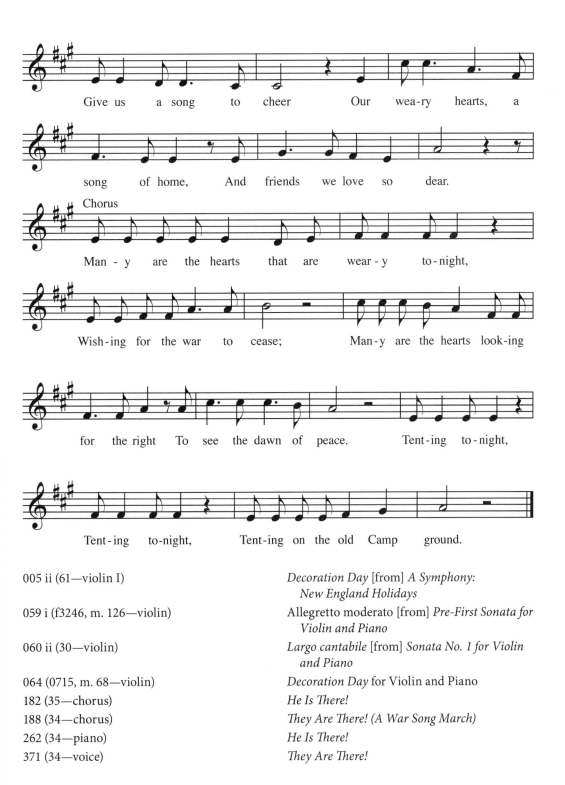

Give us a song to cheer Our wea-ry hearts, a

song of home, And friends we love so dear.

Chorus

Man - y are the hearts that are wear - y to-night,

Wish-ing for the war to cease; Man-y are the hearts look-ing

for the right To see the dawn of peace. Tent-ing to-night,

Tent-ing to-night, Tent-ing on the old Camp ground.

005 ii (61—violin I)	*Decoration Day* [from] *A Symphony: New England Holidays*
059 i (f3246, m. 126—violin)	*Allegretto moderato* [from] *Pre-First Sonata for Violin and Piano*
060 ii (30—violin)	*Largo cantabile* [from] *Sonata No. 1 for Violin and Piano*
064 (0715, m. 68—violin)	*Decoration Day* for Violin and Piano
182 (35—chorus)	*He Is There!*
188 (34—chorus)	*They Are There! (A War Song March)*
262 (34—piano)	*He Is There!*
371 (34—voice)	*They Are There!*

89

TRAMP, TRAMP, TRAMP

("In the prison cell I sit, thinking, Mother dear, of you")

SOURCE: Root and Cady publication of 1864

George Frederick Root, 1864   GEORGE FREDERICK ROOT, 1864

In the pris - on cell I sit, Think - ing, Moth - er dear, of you, And our

bright and hap - py home so far a - way, And the

tears they fill my eyes Spite of all that I can do, Tho' I

try to cheer my com - rades and be gay.

Chorus

Tramp, tramp, tramp, the boys are march - ing Cheer up com - rades they will

come, And be - neath the star - ry flag We shall breathe the air a-gain, Of the

free - land in our own be - lov - ed home.

004 ii (35—trombone)	Allegretto [from] *Symphony No. 4*
005 iii (69—piccolo)	*The Fourth of July* [from] *A Symphony: New England Holidays*
009 ii (p. 20: n3005, staff 8)	*An Afternoon or During Camp Meetin' Week One Secular Afternoon (In Bethel)* [from] *Orchestral Set No. 3* [incomplete]

010 v (22—clarinet)	*Calcium Light Night* [from] *Set No. 1 for Chamber Orchestra*
024 (53—flute)	*Overture and March "1776"*
059 ii (30—piano)	Largo [from] *Pre-First Sonata for Violin and Piano*
060 ii (31—piano)	Largo cantabile [from] *Sonata No. 1 for Violin and Piano*
116 (f4846, staff 1)	*The Celestial Railroad*
182 (23—chorus)	*He Is There!*
188 (23—chorus)	*They Are There! (A War Song March)*
262 (23—voice)	*He Is There!*
371 (23—voice)	*They Are There!*

90
WASHINGTON POST MARCH

SOURCE: Carl Fischer publication of 1889

JOHN PHILIP SOUSA, © 1889

| 004 ii (56—tuba) | Allegretto [from] *Symphony No. 4* |
| 034 (103—piano II) | *Central Park in the Dark* |

91
WHEN JOHNNY COMES MARCHING HOME
("When Johnny comes marching home again")

SOURCE: Henry Johnson publication of 1863

PATRICK SARSFIELD GILMORE, © 1863

When John-ny comes march-ing home a-gain, Hur-rah!___ Hur-rah,___ We'll give him a heart-y wel-come then, Hur-rah,___ Hur-rah;___ The men will cheer, the boys will shout, The la-dies, they will all turn out, And we'll all feel gay when John-ny comes march-ing home!___

047 (2—winds)

Take-Off No. 7: Mike Donlin-Johnny Evers
[incomplete]

YANKEE DOODLE

("Fath'r and I went down to camp")

SOURCE: *Twice 55 Community Songs,* no. 95

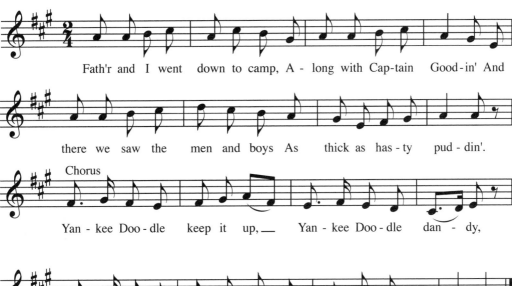

Fath'r and I went down to camp, A - long with Cap-tain Good-in' And

there we saw the men and boys As thick as has - ty pud - din'.

Chorus

Yan - kee Doo - dle keep it up, ___ Yan - kee Doo - dle dan - dy,

Mind the mu - sic and the step, And with the girls be han - dy.

004 ii (232—piccolo)	Allegretto [from] *Symphony No. 4*
005 iii (99—xylophone)	*The Fourth of July* [from] *A Symphony: New England Holidays*
007 ii (35—violin I)	*Putnam's Camp, Redding, Connecticut* [from] *Orchestral Set No. 1: Three Places in New England*
008 ii (43—flute)	*The Rockstrewn Hills Join in the People's Outdoor Meeting* [from] *Orchestral Set No. 2*
024 (67—oboe)	*Overture and March "1776"*
036 (59—cornet)	*"Country Band March"* [incomplete]
116 (203)	*The Celestial Railroad*
182 (24—piccolo)	*He Is There!*
188 (24—flute)	*They Are There! (A War Song March)*
262 (24—obligato)	*He Is There!*
371 (24—obligato)	*They Are There!*

Possible borrowing:

005 ii (46—violin I)	*Decoration Day* [from] *A Symphony: New England Holidays*
064 (f0714, m. 46—piano)	*Decoration Day* for Violin and Piano

[3]

Popular Songs

One of the people whom Ives admired greatly was George Felsburg, the piano player at Poli's Theatre in New Haven and the man Ives "spelled" from time to time. Ives remarked that Felsburg "could read a newspaper and play the piano better than some pianists could play the piano without any newspaper at all."[1] To have given Felsburg a break from his piano-playing chores meant that Ives had certain pianistic skills beyond those required for success in the world of classical music.

Many classically trained pianists, when faced with the sheet music of a popular song, can do no more than give a literal, stiff rendition of that music. Although they may be very much at home in interpreting Chopin with appropriate rubato, for example, the necessary skill to flexibly "swing" a rhythm in playing popular music is beyond them. How did Ives learn to play popular music, to "nudge" the rhythms here and there, to slough off certain notes and to emphasize others—a few of the elements that give a certain "feel" to popular music?

To be able to "spell" a piano player meant that Ives had to know a wide range of popular songs and instrumental music; it meant having an internal sense of rhythm that provided a rock-solid foundation for the correct unfolding of a piece of popular music, especially music in a spirited tempo. It meant having the ability to read music at sight and being able to play a performance with little rehearsal. Above all, it meant having the ability to improvise, to move away from the printed page to a free interpretation of the music, where the original harmonies and melodies became springboards for inspiration and invention. Although we cannot document precisely where and when Ives gained these experiences, the breadth and depth of his musical background prepared him well for being able to substitute for Felsburg.

Some of Ives's knowledge of the repertoire of popular music of the time probably came from playing from sheet music, but as many piano players who have that innate gift for playing popular piano can attest, one learns mostly by ear, rather than from the printed page. It's certain that Ives's ear must have picked up any number of popular songs and styles of piano music that he heard Felsburg and others play, but what were some other sources? As a musically impressionable youngster, Ives would have hummed or whistled tunes he heard people singing or playing; soon, he picked out the tunes on the piano. The melody being secure, he could then fit it with the harmonies he heard, or work out new ones that came to him.

Apparently, rhythms gave young Ives but few problems. Playing drums in his father's band certainly instilled in his playing precision when it came to keeping the beat, and he claimed that he could

> keep five, and even six, rhythms going in my mind at once, so that I can hear each one naturally by leaning toward it, changing the ear in each measure—and I think this is the more natural way of hearing and learning the use of and feeling for rhythms, than by writing them and playing from them on paper . . .[2]

Admittedly, this is not the same as the sort of rhythmic "feel" that one needs to interpret popular music, but it goes a long way to providing a certain rhythmic flexibility that one has to have.

An essential skill marking the good interpreter of popular music—and especially the theatre pianist—is the ability to improvise. Ives was active as a church musician in an era when improvisation was a requisite skill that any good organist had to possess.[3] Some of his abilities here undoubtedly transferred to his piano playing although the models on which an organist improvises and the style of that improvisation and its harmonic language are somewhat different from those of popular music. Nevertheless, Ives's versatility as a practical musician enabled him to make the adjustments needed to create the correct result.[4]

While popular music is sprinkled among a number of works, it is found most often in *Central Park in the Dark,* in the second movement of the *Trio for Violin, Violoncello, and Piano,* and in the second movement of *Symphony No. 4.* In the latter two works, borrowing never becomes more than a surface element, a veneer, but in *Central Park* it achieves a substantial depth, integrated, as it is, into the total sound fabric.

Two additional works in which citations of popular music show considerable promise for development are the second movement of *Orchestral Set No. 3* and *The General Slocum.* Regrettably, Ives left both compositions unfinished. Work on *Orchestral Set No. 3* began in the year after Ives's illness of 1918,[5] and continued in starts and stops during the time when he was busy setting his musical house in order with the publication of the "Concord" Sonata and *114 Songs.* Planned as a three-movement work (hymn-tune movements surrounding one given over to popular music), Ives finally abandoned the project in 1926, some time after composing had become scarcely more than a sporadic activity for him.

The General Slocum was a different matter. On June 15, 1904, the excursion boat *General Slocum,* crowded with passengers going on a church outing, exploded and burned in New York's East River; one thousand and thirty died—the greatest loss of life in New York City until the terrorist attacks ninety-seven years later. A month after the Slocum burned, Ives jotted down some ideas for a work that he thought of titling *Tragic Tone Poem: The General Slocum Disaster.* Only in 1906 did he go beyond his initial work but he soon gave it all up, recalling:

"This awful catastrophe got on everybody's nerves. I can give no other reason for attempting to put it to music, and I'm glad to look back and see the sketch is hardly more than a page."[6]

The physical act of putting some music on paper undoubtedly provided a catharsis for Ives. The sketches begin, as the people, reflecting the gaiety of the moment, sing from some of the popular tunes one might have heard at any social gathering of the day: here are *Little Annie Rooney, Ma Blushin' Rosie, The Sidewalks of New York,* and *Violets.* The deck orchestras join in, accompanying the singers, but the celebrations are shattered once and for all by a violent explosion: citations from the carefree tunes are replaced by the musical prayers of supplication in *Bethany* ("Nearer, my God, to Thee") and *Throw Out the Life-Line* with its metaphorical and literal message: "Throw out the Life-Line! Someone is sinking today." One wonders how substantial the working out of the borrowings would have been in these works had Ives been able, or chosen, to finish them.

Finally, mention must be made of *Streets of Cairo,* remembered by many as the "Hootchy-Kootchy Dance." *Streets of Cairo'*s parentage is a bit confusing. An edition, copyrighted in 1895, and giving the title as *Streets of Cairo* or *The Poor Little Country Maid,* lists James Thornton as the composer.[7] Sol Bloom, one of the shrewdest, and youngest, of the many entrepreneurs involved with the Columbian Exposition, claimed that he wrote the music for a performance of the *danse du ventre* at Chicago's global extravaganza. The famous—or infamous—"Hootchy-Kootchy" tune is an eight-measure verse to the song that ends with a rather undistinguished chorus of eight measures. The verse is set in a minor key, contrasting with the major tonality of the chorus. Ives quotes only twice from "Hootchy-Kootchy"—in his *Scherzo for String Quartet* and in *A Set of Three Short Pieces,* whose second movement is derived from this *Scherzo.* The citation follows *Bringing in the Sheaves, Massa's in de Cold Ground, My Old Kentucky Home,* and *College Hornpipe*—the entire experience truly serving as a marvelous example of Ives's belief in the transcendent power of different kinds of music to create a unity.

Ives's world of popular music embraced styles as different from one another as the genteel effusions of Stephen Foster and the insouciant rhythms of ragtime music. His usable past of popular melodies from an earlier era—songs he heard, sang, whistled, and played as a youngster—included *Araby's Daughter* ("The Old Oaken Bucket"), *The Girl I Left Behind Me, Home! Sweet Home!,* and *Long, Long Ago.* But it was especially the "Ethiopian melodies" of Stephen Collins Foster that held a special appeal for him: *Oh! Susanna, De Camptown Races, Old Folks at Home, Massa's in de Cold Ground, My Old Kentucky Home,* and *Old Black Joe* provided Ives with music on nearly forty occasions.[8]

Ives's first exposure to ragtime music was probably "at the Danbury Fair before coming to New Haven, which must have been before 1892."[9] Later, in New Haven, he heard "black-faced comedians . . . ragging their songs."[10] In August 1893, a year before he entered Yale, nineteen-year-old Charles accompanied his uncle Lyman Brewster to Milwaukee where Brewster attended the National Conference of the American Bar Association.[11] On the twentieth of August, when the meetings were over, the two traveled to Chicago to attend the Columbian Exposition. We don't know for certain that Ives heard Scott Joplin—or any other ragtime pianist—play this new music on the Midway that summer, but it is tantalizing to imagine the two of them listening to it then.[12] Once Ives had absorbed the formal and stylistic implications of ragtime, it became part of his maturing style. In the epilogue to his

Essays Before a Sonata, written after he had concluded his own experiments using ragtime in his own music, Ives shows that he had given considerable thought to this new music:

> Ragtime, as we hear it, is, of course, more (but not much more) than a natural dogma of shifted accents, or a mixture of shifted and minus accents.

He continues with a marvelous visual image,

> It is something like wearing a derby hat on the back of the head, a shuffling lilt of a happy soul just let out of a Baptist church in old Alabama.

And, knowing full well that ragtime was not the be-all and end-all of music, he shows the reader his analytical side:

> Ragtime has its possibilities. But it does not "represent the American nation" any more than some fine old senators represent it. Perhaps we know it now as an ore before it has been refined into a product. It may be one of nature's ways of giving art raw material. Time will throw its vices away and weld its virtues into the fabric of our music.[13]

It probably took Ives but a short time to master the rhythmic intricacies of ragtime; he was already adept at keenly observing, playing, and later writing down what he heard at the camp meetings he attended. There people sang their hymns with that intense, "let-out" fervor of the converted—the rhythms nudged ahead or pulled back here and there, the melody certainly recognizable, but altered as the spirit moved the singers. In his *Memos,* Ives remembered "hearing hymns written in rather even time sung with the off-accent. One that Grandma Parmelee used to sing [and] hum around some".[14]

There's no hope with - out Je-sus, The sin-ner's on - ly friend.

An increasing number of titles of some early works betray the content of the music: *Four Ragtime Dances, Nine Ragtime Dances, Three Ragtime Dances, Ragtime Dances for Two Pianos.* Ragtime elements are prominent in some pieces even when their titles give no hint of that. A short list of works includes both piano sonatas, the *Three-Page Sonata,* a number of the *Studies* for piano, *In the Inn* (the second movement of *Set for Theatre Orchestra*), the first and third sonatas for violin and piano, *Central Park in the Dark,* and the second movement of *Symphony No. 4.*

The examples presented here were copied from original nineteenth- and twentieth-century editions or from various anthologies of popular music.

AFTER THE BALL

("A little maiden climbed an old man's knee")

SOURCE: Charles K. Harris publication of 1892

Charles K. Harris, 1892   CHARLES K. HARRIS, 1892

020 ii (29—violin)   *In the Inn (Potpourri)* [from] *Set for Theatre Orchestra*

94

ALEXANDER

("Look here, Alexander, I was only fooling")

SOURCE: *Songs of the Gilded Age,* pp. 58–61

Andrew B. Sterling

HARRY von TILZER, 1904

009 ii (p. 17, n3003, section 8, staff 2)

104 (83)

*An Afternoon or During Camp Meetin' Week—
One Secular Afternoon (In Bethel)* [from]
Orchestral Set No. 3 [incomplete]

Study No. 20: March

ANNIE LISLE

(Far above Cayuga's waters)

("Down where the waving willows")

SOURCE: C. Sheard publication (n.d.)

H. S. THOMPSON, 1857

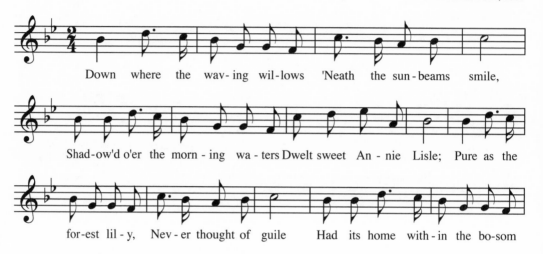

Down where the wav-ing wil-lows 'Neath the sun-beams smile,

Shad-ow'd o'er the morn-ing wa-ters Dwelt sweet An-nie Lisle; Pure as the

for-est lil-y, Nev-er thought of guile Had its home with-in the bo-som

Chorus

of sweet An-nie Lisle. Wave wil-lows, mur-mur wa-ters, Gold-en sun-beams,

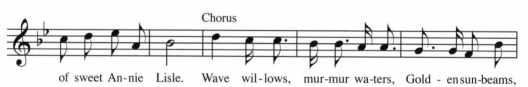

smile! Earth-ly mu-sic can-not wa-ken Love-ly An-nie Lisle.

054 (27—trombone) *March "Intercollegiate," with "Annie Lisle"*
112 (28) *March No. 5 for Piano, with "Annie Lisle"*
315 (37—voice) *Old Home Day*

96

ARABY'S DAUGHTER

(The Old Oaken Bucket)

("How dear to this heart are the scenes of my childhood")

SOURCE: Oliver Ditson publication (n.d.)

Samuel Woodworth, 1817

GEORGE KIALLMARK, 1822

How dear to my heart are the scenes of my child-hood. When

fond re-col-lec-tion pre-sents them to view, The or-chard, the mead-ow, the

deep tang-led wild-wood, And ev-'ry lov'd spot which my in-fan-cy knew.

The wide-spread-ing stream, ___ the

mill that stood near it, The bridge and the rock where the cat-a-ract fell; the

cot of my fa-ther, the dai-ry house by it, And e'en the rude buck-et that

Chorus

hung in the well. The old oak-en buck-et, the

i - ron - bound buck - et, The moss - cov-er'd buck - et that hung in the well.

059 ii (1—violin)   Largo [from] *Pre-First Sonata for Violin and Piano*

060 i (146—violin)   Andante-Allegro vivace [from] *Sonata No. 1 for Violin and Piano*

060 ii (1—violin)   Largo cantabile [from] *Sonata No. 1 for Violin and Piano*

286 (7—voice)   *The Last Reader*

378 (2—voice)   *Tom Sails Away*

Possible borrowing:

011 iii (f2698, staff 3, last measure)   *Andante: The Last Reader* [from] *Set No. 2*

018 i (f2747, m. 6—English horn)   *Andante con moto: The Last Reader* [from] *Set No. 9 of Three Pieces*

97

ARE YOU THE O'REILLY

("I'm Terence O'Reilly, I'm a man of renown")

SOURCE: *Songs of the Gilded Age,* pp. 127–29

Pat Rooney   PAT ROONEY, © 1882

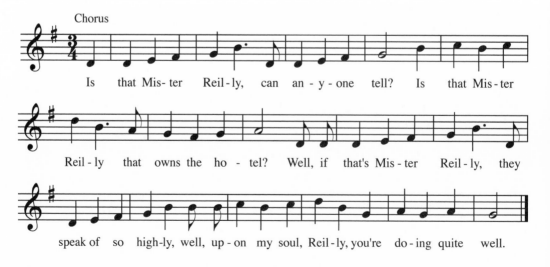

Chorus

Is that Mis- ter Reil - ly, can an- y - one tell? Is that Mis- ter

Reil - ly that owns the ho - tel? Well, if that's Mis - ter Reil - ly, they

speak of so high-ly, well, up - on my soul, Reil - ly, you're do - ing quite well.

348 (2—voice)   *The Side Show*

98

AULD LANG SYNE

("Should auld acquaintance be forgot")

SOURCE: *The Golden Book of Favorite Songs,* p. 37

earliest version of 1st-stanza words: 1711

parts of melody as early as 1687
1st appearance of traditional words and music: 1799

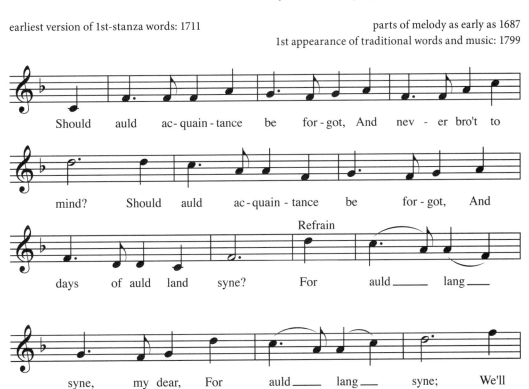

315 (33—obligato)
320 (20—piano)

Old Home Day
On the Counter

99
BEN BOLT

("Oh! don't you remember sweet Alice, Ben Bolt")

SOURCE: W. C. Peters publication of 1843

Thomas Dunn English

NELSON KNEASS, © 1843

Oh! don't you re-mem-ber sweet Al - ice, Ben Bolt Sweet Al-lice with hair____ so brown; she wept with de-light when you gave her a smile, And trem-bled with fear____ at your frown. In the old church yard, in the val-ley, Ben Bolt, In a cor-ner ob-scure and a-lone They have fit-ted a slab of___ gran-ite so gray, And sweet Al - ice lies un - der the stone. They have fit-ted a slab of __ gra-nite so gray, And sweet Al-ice lies un - der the stone.

034 (12—clarinet)

Central Park in the Dark

100

DE CAMPTOWN RACES

("De Camptown ladies sing dis song")

SOURCE: F. D. Benteen publication of 1850

Stephen Collins Foster

STEPHEN COLLINS FOSTER, © 1850

De Camp-town la-dies sing dis song Doo-dah! doo-dah! De

Camp-town race-track five miles long Oh! doo-dah-day! I

come down dah wid my hat caved in Doo-dah! doo-dah! I

go back home wid a pock-et full of tin Oh! doo-dah day!

Gwine to run all night! Gwine to run all day! I'll

bet my mon-ey on the bob-tail nag Some-bod-y bet on de bay.

002 v (7—violin)	Allegro molto vivace [from] *Symphony No. 2*
004 ii (75—clarinet)	Allegretto [from] *Symphony No. 4*
005 i (86—horn)	*Washington's Birthday* [from] *A Symphony: New England Holidays*

100-a

EVER OF THEE

("Ever of thee, I'm fondly dreaming")

SOURCE: *The Book of a Thousand Songs*

George Linley

FOLEY HALL, 1860

Ev - er of thee I'm fond - ly __ dream-ing, Thy gen-tle voice my

spir - it can cheer; Thou art the star that, mild - ly __ beam-ing,

Shone o'er my path when all was dark and drear. Still in my heart thy

form I __ cher - ish, Ev - 'ry kind tho't like a bird flies to thee. Ah!

nev - er till life and mem - 'ry __ per - ish, Can I for-get how

dear thou art to me; Morn, noon and night, wher - e'er I may be,

Fond - ly I'm dream - ing __ ev - er of thee;

Fond - ly I'm dream - ing____ ev - er of thee.

100-b
CORNET FANTASY ON EVER OF THEE

CARL FOEPPL

Possible borrowing:
089 (Foeppl—41)

Three-Page Sonata

101
FOR HE'S A JOLLY GOOD FELLOW

(Malbrook)

("We Won't Go Home Until Morning!")

("The Bear Went Over the Mountain")

("For he's a jolly good fellow")

SOURCE: *All-American Song Book*, p. 135

Words probably from 19th century

French nursery song of 17th or 18th century
first appearance of melody: ca. 1762–78

For He's A Jol- ly Good Fel - low, For He's A Jol - ly Good Fel - low, For

He's A Jol- ly Good Fel - low, Which no - bod - y can de -

ny. _____ Which no-bod-y can de - ny. _____

005 i (99—flute)   *Washington's Birthday* [from] *A Symphony:*
                                          New England Holidays

102

THE GIRL I LEFT BEHIND ME

("I'm lonesome since I cross'd the hill")

SOURCE: *The New Blue Book of Favorite Songs*, p. 221

earliest known printing of words: 1808   English or Irish origin?
                                    earliest known version of melody with this title: ca. 1810

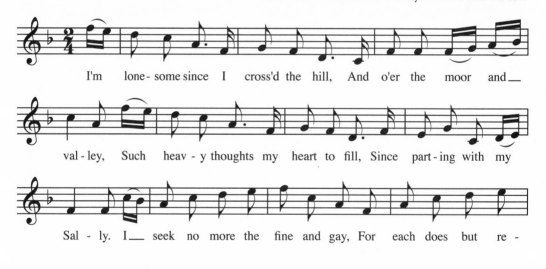

I'm lone-some since I cross'd the hill, And o'er the moor and___

val - ley, Such heav - y thoughts my heart to fill, Since part - ing with my

Sal - ly. I___ seek no more the fine and gay, For each does but re -

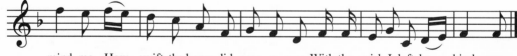

mind me How swift the hours did pass a - way With the girl I left be - hind me.

005 iii (71—piccolo)   *The Fourth of July* [from] *A Symphony: New*
                                          England Holidays

008 ii (50—trumpet)   *The Rockstrewn Hills Join in the People's*
                                          Outdoor Meeting [from] *Orchestral*
                                          Set No. 2

009 ii (p. 19, n3004, staff 7, fife)	*An Afternoon or During Camp Meetin' Week—One Secular Afternoon (In Bethel)* [from] *Orchestral Set No. 3* [incomplete]
020 ii (101—clarinet)	*In the Inn (Potpourri)* [from] *Set for Theatre Orchestra*
036 (26—flute)	*"Country Band" March* [incomplete]
104 (77)	*Study No. 20: March* (Slow Allegro or Fast Andante)
315 (25—obligato)	*Old Home Day*

103

GIT ALONG LITTLE DOGIES

("As I was a-walking one morning for pleasure")

SOURCE: *Cowboy Songs and Other Frontier Ballads,* p. 89

ca. 1860s
collected by JOHN A. LOMAX

long___ lit-tle do-gies, For you know Wy-o-ming will be your new home.

014 iii (f6164, staff 1, m. 1—piano)

Charlie Rutlage [from] *Set No. 5: The Other Side of Pioneering, or Side Lights on American Enterprise*

226 (24—piano)

Charlie Rutlage

104

GOODNIGHT, LADIES

("Goodnight, ladies! Goodnight, ladies!")

SOURCE: *All American Song Book,* p. 136

music and words of first part of song
by EDWIN P. CHRISTY, © 1847
first known publication of full song: 1867

Good - night, la - dies! ___ Good - night, la - dies! ___

Good - night, la - dies! ___ we're going to leave you now. ___

Mer - ri - ly we roll a - long. Roll a - long, roll a - long,

Mer - ri - ly we roll a - long, O - ver the dark blue sea.

005 i (178—flute)

Washington's Birthday [from] *A Symphony: New England Holidays*

105

GRANDFATHER'S CLOCK

("My grandfather's clock was too large for the shelf")

SOURCE: C. M. Cady publication of 1876

Henry Clay Work

HENRY CLAY WORK, 1876

My grand - fa - ther's clock was too large for the shelf, So it stood nine - ty years on the floor; It was tall - er by half than the old man him - self, Though it weighed not a pen - ny - weight more. It was bought on the morn of the day that he was born, And was al - ways his treas - ure and pride; But it stopp'd short

Chorus

nev - er to go a - gain When the old man died, Nine - ty years, with - out slum - ber - ing (tick, tick, tick, tick), His life - sec - onds num - ber - ing (tick, tick, tick, tick), It stopp'd short

nev - er to go a - gain When the old man died.

009 ii (p. 16: n3001, section 6, staff 8, trombone) *An Afternoon or During Camp Meetin' Week—*
One Secular Afternoon (In Bethel) [from]
Orchestral Set No. 3 [incomplete]

106

HAS ANYBODY HERE SEEN KELLY?

("Has anybody here seen Kelly?")

SOURCE: T. B. Harms and Francis, Day and Hunter ed., 1909

C. W. MURPHY and WILL LETTERS
Adapted by WILLIAM C. McKENNA, 1909

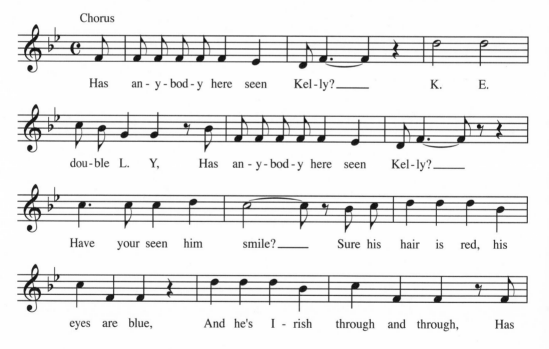

Chorus

Has an - y - bod - y here seen Kel - ly?_____ K. E.

dou - ble L. Y, Has an - y - bod - y here seen Kel - ly?_____

Have your seen him smile?_____ Sure his hair is red, his

eyes are blue, And he's I - rish through and through, Has

an-y-bod-y here seen Kel-ly?___ Kel-ly from the Emer-ald Isle. ___

009 ii (p. 15: n3002, staff 9,
   reading upside down)

An Afternoon or During Camp Meetin' Week—
One Secular Afternoon (In Bethel) [from]
Orchestral Set No. 3 [incomplete]

107

HELLO! MA BABY

("I'se got a little baby, but she's out of sight")

SOURCE: T. B. Harms publication of 1899

Ida Emerson, 1899

JOSEPH E. HOWARD, © 1899

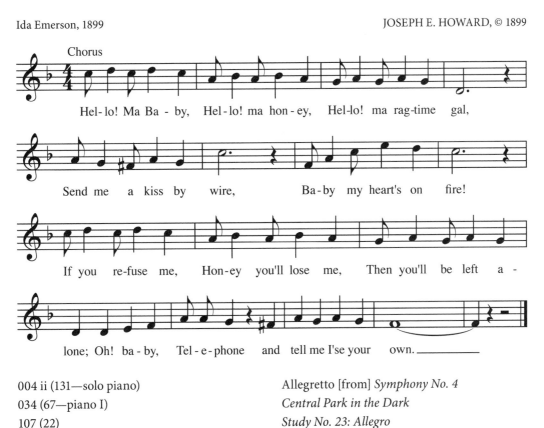

Chorus

Hel-lo! Ma Ba - by, Hel-lo! ma hon-ey, Hel-lo! ma rag-time gal,

Send me a kiss by wire, Ba-by my heart's on fire!

If you re-fuse me, Hon-ey you'll lose me, Then you'll be left a -

lone; Oh! ba - by, Tel-e-phone and tell me I'se your own. ___

004 ii (131—solo piano)
034 (67—piano I)
107 (22)
116 (f4857, staff 1)

Allegretto [from] *Symphony No. 4*
Central Park in the Dark
Study No. 23: Allegro
The Celestial Railroad

HOME! SWEET HOME!

("'Mid pleasures and palaces though we may roam")

SOURCE: *The Golden Book of Favorite Songs*, p. 24

John Howard Payne

HENRY ROWLEY BISHOP, © 1821

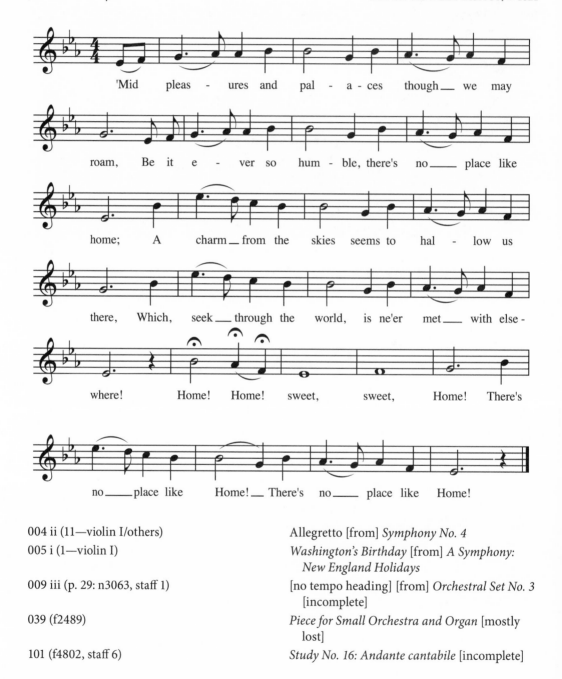

004 ii (11—violin I/others)	Allegretto [from] *Symphony No. 4*
005 i (1—violin I)	*Washington's Birthday* [from] *A Symphony: New England Holidays*
009 iii (p. 29: n3063, staff 1)	[no tempo heading] [from] *Orchestral Set No. 3* [incomplete]
039 (f2489)	*Piece for Small Orchestra and Organ* [mostly lost]
101 (f4802, staff 6)	*Study No. 16: Andante cantabile* [incomplete]

108-a

IT'S RAINING, IT'S POURING

("It's raining, it's pouring, the old man is snoring")

SOURCE: children's nursery rhyme

It's rain - ing, it's pour - ing, the old man is snor - ing. He

went to bed and he bumped his head, and he would - n't get up in the morn - ing.

180 (f5794, staff 12, last measure)
313 (22—voice)

An Election
Nov. 2, 1920 (An Election)

109

I'VE BEEN WORKING ON THE RAILROAD

(Levee Song)

("Oh, I was born in Mobile town")

SOURCE: *Twice 55 Community Songs,* no. 57

first appearance of song: 1894

Chorus

I've been work - in' on the rail - road, All the live - long

day;____ I've been work - in' on the rail - road, To

pass the time a - way.____ Don't you hear the whis - tle

blow - in', Rise up so ear - ly in the morn; —

Don't you hear the cap-'n shout - in', "Di - nah, blow your horn!" —

009 ii (p. 20: n3005, staff 10, male chorus or trombones)	*An Afternoon or During Camp Meetin' Week— One Secular Afternoon (In Bethel)* [from] *Orchestral Set No. 3* [incomplete]
104 (75)	*Study No. 20: March* (Slow Allegro or Fast Andante)
259 (16—voice)	*The Greatest Man*

110

JINGLE, BELLS

("Dashing through the snow in a one horse open sleigh")

SOURCE: *The Golden Book of Favorite Songs,* p. 120

James S. Pierpont, 1857   JAMES S. PIERPONT, © 1857

Dash - ing thro' the snow In a one horse o - pen sleigh

O'er the fields we go, Laugh-ing all the way; Bells on bob-tail ring,

Mak-ing spir-its bright, What fun it is to ride and sing A

009 ii (p. 21: n3144, staff 9)

An Afternoon or During Camp Meetin' Week—
One Secular Afternoon (In Bethel) [from]
Orchestral Set No. 3 [incomplete]

086 ii (50—violin)

Presto ("TSIAJ" or Medley on the Fence [or] on
the Campus!) [from] *Trio for Violin,*
Violoncello, and Piano

111

JUST BEFORE THE BATTLE, MOTHER

("Just before the battle, Mother")

SOURCE: Root and Cady publication of 1863

George Frederick Root

GEORGE FREDERICK ROOT, © 1863

With the en-e-my in view, Com-rades brave are round me ly-ing, Fill'd with tho'ts of home and God; For well they know that on the mor-row, Some will sleep be-neath the sod.

Chorus

Fare - well, Moth - er, you may nev-er Press me to your heart a - gain; But O, you'll not for-get me, Moth - er, If I'm num-ber'd with the slain.

112

KATHLEEN MAVOURNEEN

=former Unknown Tune 219

see also David 13-b or Hexham 28-a

("Kathleen Mavourneen, the gray dawn is breaking")

SOURCE: *The Golden Book of Favorite Songs,* pp. 48–49

Annie Barry Crawford   FREDERICK WILLIAM NICHOLLS CROUCH, 1840

Kath - leen Ma - vour - neen, the gray dawn is break - ing The

horn of the hun-ter is heard on the hill, The lark from her

light wing the bright dew is shak - ing, Kath - leen Ma -

vour-neen! What, slum - b'ring still? Oh! hast thou for - got - ten how

soon we must sev-er? Oh! hast thou for - got-ten this day we must

part? It may be for years, and it may be for - ev-er; Oh!

why art thou si - lent, thou voice of my heart? It may be for

years and it may be for-ev-er; Then why ___ art thou si-lent,

Kath - leen Ma - vour - neen?

016 iii (1—horn)	*The Pond* [from] *Set No. 7: Water Colors*
[This may be *David* or *Hexham*]	
040 (3—voice or trumpet)	*The Pond*
Possible borrowing:	
084 i (21—solo cello)	Largo cantabile: *Hymn* [from] *A Set of Three Short Pieces*
[This may be *David* or *Hexham*]	
267 (15—voice)	*Hymn*
[This may be *David* or *Hexham*]	
332 (1—voice)	*Remembrance*
[This may be *David* or *Hexham*]	

113

KATY DARLING

("Oh, they tell me thou art dead, Katy darling")

SOURCE: Oliver Ditson publication of 1851

Oh, they tell me thou art dead, Ka-ty Dar - ling, That thy

smile I may nev-er more be-hold! Did they tell thee I was false, Ka-ty

Dar - ling, Or my love for thee had e'er grown cold? Oh they

know not thy lov-ing Of the hearts of E - rin's sons; When a

love like to thine Ka-ty Dar - ling, Is the goal to the race that he

runs. Oh, hear me, sweet Ka-ty, For the

wild flowers greet me, Ka - ty Dar - ling, And the love - birds are sing-ing on each

tree; Wilt thou nev-er more hear me, Ka-ty Dar - ling; Be -

hold, love, I'm wait - ing for thee.

005 iii (99—piccolo)

The Fourth of July [from] *A Symphony: New England Holidays*

KINGDOM COMING

("Say, darkeys, hab you seen de massa")

SOURCE: Root and Cady publication of 1862

Henry Clay Work

HENRY CLAY WORK, 1862

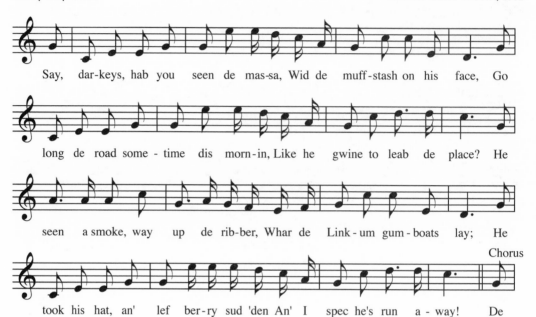

Say, dar-keys, hab you seen de mas-sa, Wid de muff-stash on his face, Go

long de road some-time dis morn-in, Like he gwine to leab de place? He

seen a smoke, way up de rib-ber, Whar de Link-um gum-boats lay; He

Chorus

took his hat, an' lef ber-ry sud 'den An' I spec he's run a-way! De

mas-sa run? ha, ha! De dar-key stay! ho, ho! It mus' be now de

king-dom com-in' An' de year ob Ju-bi-lo!

005 iii (110—piccolo)	*The Fourth of July* [from] *A Symphony: New England Holidays*
009 ii (p. 16: n3002, section 6, staff 8, solo trombone)	*An Afternoon or During Camp Meetin' Week— One Secular Afternoon (In Bethel)* [from] *Orchestral Set No. 3* [incomplete]

LITTLE ANNIE ROONEY

("A winning way, a pleasant smile")

SOURCE: Hitchcock Music Stores publication (n.d.)

Michael Nolan, 1890   MICHAEL NOLAN, 1890

037 (f2210, brace 2)   *The General Slocum* [incomplete]
385 (1—piano)   *Waltz*

116

LITTLE BROWN JUG

("My wife and I live all alone")

SOURCE: *America Sings*, p. 88

Joseph Eastburn Winner, 1869

JOSEPH EASTBURN WINNER, © 1869

My wife and I live all a-lone in a lit-tle brown hut we call our own.

She loves gin, and I love rum, Tell you what it is, Don't we have fun?

Refrain

Ha! Ha! Ha! 'tis you and me, Lit-tle Brown Jug Don't I love thee

Ha! Ha! Ha! 'tis you and me, Lit-tle Brown Jug Don't I love thee.

009 ii (p. 16: n3002, section 7, staff 10)

An Afternoon or During Camp Meetin' Week—
One Secular Afternoon (In Bethel) [from]
Orchestral Set No. 3 [incomplete]

117

DE LITTLE CABINS ALL AM EMPTY NOW

("Oh, dis heart ob mine am breaking")

SOURCE: W. F. Shaw publication of 1881

Thomas P. Westendorf

THOMAS P. WESTENDORF

Oh, I hear de owl a hoot-in' in de dark-ness ob de night, And it

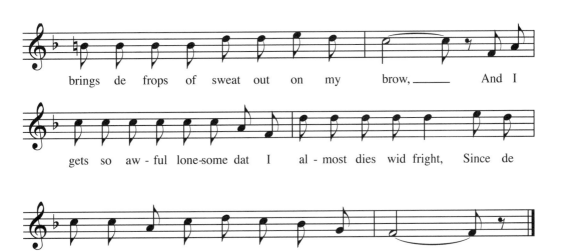

brings de frops of sweat out on my brow,⸻ And I

gets so aw-ful lone-some dat I al-most dies wid fright, Since de

lit - tle cab - ins all am emp - ty now.⸻

020 iii (3—horn)   *In the Night* [from] *Set for Theatre Orchestra*

117-a
LOCH LOMOND
("By yon bonnie banks, And by yon bonnie braes")

SOURCE: *The New Blue Book of Favorite Songs,* p. 36

Old Scotch Air

By⸻ yon bon - nie banks, And by yon bon - nie braes, Where the

sun shines bright on Loch Lo - mond, Where me and my true love were

Refrain

ev - er wont to gae, On the bon - nie, bon - nie banks of Loch Lo - mond. Oh!

Ye'll take the high road, and I'll take the low road And I'll be in Scot-land a-

fore ye, But me and my true love will nev - er meet a - gain On the

bon - nie, bon - nie banks of Loch Lo - mond.

088 iii (p. 55, staff 4, m. 2)   *The Alcotts* [from] *Sonata No. 2 for Piano:*
Concord, Mass., 1840–60

118

LONDON BRIDGE

("London bridge is falling down")

SOURCE: *Traditional Music of America*, p. 262

first appearance of text in print, ca. 1744   first printing of melody with traditional words: 1879

Lon- don Bridge is fall - ing down, fall - ing down, fall - ing down,

Lon - don Bridge is fall - ing down, My fair la - dy.

005 iii (74—piccolo)   *The Fourth of July* [from] *A Symphony: New*
England Holidays

036 (24—flute)   *"County Band" March* [incomplete]

428 (f7440, staff 1, m. 1)   *Burlesque Harmonization of "London Bridge"*

119

LONG, LONG AGO

("Tell me the tales that to me were so dear")

SOURCE: Firth and Hall publication (n.d.)

Thomas Haynes Bayly

THOMAS HAYNES BAYLY
possibly as early as ca. 1835

Tell me the tales that to me were so dear, Long long a-go,
long, long a-go: Sing me the songs I de-light-ed to hear,
Long, long a-go long a-go: Now you are come my
grief is re-mov'd, Let me for-get that so long you have rov'd,

Let me be-lieve that you love as you lov'd, Long long a-go, long a - go.

002 v (70—flute I)	Allegro molto vivace [from] *Symphony No. 2*
004 ii (178—orchestra piano II)	Allegretto [from] *Symphony No. 4*
086 ii (120—violin)	Presto ("TSIAJ" or Medley on the Fence [or] on the Campus!) [from] *Trio for Violin, Violoncello, and Piano*

120
MA BLUSHIN' ROSIE
("Dar's a colored bud ob beauty")

SOURCE: M. Witmark publication of 1900

Edgar Smith

JOHN STROMBERG, © 1900

Refrain

Ro - sie, ___ you are my po - sie, ___ You are ___ ma heart's bo-

quet; ___ Come out ___ heah in de moon - light ___ Dar's sum' fin

sweet lub ___ I wants ter say ___ Your hon - ey boy am

wait - in' ___ Dose ru - by lips ter greet ___ Don' be ___ so ag - gra-

vat - in' ___ Ma blush - in' Ros - ie ___ ma pos - ie sweet. ___

037 (f2210, brace 3)

The General Slocum [incomplete]

121

MASSA'S IN DE COLD GROUND

("Round de meadows am a-ringing")

SOURCE: Firth, Pond and Co. publication of 1852

Stephen Collins Foster   STEPHEN COLLINS FOSTER, 1852

Round de mead-ows am a - ring - ing De dark-ey's mourn - ful

song, While de mock-ing bird am sing - ing,

Hap-py as de day am long. Where de i - vy am a - creep - ing

O'er de gras - sy mound. Dare old Mas-sa am a - sleep - ing,

Chorus

Sleep - ing in de cold, cold ground. Down in de corn - field

Hear dat mourn - ful sound; All de dark - eys am a -

weep - ing, Mas-sa's in de cold, cold ground.

002 i (7—violin I)	Andante moderato [from] *Symphony No. 2*
002 ii (84—violin I)	Allegro [from] *Symphony No. 2*
002 iii (59—flute)	Adagio cantabile [from] *Symphony No. 2*
002 v (228—flute)	Allegro molto vivace [from] *Symphony No. 2*

004 ii (96—flute)	Allegretto [from] *Symphony No. 4*
005 i (116—flute)	*Washington's Birthday* [from] *A Symphony: New England Holidays*
007 i (72—violin I)	*The "St. Gaudens" in Boston Common (Col. Shaw and his Colored Regiment)* [from] *Orchestral Set No. 1: Three Places in New England*
007 ii (27—flute)	*Putnam's Camp, Redding, Connecticut* [from] *Orchestral Set No. 1: Three Places in New England*
008 i (24—flute)	*An Elegy to Our Forefathers* [from] *Orchestral Set No. 2*
008 ii (153—trumpet)	*The Rockstrewn Hills Join in the People's Outdoor Meeting* [from] *Orchestral Set No. 2*
008 iii (83—viola)	*From Hanover Square North, at the End of a Tragic Day, the Voice of the People Again Arose* [from] *Orchestral Set No. 2*
020 iii (10—high bells)	*In the Night* [from] *Set for Theatre Orchestra*
021 (f2488)	*Alcott Overture* [mostly lost]
036 (44—flute)	*"Country Band" March* [incomplete]
058 ii (101—violin I)	*Arguments* [from] *String Quartet No. 2*
084 ii (5—cello)	*Scherzo: Holding Your Own!* [from] *A Set of Three Short Pieces*
088 iv (p. 62, staff 1)	*Thoreau* [from] *Sonata No. 2 for Piano Concord, Mass., 1840–60*
105 (2)	*Study No. 21: Some Southpaw Pitching*
116 (f4848, staff 9)	*The Celestial Railroad*
373 (53—piano)	*Thoreau*
Possible borrowing:	
002 ii (84—violin I)	Allegro [from] *Symphony No. 2*
006 (section A: f1835, 5 staves from bottom of page)	*Universe Symphony*

122

MY BONNIE LIES OVER THE OCEAN

("My Bonnie lies over the ocean")

SOURCE: *The Golden Book of Favorite Songs,* p. 121

H. J. Fulmer

H. J. FULMER

447 (f0001, staff 4)

Sinclair: Two chords, etc., headed "Sun Rise Chord / over East Rock / last time up / in 1896 / Amos sings / Bring / [back my bonnie to me]"

123

MY OLD KENTUCKY HOME

("The sun shines bright in the Old Kentucky home")

SOURCE: Firth, Pond and Co. publication of 1853

Stephen Collins Foster

STEPHEN COLLINS FOSTER, © 1853

The sun shines bright in the old Ken-tuck-y Home, 'Tis

sum-mer, the dark-ies are gay, The corn top's ripe and the

mead-ow's in the bloom, While the birds make mu-sic all the day; The

young folks roll on the lit-tle cab-in floor All mer-ry, all hap-py and

bright: B'yn by Hard Times comes a knock-ing at the door, Then my

Chorus

old Ken-tuck-y Home, good - night! Weep no more, my

la - dy, Oh! weep no more to - day! We will sing one song for the

old Ken-tuck-y Home, For the old Ken-tuck-y Home, far a - way.

123-a

NANCY LEE

("Of all the wives as e'er you know")

SOURCE: Norman L. Munro publication (n.d.)

Fred Weatherly

STEPHEN ADAMS
(pseudonym of Michael Maybrick)

ho! See there she stands an' waves her hands up-

on___ the quay, An' ev'-ry day when I'm a-way, She'll

watch__ for__ me, An' whis-per low, when tem-pests blow, for

Jack__ at sea, Yeo ho!__ lads, ho!__ yeo ho!

The sai - lor's wife, the sai-lor's star__ shall be, Yeo

ho!__ we go a - cross__ the sea, __ The sai - lor's

wife, the sai - lor's star___ shall be, The

sai - lor's wife, his star shall be.___

009 ii (p. 17: n3003, staff 1, trumpet-cornet)   *An Afternoon or During Camp Meetin' Week—*
One Secular Afternoon (In Bethel) [from]
Orchestral Set No. 3 [incomplete]

124

NELLY BLY

("Nelly Bly! Nelly Bly! bring de broom along")

SOURCE: Firth, Pond and Co. publication of 1849 (cover); 1850 (first page of music)

Stephen Collins Foster

STEPHEN COLLINS FOSTER, 1849

Note: Ives does not borrow from this tune.

125

OH, DEM GOLDEN SLIPPERS

("Oh, my golden slippers am laid away")

SOURCE: John F. Perry publication of 1879

James A. Bland

JAMES A. BLAND, 1879

Oh, my gol - den slip-pers am ___ laid a - way, Kase I don't 'spect to wear 'em till my wed-din' day, And my long - tail'd coat, dat I loved so well, I will wear up in de char-iot in de morn; And my long, white robe dat I bought last June, I'm gwine to git changed Kase it fits too soon, And de ole grey hoss dat I used to drive, I will

hitch him to de char - iot in de morn. Oh, dem gold - en slip-pers! Oh, dem

gold-en slip-pers! Gold-en slip-pers I'm gwine to wear, be - cause dey look so

neat; Oh, dem gold - en slip-pers! Oh, dem gold - en slip-pers!

Gold - en slip-pers Ise gwine to wear, To walk de gold - en street.

| 181 (51—piano) | *General William Booth Enters into Heaven* |
| 255 (51—piano) | *General William Booth Enters into Heaven* |

126

OH, MY DARLING CLEMENTINE

("In a cavern, in a canyon")

SOURCE: Oliver Ditson publication of 1884

traditional words and music
© 1884 by PERCY MONTROSE
reissued in 1885, with some change in music, as "Clementine,"
credited to BARKER BRADFORD

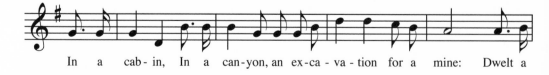

In a cab - in, In a can-yon, an ex-ca - va - tion for a mine: Dwelt a

miner, a For-ty - ni - ner, And his daugh-ter Cle-men - tine. Oh my

dar - ling, Oh my dar - ling, Oh my dar - ling Cle-men - tine, You are

lost and gone for - ev - er, Dref - ful sor - ry, Cle - men - tine.

038 (13—flute)   *The Gong on the Hook and Ladder or Firemen's*
Parade on Main Street

070 (13—flute)   *The Gong on the Hook and Ladder or Firemen's*
Parade on Main Street

127

OH! SUSANNA

("I came from Alabama wid my banjo on my knee")

SOURCE: C. Holt, Jr., publication of 1848

Stephen Collins Foster   STEPHEN COLLINS FOSTER, 1848

I__ came from Al - a - ba-ma wid my ban-jo on my knee I'm

gwan to Lou - si - an-na, My__ true love for to see, It__ raind all night the

day I left the weath-er it was dry, The sun so hot I frose to death Sus-

an-na dont you cry. Oh! Sus - an-na Oh! dont you cry for me I've

come from Al - a - ba - ma wid mi ban - jo on my knee.

061 i (19—violin)

Autumn [from] *Sonata No. 2 for Violin and Piano*

128

OLD BLACK JOE

("Gone are the days when my heart was young and gay")

SOURCE: Firth, Pond and Co. publication of 1860

Stephen Collins Foster

STEPHEN COLLINS FOSTER, © 1860

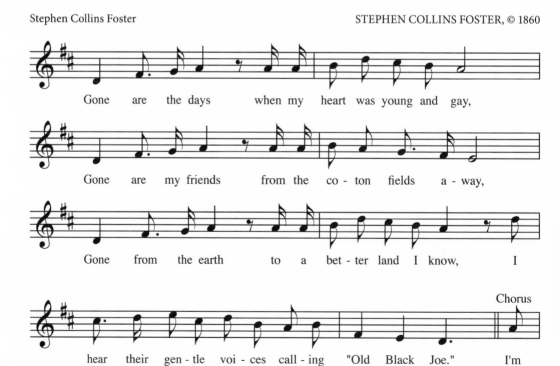

Gone are the days when my heart was young and gay,

Gone are my friends from the co - ton fields a - way,

Gone from the earth to a bet - ter land I know, I

hear their gen - tle voi - ces call - ing "Old Black Joe." I'm

com - ing, I'm com - ing, for my head is bend - ing low: I

hear those gen - tle voi - ces call - ing, "Old Black Joe."

004 ii (112—solo piano)	Allegretto [from] *Symphony No. 4*
007 i (1—flute)	*The "St. Gaudens" in Boston Common (Col. Shaw and his Colored Regiment)* [from] *Orchestral Set No. 1: Three Places in New England*
008 i (3—zither)	*An Elegy to Our Forefathers* [from] *Orchestral Set No. 2*
116 (65)	*The Celestial Railroad*

Possible borrowing:

002 v (65—horns)	Allegro molto vivace [from] *Symphony No. 2*
007 i (2—bass), see also *Jesus Loves Me* 30	*The "St. Gaudens" in Boston Common (Col. Shaw and his Colored Regiment)* [from] *Orchestral Set No. 1: Three Places in New England*

129

OLD FOLKS AT HOME

("'Way down upon de Swanee Ribber")

SOURCE: Firth, Pond and Co. publication of 1851

Stephen Collins Foster   STEPHEN COLLINS FOSTER, 1851

'Way down up- on the Swa-nee rib-ber, Far, far a - way,

Dere's wha my heart is turn - ing eb-ber, Dere's wha de old folks

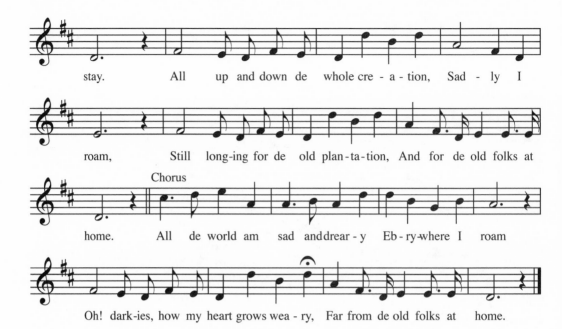

stay. All up and down de whole cre - a - tion, Sad - ly I

roam, Still long-ing for de old plan - ta - tion, And for de old folks at

Chorus

home. All de world am sad and drear - y Eb - ry where I roam

Oh! dark-ies, how my heart grows wea - ry, Far from de old folks at home.

005 i (7—horn)

Washington's Birthday [from] *A Symphony: New England Holidays*

130

ON THE BANKS OF THE WABASH, FAR AWAY

("Round my Indiana homestead wave the cornfield" [*sic*])

SOURCE: Howley, Haviland and Co. publication of 1897

Paul Dresser

PAUL DRESSER, © 1897

Oh, the moon- light's fair to-night a-long the Wa-bash, From the

fields there comes the breath of new mown hay._____ Thro' the

syc - a - mores   the   can - dle   lights   are   gleam - ing,   On   the

banks   of   the   Wa-bash,   far   a - way.

039 (f2490)	*Piece for Small Orchestra and Organ* [mostly lost]
049 iii (f2721) [appears only in sketch; does not appear in actual score]	*Tone Roads No. 3* [from] *Tone Roads et al.*
259 (9—voice)	*The Greatest Man*
372 (6—voice)	*The Things Our Fathers Loved*

130-a

PETER, PETER PUMPKIN EATER

=possibly former Unknown Tune 201

("Peter, Peter pumpkin eater,

Had a wife but couldn't keep her,

So he put her in a pumpkin shell,

And there he kept her very well.")

SOURCE: English nursery rhyme

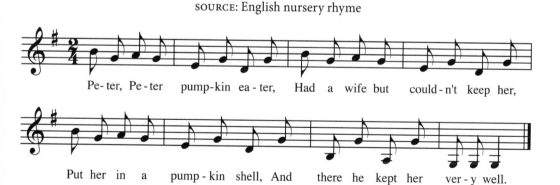

Pe - ter, Pe - ter   pump-kin ea - ter,   Had a wife but   could - n't keep her,

Put her in a   pump - kin shell, And   there he kept her   ver - y well.

004 ii (72—orchestra piano primo and solo piano)	Allegretto [from] *Symphony No. 4*

088 ii (p. 23, staff 2, right hand)

Hawthorne [from] *Sonata No. 2 for Piano: Concord, Mass., 1840–60*

116 (f4846, staff 14)

The Celestial Railroad

130-b

PUSH DEM CLOUDS AWAY

=former Unknown Tune 194

SOURCE: T. B. Harms publication of 1892

PERCY GAUNT, 1892

If you want to git to Hea-ven on de nick-el-plat-ed road, Just __ push dem clouds a - way! __ Bring a - long all yer bag-gage and __ check it to de Lord, When you push dem clouds a - way! __ If de train am a-speed-in' an' you can't catch __ on, __ When you push dem clouds a - way! __ You're a coon dat's gone, and __ wuss dan __ none, When you push dem clouds a - way! Just

Chorus

push! Don't shove! Just push dem clouds a -

way! _____ Keep a-push - in' an' a-shov - in' an' a-

push - in' an' a-shov - in', 'Till you push dem clouds a - way!

020 ii (86—violin)   *In the Inn* [from] *Set for Theatre Orchestra*

131

REUBEN AND RACHEL

("Reuben, I have long been thinking")

SOURCE: White, Smith, and Perry publication of 1871

Harry Birch   WILLIAM GOOCH, pub. 1871

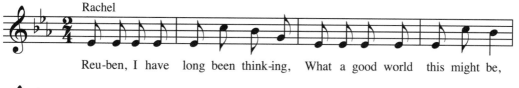

Reu-ben, I have long been think-ing, What a good world this might be,

If the men were all trans-por-ted Far be-yond the North-ern Sea.

Ra-chel, I have long been think-ing, What a fine world this might be,

If we had some more young la-dies On this side the North-ern Sea.

131-a

RIDING DOWN FROM BANGOR

("Riding down from Bangor on an eastbound train")

SOURCE: Oliver Ditson publication of 1881

LOUIS SHREVE OSBORNE, 1881

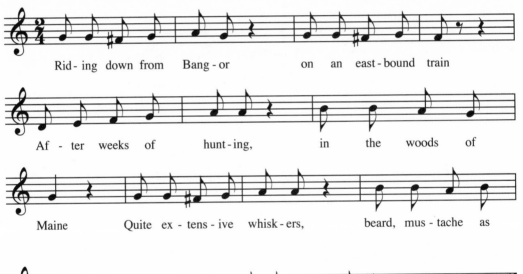

Rid - ing down from Bang - or on an east - bound train

Af - ter weeks of hunt - ing, in the woods of

Maine Quite ex - tens - ive whisk - ers, beard, mus - tache as

well Sat a stu - dent fel - low, tall and slim and swell.

132

ROCK-A-BYE BABY

("Rock-a-bye, baby, on the tree top")

SOURCE: Charles D. Blake publication of 1887

words first published 1761 in *Mother Goose's Melody* as
"Hush-a-bye, Baby"; changed to current text by Effie I. Crockett   EFFIE I. CROCKETT, ca. 1872

Rock - a-bye, ba - by, on the tree top, When the wind

blows the cra - dle will rock, When the bough

breaks the cra - dle will fall, And

down will come ba - by, cra - dle and all.

008 ii (127—flute)   *The Rockstrewn Hills Join in the People's
                    Outdoor Meeting [from] Orchestral Set No. 2*

133

THE SIDEWALKS OF NEW YORK

("Down in front of Casey's old brown wooden stoop")

SOURCE: Howley, Haviland and Co. publication of 1894

James W. Blake and Charles B. Lawlor   JAMES W. BLAKE and CHARLES B. LAWLOR, © 1894

East   side,   West   side,   all   a - round   the

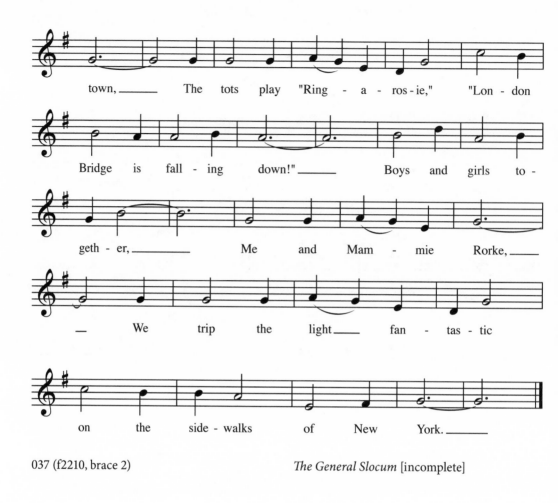

town, _____ The tots play "Ring - a - ros - ie," "Lon - don

Bridge is fall - ing down!" _____ Boys and girls to -

geth - er, _____ Me and Mam - mie Rorke, _____

— We trip the light ____ fan - tas - tic

on the side - walks of New York. _____

037 (f2210, brace 2)   *The General Slocum* [incomplete]

134

SILVER THREADS AMONG THE GOLD

("Darling, I am growing old")

SOURCE: Charles W. Harris publication of 1873

Eben Eugene Rexford   HART PEASE DANKS, © 1873

Dar - ling, I am grow-ing old, _____ Sil - ver threads a-mong the

gold, Shine up-on my brow to - day; _____ Life is fad-ing fast a-

way;   But   my dar - ling, you will   be,   will be

Al - ways young and fair to me,   Yes!   my dar-ling, you will

be_____   Al - ways young and fair   to me.

Chorus

Dar - ling, I am grow-ing, grow - ing old,   Sil - ver threads a-mong the

gold,   Shine up-on my brow to - day; __ Life   is fad-ing fast a - way.

009 ii (p. 16: n3002, section 7, staff 11)

An Afternoon or During Camp Meetin' Week—
One Secular Afternoon (In Bethel) [from]
Orchestral Set No. 3 [incomplete]

135

THE SON OF A GAMBOLIER

("I'm a rambling wretch of poverty")

SOURCE: Spaeth, *Read 'Em and Weep,* p. 89

first appearance of tune with words
"A Song of a Gambolier," © 1873

Chorus:
Then combine your humble ditties,
As from tavern to tavern we steer,
Like ev'ry honest fellow,

I drinks my lager beer,
Like ev'ry jolly fellow,
I takes my whisky clear,
I'm a rambling wreck of poverty,
And the son of a gambolier.

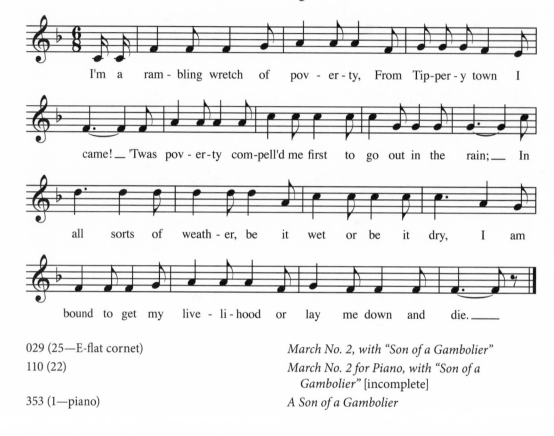

I'm a ram - bling wretch of pov - er - ty, From Tip-per-y town I
came! __ 'Twas pov - er - ty com-pell'd me first to go out in the rain; __ In
all sorts of weath - er, be it wet or be it dry, I am
bound to get my live - li - hood or lay me down and die. __

029 (25—E-flat cornet)   *March No. 2, with "Son of a Gambolier"*
110 (22)   *March No. 2 for Piano, with "Son of a*
                                Gambolier" [incomplete]
353 (1—piano)   *A Son of a Gambolier*

136

STOP THAT KNOCKING AT MY DOOR

("I once did lub a colord Gal")

SOURCE: G. P. Reed publication of 1847

Anthony F. Winnemore, 1843   ANTHONY F. WINNEMORE, 1843

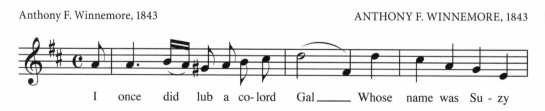

I once did lub a co-lord Gal__ Whose name was Su - zy

Brown, She came from old Vir - gin - ny, She was de fair - est in de town, Her eyes so bright dey shine at night when de moon am gone a - way, She used to call his dark - ey up Just a fore de broke of day: wid a who dar? who dar? who dar? An a who dar a knock-ing at my door? Am dat you Sam? Am dat you Sam? No, you bet - ter stop dat knock-ing at my door.

088 iii (p. 56, staff 1)

The Alcotts [from] *Sonata No. 2 for Piano: Concord, Mass., 1840–60*

137
STREETS OF CAIRO

(The Poor Little Country Maid)

(The Hootchy-Kootchy Dance)

("I will sing you a song, And it won't be very long")

SOURCE: Frank Harding publication of 1895

James Thornton

JAMES THORNTON, pub. 1895
also claimed by SOL BLOOM, 1893

I will sing you a song, And it won't be ve - ry long, 'Bout a

maid - en sweet, And she nev - er would do wrong,

Ev - 'ry - one said she was pret - ty, She was not long in the ci - ty,

Chorus

All a - lone, oh, what a pit - ty, Poor lit - tle maid. She nev - er

saw the streets of Cai - ro, On the Mid - way she had nev - er strayed,

She nev - er saw the kutch - y, kutch - y, Poor lit - tle coun - try maid. __

083 (17—violins)
084 ii (17—violins)

Scherzo for String Quartet
Scherzo: Holding Your Own! [from] *A Set of Three Short Pieces*

138

SWEET ROSIE O'GRADY

("Just down around the corner of the street where I reside")

SOURCE: Joseph W. Stern publication of 1896

Maude Nugent, 1896

MAUDE NUGENT, 1896

Note: Ives does not borrow from this tune.

139

TAMMANY

("Hiawatha was an Indian, so was Navajo")

SOURCE: M. Witmark publication of 1905

Vincent P. Bryan, 1905

GUS EDWARDS, 1905

Hi-a-wa-tha was an In-dian, so was Nav-a-jo, Pale-face or-gan-grind-ers killed them man-y moons a-go. But there is a band of In-dians, that will nev-er die. When they're at the In-dian club, this is their bat-tle cry: Tam-ma-ny, Tam-ma-ny, Big Chief sits in his te-pee, cheer-ing braves to vic-to-ry. Tam-ma-ny, Tam-ma-

ny,   Swamp 'em Swamp 'em   get   the "wam-pum,"   Tam - ma - ny.

010 iii (7—piccolo)	*The Ruined River* [from] *Set No. 1 for Chamber Orchestra*
014 i (f6157, staff 1, m. 3—piano)	*The New River* [from] *Set No. 5: The Other Side of Pioneering, or Side Lights on American Enterprise*
186 (7—piccolo)	*The New River*
Possible borrowing:	
017 i (f2781, score 1, m. 3—voice)	*The New River* [from] *Set No. 8: Songs Without Voices*

140

TA-RA-RA BOOM-DE-AY!

("A sweet tuxedo girl you see")

SOURCE: Leo Feist publication of 1922 (as "Ta-ra-ra Boom-der-é")

Henry J. Sayers   HENRY J. SAYERS, © 1891

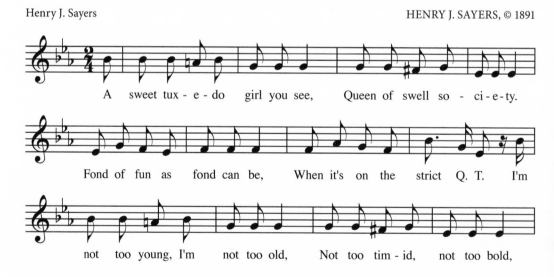

A   sweet tux - e - do   girl you see,   Queen of swell so - ci - e - ty.

Fond of fun as   fond can be,   When it's on   the   strict Q. T.   I'm

not   too young, I'm   not too old,   Not too tim - id,   not too bold,

Just the kind you'd like to hold, Just the kind for sport I'm told. Ta-ra-ra

Boom-der-é Ta-ra-ra Boom-der-é Ta-ra-ra Boom-der-é Ta-ra-ra

Boom-der-é Ta-ra-ra Boom-der-é Ta-ra-ra Boom-der-é

Ta - ra - ra Boom - der - é Ta - ra - ra Boom - der - é.

010 iii (13—cornet)	*The Ruined River* [from] *Set No. 1 for Chamber Orchestra*
014 i (f6158, m. 1—voice)	*The New River* [from] *Set No. 5: The Other Side of Pioneering, or Side Lights on American Enterprise*
017 i (f2782, score 2, voice)	*The New River* [from] *Set No. 8: Songs Without Voices*
020 ii (74—violin)	*In the Inn (Potpourri)* [from] *Set for Theatre Orchestra*
047 (1—winds)	*Take-Off No. 7: Mike Donlin-Johnny Evers* [incomplete]
086 ii (130—violin)	Presto ("TSIAJ") or Medley on the Fence [or] on the Campus!) [from] *Trio for Violin, Violoncello, and Piano*
186 (13—voices)	*The New River*

141

THAT OLD CABIN HOME UPON THE HILL

("Far away in the South among the cotton fields")

SOURCE: G. Schirmer publication of 1918

Frank Dumont

FRANK DUMONT, © 1880

086 ii (68—cello)

Presto ("TSIAJ" or Medley on the Fence [or] on the Campus!) [from] *Trio for Violin, Violoncello, and Piano*

109 (65)

March No. 1 for Piano, with "Year of Jubilee"

142

THERE'S MUSIC IN THE AIR

("There's music in the air, when the infant morn is nigh")

SOURCE: *Carmina Yalensia*, p. 55

Frances Jane Crosby

GEORGE FREDERICK ROOT, 1854

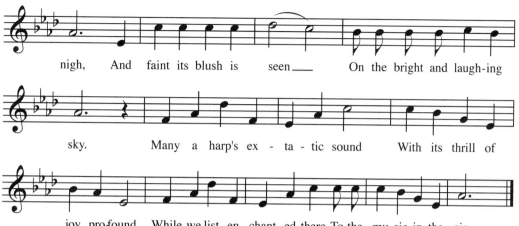

nigh, And faint its blush is seen___ On the bright and laugh-ing

sky. Many a harp's ex - ta - tic sound With its thrill of

joy pro-found, While we list en chant-ed there To the mu-sic in the air.

003 ii (64—flute)   *Children's Day* [from] *Symphony No. 3*

143

VIOLETS

("Ev'ry morn I send thee violets")

SOURCE: Boosey publication of 1900

Julian Fane

ELLEN WRIGHT, © 1900
words adapted from Heinrich Heine

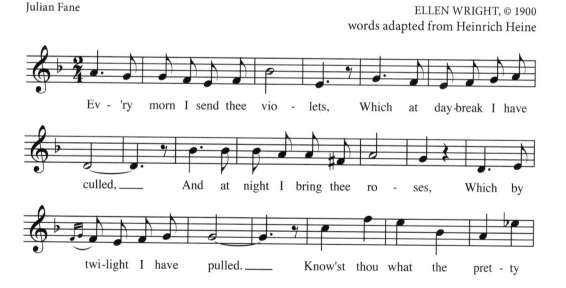

Ev - 'ry morn I send thee vio - lets, Which at day-break I have

culled,___ And at night I bring thee ro - ses, Which by

twi-light I have pulled.___ Know'st thou what the pret - ty

flow-ers Ten - der se-cret-ly would say?_____ Ah!_____

Ah!_____ Thou shalt dream of me the night long, And be true to

me by day. Ah!_____ Ah!_____

Thou shalt dream of me the night long And be true to me by day.__

WAKE NICODEMUS

("Nicodemus, the slave, was of African birth")

SOURCE: Root and Cady publication of 1864

Henry Clay Work   HENRY CLAY WORK, © 1864

Nic - o - de - mus, the slave, was of Af - ri - can birth, And was bought for a bag - ful of gold; He was rec - on'd as part of the salt of the earth; But he died years a-go, ver - y old. 'Twas his last sad re-quest so we laid him a-way In the trunk of an old hol - low tree. "Wake me up!" was his charge, "at the first break of day, Wake me up for the great Ju - bi - lee!"

Chorus

The "Good Time Com-ing" is al-most here! It was long, long, long on the way! Now run and tell E - li - jah to hur-ry up Pomp, And meet us at the gum-tree down in the swamp, To wake Nic - o - de-mus to - day.

144-a

WHERE DID YOU GET THAT HAT?

SOURCE: Harding's Music Office publication

Joseph J. Sullivan, 1888   JOSEPH J. SULLIVAN, 1888

Now how I came to get this hat 'tis ve-ry strange and fun-ny;

grand-fa-ther died and left to me his prop-er-ty and mon-ey. And

when the will it was read out, they told me straight and flat; If

I would have his mon-ey, I must al-ways wear his hat!

Chorus

Where did you get that hat? Where did you get that tile?

Is-n't it a nob-by one, and just the prop-er style? I should like to have one

just the same as that! Where-e'er I go they shout:"Hel-lo! Where did you get that hat?"

An Afternoon or During Camp Meetin' Week—
One Secular Afternoon (In Bethel) [from]
Orchestral Set No. 3 [incomplete]

145

YEAR OF JUBILEE

(Kingdom Has Come!)

("I come up Norf, on a little bender")

SOURCE: H. M. Higgins publication of 1862

"Sambo"

I come up Norf, on a lit-tle ben-der, Left Mis-sus at home wid

no one to tend her, Ole Mas-sa's gone, I dun-no whar to:

Chorus

Sam-bo pret-ty sure he don't much care to. Den sound de horn,____

beat de drum,____ Sound de horn and beat de drum, De

year ob ju-bi-lee am come. Sound de horn and

beat de drum, De year ob ju-bi-lee am come.

109 (17) *March No. 1 for Piano*

[4]

College Music

While he was a student at Yale, Ives wrote music for a number of shows produced by Delta Kappa Epsilon, a junior fraternity to which he belonged. One might expect that these would be natural outlets for him to engage in musical pranks through the citations of music borrowed from fraternity and college songs that his classmates would recognize. This is, however, not the case, for none of these works contain borrowed music. Instead, Ives reserved his citations of fraternity and college songs for compositions that had no specific connection with his life in the social organizations of which he was a member.

College songs provided the least inspiration of all Ives's source material when one considers the number of works in which such music is used. Of the twenty-three to twenty-four movements containing college songs, only *Symphony No. 2* affords one of them more than a passing glance or cursory treatment. There, in the second movement, the lovely melodic contour of *Where, O Where Are the Verdant Freshmen?* based on David Walker's *The Hebrew Children,* provides moments of considerable substance with its gentle citations.

In *Johnny Poe,* a work for male chorus and orchestra, Ives recalled the exploits of one of Princeton's legendary students.[1] While Ives's borrowings from the song *Old Nassau* are not extensive, they are sufficient to evoke the university and her athlete-war hero.

The remaining works consist of four marches, in which Ives's use of his borrowed sources was less ambitious in scope, and in the second movement of the *Trio for Violin, Violoncello, and Piano,* marked "TSIAJ" (for "this scherzo is a joke"), where *A Band of Brothers in DKE; Hold the Fort, McClung Is Coming; Few Days;* and *Freshmen in the Park* are not terribly important, being only four of at least twenty-four borrowings. Only *The Gods of Egypt Bid Us Hail!* is afforded a lengthy citation.[2] In *Calcium Light Night,* the fifth movement of his first set for chamber orchestra, and in the incomplete *Yale-Princeton Football Game,* where borrowing is of greater consequence than in most of Ives's other music citing such material, Ives provides memos of words and tunes of fraternity and college songs that he uses.

The citation of college and fraternity songs had, and has, a decided significance for the insider, the Yale man, the connoisseur, but there is a certain limited appeal to this music. Ives undoubtedly saw it as somewhat frivolous, containing none of the universal elements that he found, for example, in the hymn tunes and patriotic and military music of the common man. Thus, borrowed college tunes saw only limited use as a vehicle for Ives's thoughts and creativity.

146

A BAND OF BROTHERS IN DKE

(Phi Marching Song)

("A band of brothers in DKE, we march along tonight")

SOURCE: *100 Songs of DKE,* pp. 36–37

Hugh A. Boyne   re-arranged by WILLIAM G. HARRIS

A band of broth-ers in D K E, we march a-long to - night. __

Two by two with arms locked firm and tight; ___ Our

lead - er sig-nals with hat in hand, as we go march-ing by, ___

Chorus

Sing - ing Del - ta Kap-pa Ep - si - lon. So mer-ri-ly sing we

all to D K E, ___ The moth - er of jol - li-ty, ___

__ Whose chil-dren are gay and free, ___ We'll sing to Phi, and

then we'll sing to dear __ old Del - ta Kap-pa Ep-si - lon. __

010 v (12—clarinet)   *Calcium Light Night* [from] *Set No. 1 for*
                                        Chamber Orchestra

086 ii (16—violin)   Presto ("TSIAJ" or Medley on the Fence [or] on the Campus!) [from] *Trio for Violin, Violoncello, and Piano*

147

BATTELL CHAPEL CHIMES

SOURCE: Taken from Ives's *The Bells of Yale,* mm. 24–31

192 (24—piano)
440 (16—bells)

The Bells of Yale
E. Ives: *A Christmas Carol*

148

BINGO

("Here's to good old Yale, drink it down")

SOURCE: *Carmina Yalensia,* p. 24

first appeared as "Brandy and Water"
JULIEN CARLE, 1853

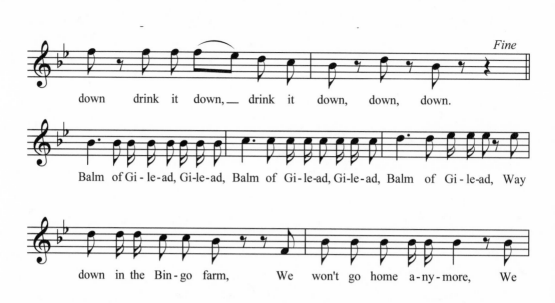

down drink it down, — drink it down, down, down.

Balm of Gi-le-ad, Gi-le-ad, Balm of Gi-le-ad, Gi-le-ad, Balm of Gi-le-ad, Way

down in the Bin-go farm, We won't go home a-ny-more, We

won't go home a-ny-more, We won't go home a-ny-more, Way

down on the Bin-go farm, Bin-go, Bin-go, Bin-go, Bin-go,

D.C. al Fine

B I

N G O

(spoken)

Bin-go, Bin-go, Way down on the Bin-go farm.

113 (41)

Possible borrowing:

    426 (1—piano); or *Lebanon* 33

March No. 6 for Piano, with "Here's to Good Old Yale"

Burlesque Harmonization in C

148-a

BREKEKE-KEK, KO-AX, KO-AX

[from *THE FROGS*]*

*translation has Brekekekex, coax, coax

ARISTOPHANES

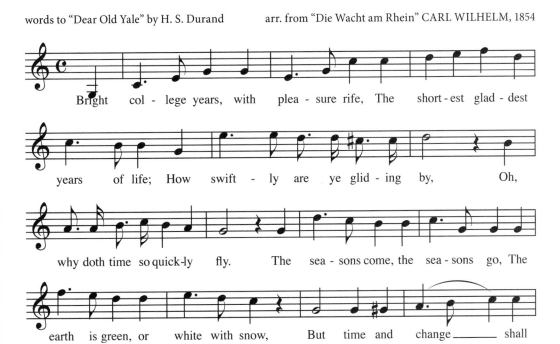

Bre - ke - ke - kek, ko - ax, ko - ax

051 (f2203, m. 6)   *Yale-Princeton Football Game* [incomplete?]

149

DEAR OLD YALE

(Bright College Years)

(Die Wacht am Rhein)

SOURCE: *Yale Songs: A Collection of Songs in Use by the Glee Club
and Students of Yale College*

words to "Dear Old Yale" by H. S. Durand   arr. from "Die Wacht am Rhein" CARL WILHELM, 1854

Bright col - lege years, with plea - sure rife, The short - est glad - dest

years of life; How swift - ly are ye glid - ing by, Oh,

why doth time so quick-ly fly. The sea - sons come, the sea - sons go, The

earth is green, or white with snow, But time and change_____ shall

nought a - vail, To break the friend - ships, formed at Yale

051 (f2203, bottom staff)   *Yale-Princeton Football Game* [incomplete?]

150

FEW DAYS

(The College Chorus)

("Come, brothers, and song we'll sing, Psi U")

SOURCE: *Yale Glees,* p. 9

W. H. Boughton   GEORGE MORRIS, © 1854

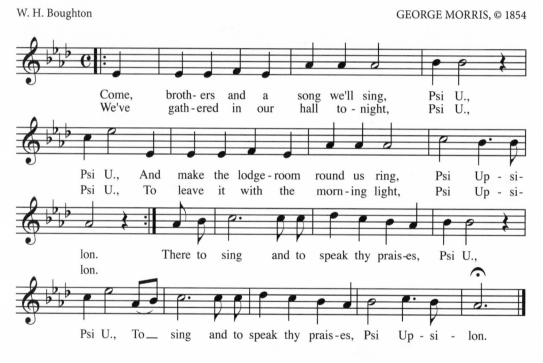

Come, broth- ers and a song we'll sing, Psi U.,
We've gath - ered in our hall to - night, Psi U.,

Psi U., And make the lodge - room round us ring, Psi Up - si-
Psi U., To leave it with the morn - ing light, Psi Up - si-

lon. There to sing and to speak thy prais - es, Psi U.,
lon.

Psi U., To__ sing and to speak thy prais - es, Psi Up - si - lon.

010 v (4—trombone)   *Calcium Light Night* [from] *Set No. 1 for Chamber Orchestra*

038 (20—trumpet)   *The Gong on the Hook and Ladder or Firemen's Parade on Main Street*

070 (20—flute)   *The Gong on the Hook and Ladder or Firemen's Parade on Main Street*

086 ii (47—violin)   *Presto ("TSIAJ") or Medley on the Fence* [or] *on the Campus!) from Trio for Violin, Violoncello, and Piano*

150-a

FRESHMEN IN THE PARK

=model for "The Worms Crawl In"

The worms crawl in, the worms crawl out, the

ants play pi - noch - le on your snout

034 (95—piano II)
086 ii (65—violin)

Central Park in the Dark
Presto ("TSIAJ" or Medley on the Fence [or]
on the Campus!) [from] *Trio for Violin,
Violoncello, and Piano*

150-b

GODS OF EGYPT BID US HAIL!

(Wolf's Head Anthem)

=formerly Unknown Tune 216

Note: The music for this tune was not available for copying. The version that appears below is taken from the second movement of the *Trio for Violin, Violoncello, and Piano.*

[Gods of E- gypt bid us hail!]

086 ii (178—piano)

Presto ("TSIAJ" of Medley on the Fence [or]
on the Campus!) [from] *Trio for Violin,
Violoncello, and Piano*

151

HARVARD HAS BLUE STOCKING GIRLS

("Harvard has blue stocking girls, Yale has blue stocking men")

SOURCE: The Music Manuscripts of Charles Edward Ives, microfilm f2208-09

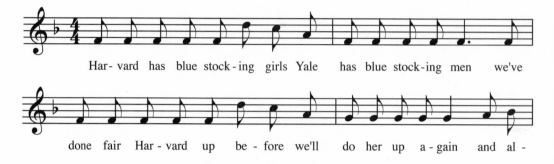

Har - vard has blue stock - ing girls Yale has blue stock - ing men we've

done fair Har - vard up be - fore we'll do her up a - gain and al -

though the Har - vard foot - ball team may try what they can do they can

ne - ver on their tin - type beat the grand old blue.

051 (f2203, 3 staves from bottom of page)   *Yale-Princeton Football Game* [incomplete?]

152

HOLD THE FORT, McCLUNG IS COMING

("Hold the fort, McClung is coming, Barbour signals still")

SOURCE: *Grand Army War Songs,* pp. 88–89

parody on the hymn "Hold the Fort"
PHILIP PAUL BLISS, © 1870

Hold the fort, Mc - Clung is com - ing Bar - bour sig - nals still

Hef - fle -fin - ger   in the cen - ter   Win   we must and   will.

051 (f2203, bottom staff)   *Yale-Princeton Football Game* [incomplete?]
086 ii (169—piano)   Presto ("TSIAJ" or Medley on the Fence [or]
                                on the Campus!) [from] *Trio for Violin,*
                                 Violoncello, and Piano

153

HY-CAN NUCK A NO

("Hy-can nuck a no, Hy-can nuck a no ko")

SOURCE: The Music Manuscripts of Charles Edward Ives, microfilm f2208-09

Hy - can nuck a no   Hy - can nuck a no ko

051 (f2203, 2 staves from bottom of page)   *Yale-Princeton Football Game* [incomplete?]

154

JOLLY DOGS

(Marching Song)

("And when in future years you trot your boy
upon your knee" = words to 3rd stanza)

SOURCE: *100 Songs of DKE* (1900), pp. 38–39

A. E. Lamb   air: "Jolly Dogs"
3rd stanza preferred by Ives

And   when in fu-ture   years you trot your boy up-on your knee,   Just

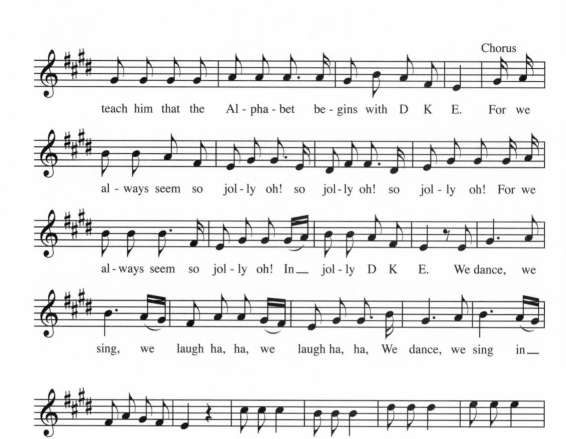

teach him that the Al - pha - bet be - gins with D K E. For we

al - ways seem so jol - ly oh! so jol - ly oh! so jol - ly oh! For we

al - ways seem so jol - ly oh! In — jol - ly D K E. We dance, we

sing, we laugh ha, ha, we laugh ha, ha, We dance, we sing in —

Jol - ly D K E. Fa la la, fal la la, fal la la, fal la la,

fal la la, fal la la, fal la la la la la la, la la la la,

Slap, bang, here we are a - gain, here we are a - gain, here we are a - gain,

Slap, bang, here we are a - gain, Hur - rah for D K E.

010 v (8—piccolo)

033 (89—voices)

Calcium Light Night [from] *Set No. 1 for Chamber Orchestra*

March: The Circus Band

196   **THE CHARLES IVES TUNEBOOK**

155

OLD NASSAU

("Tune every harp and every voice")

SOURCE: Wilford Seymour publication of 1905

Harland Page Peck

CARL LANGLOTZ, 1859

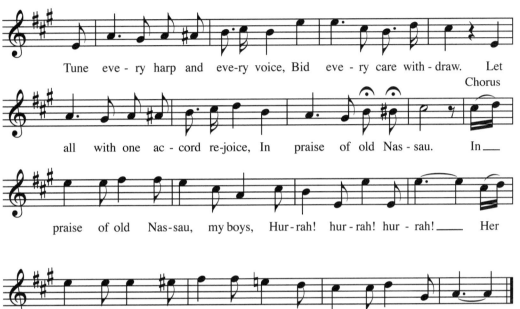

Tune eve - ry harp and eve-ry voice, Bid eve - ry care with - draw. Let
Chorus

all with one ac - cord re-joice, In praise of old Nas - sau. In

praise of old Nas-sau, my boys, Hur-rah! hur - rah! hur - rah! Her

sons will give while they shall live, Three cheers for old Nas - sau.

051 (f2203—4 staves from bottom of page)   *Yale-Princeton Football Game* [incomplete?]
183 (44—bass voice)   *Johnny Poe* [incomplete]

156

OMEGA LAMDA CHI

=parody on "Sailing, Sailing"

SOURCE: Taken from Ives's *March No. 3* (111)

053 (9—E-flat basses)
111 (3)

March in F and C, with "Omega Lambda Chi"
March No. 3 for Piano, with "Omega Lamba Chi"

157

WHERE, O WHERE

(Ganges)

("Where, O where are the verdant Freshmen?")

("Where are the Hebrew children?")

("Where, O where is pretty little Susie?")

SOURCE: *The New Blue Book of Favorite Songs,* pp. 230–31

parody on the hymn "The Hebrew Children"
DAVID WALKER, 1841

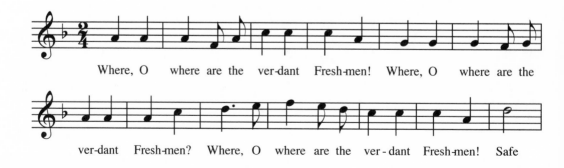

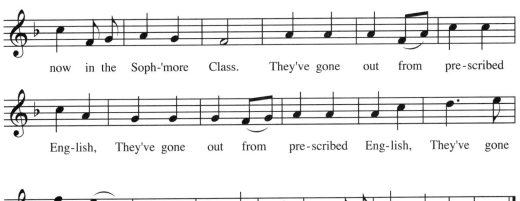

now in the Soph-'more Class. They've gone out from pre-scribed

Eng-lish, They've gone out from pre-scribed Eng-lish, They've gone

out from pre-scribed Eng-lish, Safe now in the Soph-'more Class.

002 ii (72—flute)   Allegro [from] *Symphony No. 2*
002 v (181—violin)   Allegro molto vivace [from] *Symphony No. 2*

157-a

YALE'S SHORT CHEER

(9 Rah's/3 Yale's)

f   ff   fff   ff   sf

Rah, rah, rah,   rah, rah, rah, rah,   rah rah Yale   Yale Yale

051 (f2203, m. 5)   *Yale-Princeton Football Game* [incomplete?]
193 (f6045, brace 5)   *The Boys in Blue*

[5]

Popular Instrumental Tunes

Included here are some of the dance tunes from the vast repertory of music played at barn dances and country fairs in the nineteenth century. The origins of much of this music have been lost with the passing of time, but most of the tunes share a common ancestry of purpose—that of accompanying dancing, especially in the British Isles. Such music was handed down by oral traditions and came to Ives's time with the original melodic skeletons and contours sometimes more, sometimes less, intact, and with many different titles.[1] While we might refer to these today as "fiddle" tunes, a variety of instruments, including the jew's harp, was commonly used in their performance in Ives's day.[2]

In borrowing from this music Ives divided his attention fairly evenly between tunes in the lilting 6/8 meter of *Saint Patrick's Day* and *Irish Washerwoman*, for example, and those like *Money Musk* and *College Hornpipe* that have a more squared-off character, brought about in part by their duple meter. In Ives's hands, however, these differences in character were often short lived. He frequently altered their basic rhythmic qualities by superimposing displaced accents on them and by placing the tunes in larger, multiple layers of differing metrical and/or rhythmic contexts; in doing so, a borrowed tune could end up with rhythmic accentuations at odds with its original pulses. A short example, involving *The Campbells Are Comin'*, used in *Washington's Birthday*, illustrates one level of this technique:[3]

Model

Ives

This was all in keeping with what he remembered hearing at barn dances:

> In some parts of the hall a group would be dancing a polka, while in another a waltz, with perhaps a quadrille or lancers going on in the middle.[4] Some of the players in the band would, in an impromptu way, pick up with the polka, and some with the waltz or march. Often the piccolo or cornet would throw in "asides." Sometimes the change in tempo and mixed rhythms would be caused by a fiddler who, after playing three or four hours steadily, was getting a little sleepy—or by another player who had been seated too near the hard cider barrel. Whatever the reason for these changing and sometimes simultaneously playing of different things, I remember distinctly catching a kind of music that was natural and interesting, and which was decidedly missed when everybody came down "blimp" on the same beat again.[5]

Although Ives most often used his "fiddle" tunes with the rapid tempos with which we customarily associate them, some of his settings reflect those greater varieties of tempo in "some of the old dancing and fiddle playing" that he and his father remembered. In the finale of *Symphony No. 2*, Ives spins out citations of both *Turkey in the Straw* and *Pig Town Fling* in a pace slower than one normally expects for such music; together they provide a lovely countermelody to the "part suggesting a Steve Foster tune"[6] and to a brief mention of *Long, Long Ago*, a tune entirely appropriate to the moment.

Portions of *Washington's Birthday* reflect Ives's attempt to recapture "some of the old breakdown tunes and backwoods fun and comedy and conviviality that [were] gradually being forgotten."[7] There, in a brief span of fifty-odd measures, portions of *The White Cockade, Irish Washerwoman, The Campbells Are Comin', Garryowen, Fisher's Hornpipe, Saint Patrick's Day, Money Musk,* and *Pig Town Fling* are all cited, the whole forming a miniature anthology of "fiddle" tunes.

Ability at improvisation is a given for the jazz performer; such skills were, and are, expected to be part of the interpretation of some Baroque music; so it is with these dance tunes. A printed version of the music, thus, represents hardly more than the skeleton upon which the actual performance is based. In that respect, this music shares another common bond with printed versions of some Baroque music and of jazz. In attempts to capture this music in notated form, rarely is there agreement from printed version to printed version as to what the precise notes of the tune are. Differences among printed editions can range from the omission or addition of a few notes to major alterations in all but the barest melodic contour. Nuances are entirely another thing. One can no more notate the lilt of a well-crafted, improvised jazz melodic line than to capture the swing of a fiddler's bow and placement of fingers as they nudge the melody up or down, sometimes in microtonal increments. To speak of a definitive version of this music—printed or performed—is to speak a contradiction.

Although the versions of the tunes presented here may be somewhat different from those known by Ives or the reader, each tune, nevertheless, would have been clearly recognizable to Ives and should not present any problems for the reader.

158

ARKANSAS TRAVELLER

SOURCE: Firth, Pond and Co. publication of 1851

© 1851

007 ii (27—clarinet)

Putnam's Camp, Redding, Connecticut [from]
Orchestral Set No. 1: Three Places in
New England

036 (44—cornet I)

"Country Band" March [incomplete]

315 (25—obligato)

Old Home Day

BLOW THE MAN DOWN

("As I was walking down Paradise Street")

SOURCE: *The New Blue Book of Favorite Songs*, p. 224

first known printing: 1879 with words and music,
titled "Knock [i.e., "Blow"] a Man Down"

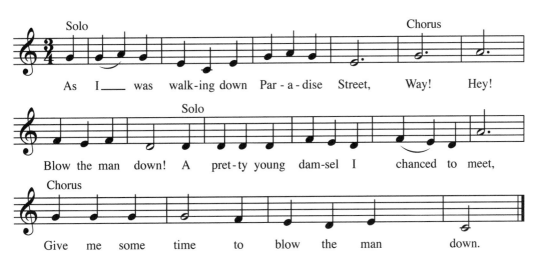

Solo

Chorus

As I___ was walk-ing down Par - a - dise Street, Way! Hey!

Solo

Blow the man down! A pret-ty young dam-sel I chanced to meet,

Chorus

Give me some time to blow the man down.

005 i (135—horn)

Washington's Birthday [from] *A Symphony:
New England Holidays*

160

THE CAMPBELLS ARE COMIN'

(Hob Nob)

("The Campbells are comin' O-ho! O-ho!")

SOURCE: G. E. Blake publication (n.d.)

first known appearance in print: ca. 1745

The Camp- bells are com-in' O - ho! O-ho! The

Camp - bells are com - in' O - ho! O - ho! The

Camp - bells are com - in' From

bon - - nie Loch Lo - - - mond, The

Fine

Camp - bells are com - in' O - ho! O - ho! The

great Ar-gyle___ he goes be - fore, ___ He makes the guns___ and

can - nons roar; Wi' sound___ of trum - pet

D.C. al Fine

pipe___ and drum, ___And ban - ners wav - ing to the sun.

COLLEGE HORNPIPE

("Sailor's Hornpipe")

("Jacks the Lad")

SOURCE: *Musician's Omnibus Complete*

earliest known printing: ca. 1796

005 i (81—flute)	*Washington's Birthday* [from] *A Symphony: New England Holidays*
005 iii (45—oboe)	*The Fourth of July* [from] *A Symphony: New England Holidays*
059 rejected iii (15—violin)	*Scherzo* [from] *Pre-First Sonata for Violin and Piano*
061 ii (14—violin)	*In the Barn* [from] *Sonata No. 2 for Violin and Piano*
083 (14—violin I)	*Scherzo for String Quartet*
084 ii (14—violin I)	*Scherzo: Holding Your Own!* [from] *A Set of Three Short Pieces*
086 ii (89—violin)	Presto ("TSIAJ" or Medley on the Fence [or] on the Campus!) [from] *Trio for Violin, Violoncello, and Piano*
125 (145)	*Waltz-Rondo*

161-a
CUCKOO'S CALL

[Cuck - oo,   Cuck - oo]

005 iii (16—piccolo)

The Fourth of July [from] *A Symphony:*
New England Holidays

162
FISHER'S HORNPIPE

SOURCE: Lee and Walker publication (n.d.)

005 i (145—piccolo)

Washington's Birthday [from] *A Symphony:*
New England Holidays

005 iii (49—piccolo)

The Fourth of July [from] *A Symphony:*
New England Holidays

125 (193)

Waltz-Rondo

163

GARRYOWEN

(Garry Owen)

SOURCE: *Musician's omnibus complete*

004 ii (252—violin I)	Allegretto [from] *Symphony No. 4*
005 i (141—horn)	*Washington's Birthday* [from] *A Symphony: New England Holidays*
005 iii (82—piano)	*The Fourth of July* [from] *A Symphony: New England Holidays*
315 (32—obligato)	*Old Home Day*

164

IRISH WASHERWOMAN

SOURCE: E. Riley publication (n.d.)

first known printing: 1792

004 ii (257—violin I)
005 i (127—horn)

Allegretto [from] *Symphony No. 4*
Washington's Birthday [from] *A Symphony:*
New England Holidays

Possible borrowing:

005 iii (97—horn)

The Fourth of July [from] *A Symphony:*
New England Holidays

165

THE KERRY DANCE

("O the days of the Kerry dancing")

SOURCE: William A. Pond and Co. publication (n.d.)

attributed to JAMES LYMAN MOLLOY, 1879, but
measures 1–8 are identical to "The Cuckoo" by
MARGARET CASSON, ca. 1790

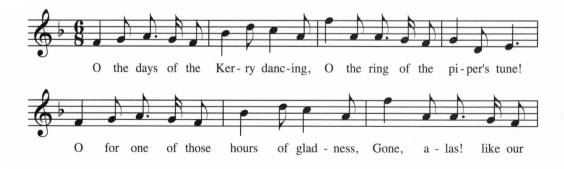

youth, too soon; When the boys be - gan to gath - er

In the glen of a sum-mer night, And the Ker - ry pi - per's tun - ing

made us long— with wild de-light. O to think of it,

O to dream of it, fills my heart with tears.

O the days of the Ker - ry danc - ing, O the ring of the

pi - per's tune! O for one of those hours of glad - ness,

Gone, a - las! like our youth, too soon.

Possible borrowing:
002 v (11—violin)

Allegro molto vivace [from] *Symphony No. 2*

166
MONEY MUSK

SOURCE: George Willig publication (n.d.)

005 i (156—piccolo)

Washington's Birthday [from] *A Symphony: New England Holidays*

059 rejected iii (15—violin)

Scherzo [from] *Pre-First Sonata for Violin and Piano*

061 ii (35—violin)

In the Barn [from] *Sonata No. 2 for Violin and Piano*

167
PIG TOWN FLING

(Warm Stuff)

(Cripple Creek)

SOURCE: *The Half-Dollar Music Series: Favorite Reels, Jigs and Hornpipes*, no. 107, p. 17

002 i (23—violin)	Andante moderato [from] *Symphony No. 2*
002 iv (17—flute)	Lento [from] *Symphony No. 2*
002 v (52—violin II)	Allegro molto vivace [from] *Symphony No. 2*
004 ii (175—bassoon)	Allegretto [from] *Symphony No. 4*
005 i (163—violin I)	*Washington's Birthday* [from] *A Symphony: New England Holidays*
042 ii (f2481, score 1, m. 3)	[2nd Ragtime Dance] [from] *Three Ragtime Dances* [mostly lost]
086 ii (118—violin)	Presto ("TSIAJ" or Medley on the Fence [or] on the Campus!) [from] *Trio for Violin, Violoncello, and Piano*

168

SAINT PATRICK'S DAY

SOURCE: Firth and Hall publication (n.d.)

004 ii (248—bassoon)	Allegretto [from] *Symphony No. 4*
005 i (145—horn)	*Washington's Birthday* [from] *A Symphony: New England Holidays*
005 iii (88—piano)	*The Fourth of July* [from] *A Symphony: New England Holidays*
024 (44—violin)	*Overture and March "1776"*
086 ii (170—violin)	*Presto ("TSIAJ" or Medley on the Fence [or] on the Campus!) [from] Trio for Violin, Violoncello, and Piano*
315 (35—obligato)	*Old Home Day*

169

TURKEY IN THE STRAW

(Zip Coon)

(Old Zip Coon)

source: *Favorite Songs of the People*, p. 128

© 1834
claimed by both BOB FARRELL and
GEORGE WASHINGON DIXON

170
WESTMINSTER CHIMES
(Westminster Quarters)

(Cambridge Quarters)

SOURCE: *Wikipedia*

probably by WILLIAM CROTCH, 1793–94

004 i (21—cello)	Prelude [from] *Symphony No. 4*
004 ii (116—celesta)	Allegretto [from] *Symphony No. 4*
004 iv (45—bell)	Largo [from] *Symphony No. 4*
058 iii (78—viola)	*The Call of the Mountains* [from] *String Quartet No. 2*
089 (49)	*Three-Page Sonata*

171
THE WHITE COCKADE

SOURCE: *Musician's omnibus complete*

005 i (109—violin I)   *Washington's Birthday* [from] *A Symphony: New England Holidays*

059 rejected iii (f3212, staff 3, piano)   Scherzo [from] *Pre-First Sonata for Violin and Piano*

061 ii (64—piano)   *In the Barn* [from] *Sonata No. 2 for Violin and Piano*

125 (148)   *Waltz-Rondo*

Possible borrowing:

    005 iii (66-a—piccolo)   *The Fourth of July* [from] *A Symphony: New England Holidays*

[6]

Classical Music

When Ives borrowed music from the "classical" tradition, he used it in one of two ways. On the one hand Ives employed his sources as models for his own student works as he was learning the art, the craft of composition. Here, melody, harmony, and rhythm are taken more or less intact from a model and imitated, creating a "new" piece of music. We can trace this method of borrowing from an isolated example in 1887, through his student days at Yale, and ending around the turn into the twentieth century. Beethoven, Donizetti, Schubert, Mendelssohn, Schumann, Robert Franz, Peter Cornelius, Brahms, Tchaikovsky, and Dvořák are among the composers whose works Ives chose to imitate. Although he would later refer to some of their music as "lollypop," as "sop," as "ta ta's and greasy ringlets,"[1] he was beholden, as a young composer, to the music of these "ladies." From their music, Ives learned the art of composing by imitation—an age-old practice that is typical of a budding composer's explorations in search of his own style. Ives's results are derivative, to be sure, but they are perfectly acceptable at that stage of his work as a student composer. A list of compositions Ives used as models for his own works, most of them dating from his student days at Yale, is found in chapter 7, "Musical Models."

During his first few weeks at Yale, Ives showed Horatio Parker, his composition teacher, some of his own music—experimental ideas that "Father had been willing for [him] to think about, discuss, and try out."[2] Here was music young Ives hoped would impress Parker, experiments that might win from Parker the sort of encouragement George Ives had given his son. Parker, however, was not prepared for what young Ives showed him. The music didn't follow "standard" practices and some of it must have sounded like pure cacophony to Parker's ears. Of the dissonances in the song *At Parting*, Parker said, "There's no excuse for that—an E flat way up there and stopping, and the nearest D natural way down two octaves—etc."[3] When Ives told his father of Parker's reaction, George had a refreshing, but typically iconoclastic, response—one of the last bits of advice he was to give his son: "Tell Parker that every dissonance doesn't have to resolve, if it doesn't happen to feel like it, any more than every horse should have to have its tail bobbed because it's the prevailing fashion."[4] One suspects that the young Ives never shared his father's comments with Parker.

George Ives's death on the 4th of November of that year, only a scant five weeks after Ives entered Yale, was a tremendous blow to his son. Now the most important figure in his young life was gone and the person Ives had opened himself to by sharing some of the music that father and son had shared—the one whom Ives naively thought would be supportive of these efforts—had summarily dismissed them. One can only imagine what a devastating blow this must have been to Ives. This same man was to continue Ives's education as a composer. At some point, Ives wrote in his *Memos:*

> Parker was a composer and widely known, and Father was not a composer and little known—but from every other standpoint I should say that Father was by far the greater man.[5]

Ives, nevertheless, continued to study composition with Parker and to learn from him (perhaps in spite of himself).

A transition phase exists between slavishly imitating what a master composer has done and finding one's own voice as a composer. That transition period for Ives meant borrowing heavily from the substance and spirit of certain symphonies of Beethoven, Schubert, Tchaikovsky, andDvořák, without, however, resorting to literal transcription of these works. Burkholder, Sinclair, and other have written about Ives's use of Dvořák's *Symphony No. 9,* movements from Schubert's *Eighth* symphony, the Beethoven *Ninth,* and Tchaikovsky's *Symphony No. 6* as models for the first symphony he composed, part of which he submitted as his senior thesis at Yale. In 1898 and 1899, Ives turned to a Horatio Parker work for guidance, using his teacher's *Hora novissima* as a model for *The Celestial Country,* one of his most ambitious efforts up to that date.[6]

When he composed his *Symphony No. 2* in 1900–1902, one of the most ambitious of his works immediately following graduation, he continued to refine the practices that had worked so well for him in his *First Symphony.* Now, he turned to the Brahms *First,* Dvořák's *Ninth,* and Tchaikovsky's *Symphony No. 4.*

Upon reaching the early years of his maturity as a composer, Ives gave up the practice of imitating entire models. He turned now to much shorter borrowed melodies—for their contours, for the ways they could be juxtaposed against other borrowings or original lines, for ways in which they might be combined contrapuntally, and, occasionally for their extra-musical possibilities. To the list of composers given above can be added the names of J. S. Bach, Handel, Rossini, Wagner, Gottschalk, Debussy, and Ethelbert Nevin.

Ives's persona as a curmudgeon with few kind words to say about composers of classical music developed over the years to the point that he expressed disdain for most such composers. He often belittled them for what he perceived as their lack of masculinity. Speaking with a self-assured certainty, he saw most of it as wanting in manly strength—in his words, "music has always been an emasculated art—at least too much—say 88⅔%."[7]

> Even those considered the greatest (Bach, Beethoven, Brahms, etc.) have too much of it, though less [than] the other rubber-stamp great men. They couldn't exactly help it—life with them was such that they had to live at least part of the time by the ladies'

smiles—they had to please the ladies or die. And that is the reason—through their influence—that no one can prove (not even the ladies) that there has been [any] great music ever composed—that is, in this world.[8]

Ives harangued about the "sugar-plum sound for the soft ears" of much of the music of the three B's, but was willing to admit that their music was among the "strongest and greatest in all art, and nothing since is stronger or greater than their strongest and greatest,"—those composers had "some manhood of their own." Not content to leave it with damning them with that faint praise, he stated that even *that* music was "not quite as strong and great as [that of] Carl Ruggles."[9]

Composers from the Romantic tradition were the special targets for his scorn:

some [music] of Chopin [is] (pretty soft, but you don't mind it in him so much because one just naturally thinks of him with a skirt on, but one which he made himself).[10]

"Lady" composers, Ives's favorite term of derision, included Grieg and Tchaikovsky ("the great Russian weeper");[11] but he saved his most vitriolic comments for "Richy" Wagner, who

had more or less of a good brain for technical progress, but he seems to put it to such weak uses—exulting, like a nice lady's purple silk dress, in fake nobility and heroism, but afraid to jump in a mill pond and be a hero. He liked instead to dress up in purple and sing about heroism—(a woman posing as a man).[12]

While he lumped Beethoven with Bach and Brahms in some of his diatribes, Ives softened his criticism when it came to Beethoven, for he thought some of his music was virile, powerful, and capable of great transcendent powers when it explored the immense profundities of existence. For Ives, the "relentlessness of fate knocking at the door," as manifested in the opening four notes of Beethoven's *Symphony No. 5,* marked that work, that particular motto, as a musical world apart from any other "classical" music. In that four-note motto—that "oracle"—that Ives borrows for use in at least eight (and perhaps nine) different compositions

lies one of Beethoven's greatest messages. We would place its translation above the relentlessness of fate knocking at the door, above the greater human message of destiny, and strive to bring it towards the spiritual message of Emerson's revelations, even to the "common heart" of Concord—the soul of humanity knocking at the door of the divine mysteries, radiant in the faith that it *will* be opened—and human become the divine![13]

In addition to illuminating a subject or a mood by underscoring it with appropriate borrowed music, Ives's musical wit surfaces in his musical punning in another way of interpreting the moment. In *The Side Show,* Ives recycles some of the melody of Pat Rooney, Sr.'s 1883 waltz song, *Are You the O'Reilly?* The ascending melodic line in the singer's part at the beginning of both Ives's and Rooney's songs match much of the ascending melody of the opening of the quintuple-metered second movement of Tchaikovsky's *Pathétique* symphony. When the words speak of O'Reilly looking "a bit like a Russian dance," Ives pulls the telling fragment of the Tchaikovsky 6th out of his tune bank, changes his song's meter to 5/4 (although it has been limping along, alternating triple with duple meter), and cites the opening two measures of the Russian composer's melody. The musical pun is obvious as one tune becomes another in Ives's sleight-of-hand manipulations. The line between the Tchaikovsky and the Rooney becomes blurred. Has the Tchaikovsky become the limping triple- and duple-metered Pat Rooney—or does the Rooney become the Tchaikovsky?

Tchaikovsky, *Symphony No. 6*, 2nd movement, mm. 9–14; transposed

Ives, *The Side Show*, mm. 18–21

In *Grantchester*, the first six, and then the first ten, notes of the opening flute solo from Debussy's *Prelude to "The Afternoon of a Faun"* are sounded in the voice as Rupert Brooke's text mentions:

> "... Nature there or Earth or such. And clever modern men have seen a Faun peeping through the grass."

As is the case with so many puns, neither of these examples is marked by subtlety; this is especially true of *Grantchester,* if one sees the musical score before hearing the music. The title reads "*Grantchester (with a quotation from Debussy)*" and permission is noted "By courtesy and special authorization of the publisher: Jean Jobert, Paris, 44 Rue du Colisée."

It is easy to find a reason for Ives to borrow from Handel for his own *Slow March* ("Inscribed to the Children's Faithful Friend"). Beginning with a citation from Handel's "Dead March" from *Saul,* Ives recounts the taking leave of a loved one, the family dog: "One evening just at sunset we laid him in the grave; Although a humble animal his heart was true and brave." One can understand the precocious twelve-year-old Ives using Handel's music to create an appropriately somber musical mood to accompany the burial of a family pet.

Punning and extra-musical reasons aside, Ives's citations of other "classical" pieces appear to have been chosen for particular melodic contours which Ives could use as subsequent springboards for his own music. He certainly did not quote from "classical" sources to give his own music respectability. Ives was too confident of his own abilities to need that kind of crutch. Whatever his intentions, snippets of "classical" melodies tended to be of little consequence, for Ives nearly always dismisses them, crowds them out with his beloved hymn tunes, patriotic, and popular songs. In its own way, Ives's dismissive attitude toward "classical" sources could be seen as a parallel—a payback—to Horatio Parker's disparaging responses to Ives's experiments.

Since some of these "classical" borrowings are so transient and rarely explored beyond their brief mention, one is tempted, if only for the moment, to adapt Kurt Stone's criticism of borrowings in *Symphony No. 4* (which I feel is unjustified for that particular work) to Ives's use of "classical" sources, and agree with his assessment that "musically speaking any other tunes would have done just as well."[14]

Ives's sources are given below alphabetically by the last name of the composer. Since nearly all the "classical" models, except George Ives's *Fugue No. 4 in B Flat* (which I have copied from the Charles Ives Manuscript Collection at Yale) are recognizable and readily available in modern editions, no specific publications are given for the models presented here.

172
SINFONIA IN A MINOR, BWV 799
mm. 49–52

JOHANN SEBASTIAN BACH, 1723

118 (20)   *Invention in D*

172-a
SINFONIA IN F MINOR, BWV 795
mm. 28–29

JOHANN SEBASTIAN BACH, 1723

002 i (93—violin I)   Andante moderato [from] *Symphony No. 2*
002 iv (34—oboe I)   Lento (maestoso) [from] *Symphony No. 2*
002 v (25—violin I)   Allegro molto vivace [from] *Symphony No. 2*
105 (p. 6, staff 1)   *Study No. 21: Some South-Paw Pitching*

172-b

FUGUE IN E MINOR, BWV 855

(*Well-Tempered Clavier*, I)

mm. 13–14, 15–17, 22

JOHANN SEBASTIAN BACH, 1722

002 v (147—violin I) Allegro molto vivace [from] *Symphony No. 2*

172-c
FUGUE IN D MINOR [FROM] *TOCCATA
AND FUGUE IN D MINOR,* **BWV 538**
mm. 21–22

JOHANN SEBASTIAN BACH, 1708–17

004 iii (21—violin I) *Fugue* [from] *Symphony No. 4*
057 i (21—violin II) *Chorale* [from] *String Quartet No. 1*

173

SYMPHONY NO. 5, OP. 67

first movement

mm. 1–2

LUDWIG VAN BEETHOVEN, 1805–1807

Strings   *ff*

022 (f2214, brace 3)	*Emerson Overture for Piano and Orchestra* [incomplete]
088 i (p. 1, staff 1)	*Emerson* [from] *Sonata No. 2 for Piano: Concord, Mass., 1840–60*
088 ii (p. 31, staff 2)	*Hawthorne* [from] *Sonata No. 2 for Piano: Concord, Mass., 1840–60*
088 iii (p. 53, staff 3)	*The Alcotts* [from] *Sonata No. 2 for Piano: Concord, Mass., 1840–60*
088 iv (p. 63, staff 4)	*Thoreau* [from] *Sonata No. 2 for Piano: Concord, Mass., 1840–60*
097 (p. 4, staff 2)	*Study No. 9: The Anti-Abolitionist Riots in the 1830s and 1840s*
116 (f4841, staff 3)	*The Celestial Railroad*
123 i (f4907, staff 3, m. 2, right hand)	Slowly [from] *Four Transcriptions from "Emerson"*
123 ii (f4910, staff 2, right hand)	Moderato [from] *Four Transcriptions from "Emerson"*
123 iv (f4919, staff 1, right hand)	Allegro agitato-Broadly [from] *Four Transcriptions from "Emerson"*

173-a

***SONATA IN F MINOR FOR PIANO*, OP. 2, NO. 1**

second movement

mm. 1–2

LUDWIG VAN BEETHOVEN, 1795

Possible borrowing:

057 ii (1—violin)

Chorale [from] *String Quartet No. 1: From the Salvation Army*

173-b

***SONATA IN B-FLAT FOR PIANO*, OP. 106**

("Hammerklavier")

first movement

mm. 1–2

LUDWIG VAN BEETHOVEN, 1817–18

088 i (p. 6, staff 3)

Emerson [from] *Sonata No. 2 for Piano: Concord, Mass., 1840–60*

173-c

ANDANTE FAVORI IN F

LUDWIG VAN BEETHOVEN, 1804

174

SYMPHONY NO. 9, OP. 125

fourth movement

mm. 92–95

LUDWIG VAN BEETHOVEN, 1817–23

Cello

058 ii (96—violin II)   *Arguments* [from] *String Quartet No. 2*

175

SYMPHONY NO. 1, OP. 68

second movement

mm. 25–27

JOHANNES BRAHMS, 1876

002 iii (16—flute)   Adagio cantabile [from] *Symphony No. 2*

175-a
SYMPHONY NO. 1, OP. 68
first movement

mm. 181–88

JOHANNES BRAHMS, 1876

Violin

002 ii (186—violin I)   Allegro [from] *Symphony No. 2*

175-b
SYMPHONY NO. 1, OP. 68
fourth movement

m. 60ff

JOHANNES BRAHMS, 1876

Violin   *poco* ***f***

002 iv (1—horn)   Lento [from] *Symphony No. 2*

175-c
SYMPHONY NO. 1, OP. 68
fourth movement

m. 273ff

JOHANNES BRAHMS, 1876

Violin

002 i (76—violin I)	Andante moderato [from] *Symphony No. 2*
002 iv (26—violins)	Lento maestoso [from] *Symphony No. 2*

175-d

SYMPHONY NO. 1, OP. 68

fourth movement

mm. 385–88

JOHANNES BRAHMS, 1876

Flute

002 iv (37—trombone)	Lento [from] *Symphony No. 2*
002 v (246—bassoon)	Allegro molto vivace [from] *Symphony No. 2*

176

SYMPHONY NO. 2, OP. 73

first movement

mm. 48–53

JOHANNES BRAHMS, 1877

Flute *mp*   *p*   Violin I

058 ii (92—violin I)   *Arguments* [from] *String Quartet No. 2*

177

SYMPHONY NO. 3, OP. 90

first movement

mm. 3–4

JOHANNES BRAHMS, 1883

Violin I   *f passionato*

002 ii (149—violin)   Allegro [from] *Symphony No. 2*

177-a

=former 192

SYMPHONY NO. 3, OP. 90

first movement

mm. 47–48

JOHANNES BRAHMS, 1883

Violin I   *espress*

002 ii (126—violin I)   Allegro [from] *Symphony No. 2*

177-b
VIER ERNSTE GESÄNG, OP. 121
third movement (*O tod, wie bitter*)

mm. 29–30

JOHANNES BRAHMS, 1896

noch zu er - war - - - - - ten —— hat!

002 iv (29—flutes)　　　　　　　Lento [from] *Symphony No. 2*

178
PRÉLUDE À "L'APRES-MIDI D'UN FAUNE"
mm. 1–3

CLAUDE DEBUSSY, 1892–94

Flute solo　*p*　*doux et expressif*

258 (4—piano)　　　　　　　*Grantchester*

178-a
"GOLLIWOG'S CAKEWALK"
[from] *CHILDREN'S CORNER*
m. 10ff

CLAUDE DEBUSSY, 1906–1908

088 ii (p. 37, staff 3, right hand)

Hawthorne [from] *Sonata No. 2 for Piano: Concord, Mass., 1840–60*

179
LUCIA DI LAMMERMOOR
Act II: Sextet
mm. 1–2

GAETANO DONIZETTI, 1835

Note: Ives uses this source as a model, rather than for the purposes of borrowing

179-a
SYMPHONY NO. 9, OP. 95
("From the New World")
first movement
m. 115ff

ANTONIN DVOŘÁK, 1893

Violin *p*

cresc.

002 v (60—violin I)

Allegro molto vivace [from] *Symphony No. 2*

179-b

SYMPHONY NO. 9, OP. 95

("From the New World")

second movement

mm. 7–18

ANTONIN DVOŘÁK, 1893

English
horn solo   *p*

001 ii (3—English horn)   Adagio molto sostenuto [from] *Symphony No. 1*

179-c

SYMPHONY IN D MINOR

first movement

mm. 6–8

CESAR FRANCK, 1886–88

Violin   *p espress*

Note: The following three songs are set to the same music

243 (16—voice and piano)   *The Ending Year*
357 (voice and piano)   *The Song of the Dead* [lost]

Note: This song appears in John Kirkpatrick's edition of *Forty Earlier Songs*. Kirkpatrick's conjecture was that this was probably the first song in a group of three Kipling songs that Ives composed. See *Forty Earlier Songs*, p. x and Sinclair's *Descriptive Catalogue*, p. 506 for more details.

382 (16—voice and piano)   *The Waiting Soul*

180

THE LAST HOPE

mm. 48–50

LOUIS MOREAU GOTTSCHALK, ca. 1853–54
[see also 36-a for arr. as *Mercy* by Edwin Pond Parker]

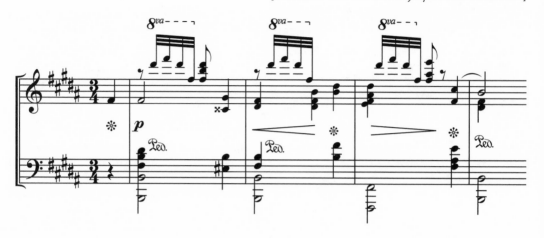

152 (46—tenor)   *Psalm 90*

181

SEE THE CONQUERING HERO COMES [from] *JUDAS MACCABEUS*

mm. 1–4

GEORGE FRIDERIC HANDEL
1st performance, 1747

See the ___ conqu'- ring he - - ro comes

Cantus I

114 (1)   *March in G and C for Piano, with "See the*
                              Conquering Hero Comes"

182

***DEAD MARCH* [from]**

SAUL

Act III, Scene 5

mm. 1–4

GEORGE FRIDERIC HANDEL, 1739

349 (1—piano) *Slow March*

182-a

***HALLELUJAH* [CHORUS]**

[from] *MESSIAH*

m. 4

GEORGE FRIDERIC HANDEL, 1742

Possible borrowing:

255 (61—voice) *General William Booth Enters into Heaven*

183

SYMPHONY NO. 94

("Surprise")

second movement

mm. 1–8

FRANZ JOSEPH HAYDN, 1791

Violin   *ten.*   *ten.*

436 (f7457, m. 1)   *Take-Off on "Surprise Symphony"*

184

FUGUE NO. 4 IN B FLAT

SOURCE: The Music Manuscripts of Charles Edward Ives

Microfilm no. 7457

GEORGE EDWARD IVES

063 i (16—piano)

Allegro [from] *Sonata No. 4 for Violin and Piano: Children's Day at the Camp Meeting*

185

NARCISSUS

[from] *WATER SCENES*

Op. 13, no. 4

mm. 5–6

ETHELBERT NEVIN

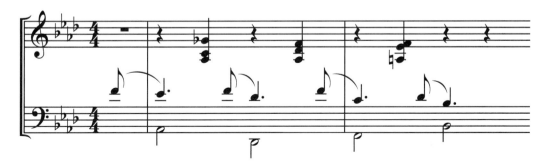

320 (18—voice)

On the Counter

186
OVERTURE [to]
WILLIAM TELL

GIOACCHINO ROSSINI, 1829

English horn

259 (21—voice)   *The Greatest Man*

187
SYMPHONY NO. 6, OP. 74
second movement
mm. 1–6

PETER ILYICH TCHAIKOVSKY, 1893

Cello

348 (18—voice)   *The Side Show*

188

SYMPHONY NO. 6, OP. 74

third movement

mm. 81–83

PETER ILYICH TCHAIKOVSKY, 1893

Oboe

001 iv (329—winds)
058 ii (87—cello)

Allegro molto [from] *Symphony No. 1*
Arguments [from] *String Quartet No. 2*

188-a

SYMPHONY NO. 6, OP. 74

third movement

mm. 221–32

PETER ILYICH TCHAIKOVSKY, 1893

Violin   *sempre* **fff**

001 iv (329—winds)

Allegro molto [from] *Symphony No. 1*

188-b
SYMPHONY NO. 4, OP. 36
third movement

mm. 1–6

PETER ILYICH TCHAIKOVSKY, 1877

002 v (1—violins)   Allegro molto vivace [from] *Symphony No. 2*

189
PRELUDE [1] [to]
TRISTAN UND ISOLDE
mm. 1–2

RICHARD WAGNER, 1859

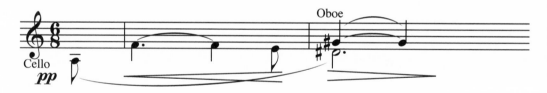

058 i (1—viola)	*Discussions* [from] *String Quartet No. 2*
123 i (f4907, staff 4, m. 1, right hand)	Slowly [from] *Four Transcriptions from "Emerson"*
123 iii (f4917, staff 1, right hand)	Largo [from] *Four Transcriptions from "Emerson"*
123 iv (f4918, staff 1, right hand)	Allegro agitato-Broadly [from] *Four Transcriptions from "Emerson"*
Possible borrowing:	
088 i (p. 13, staff 4, m. 1)	*Emerson* [from] *Sonata No. 2 for Piano: Concord, Mass., 1840–60*

190
PRELUDE [2] [to]
TRISTAN UND ISOLDE
mm. 36–38

RICHARD WAGNER, 1859

002 iii (44—violin I)   Adagio cantabile [from] *Symphony No. 2*

191
PRELUDE [3] [to]
TRISTAN UND ISOLDE
mm. 62–63

RICHARD WAGNER, 1859

002 iii (25—flute)   Adagio cantabile [from] *Symphony No. 2*

191-a
WEDDING MARCH* [from] *LOHENGRIN
Act III, Scene 1
mm. 5–12

RICHARD WAGNER, 1846–48

088 iii (p. 55, staff 3)

The Alcotts [from] *Sonata No. 2 for Piano: Concord, Mass., 184–60*

Part 2

[7]

Newly Identified and Unidentified Tunes

This section was titled "Unknown Tunes" in the first edition of the *Tunebook*. That designation was, and is, imprecise. Unless they are from Ives's fertile imagination, such tunes are certainly known to someone. I have, therefore, changed the title of this chapter to reflect those tunes that are still unidentified, including ones new to this edition, and to give titles to those borrowings that have been identified.

Many have offered suggestions as to the identity of those thirty-three "unknown" tunes.[1] Failing to see the forest for the trees, I missed some tunes whose identifications seem obvious in retrospect. Other borrowings reflect the subtle workings of Ives's creative mind in which one tune can become another, can become another, can become another in an almost kaleidoscopic labyrinth of aural sleights of hand—now you hear it, now you don't. In measures 35 through 44 in the third movement of the first string quartet, for example, the first violin plays a melodic line whose contour strongly suggests a borrowed tune:

Ives, *String Quartet No. 1*, 3rd movement, mm. 35-44; articulations omitted

Rather than being a single tune, however, it is an amalgam of *Beulah Land, Shining Shore,* and *Nettleton,* all of which contain a common rhythmic motto of two short notes, followed by a long one—precisely the pattern that dominates Ives's melody. Intervals of the 4th, 6th, and 3rd in the Ives also suggest the three hymns, whose melodies contain those intervals at important points. In laying out the line for the first violin, Ives never directly cites the melody of any of these three tunes but their presence is, nevertheless, close by. Failing to identify this "tune," I originally included it in the "Unknown Tunes" section as tune number 210. Burkholder's suggestion that this melody is actually the combination of the three hymns seems to be right on target.

Other examples come so close to a known tune that one is tempted to make the call in favor of that source: the pentatonic figuration of the following tune is such an example. Is this *Peter, Peter, Pumpkin Eater*? It certainly is very close to that nursery rhyme tune—the notes are there, but Ives skews the original ordering of them:

Ives, *Symphony No. 4*, 2nd movement, mm. 72-73

Orchestra Piano Primo

The contour's resemblance to *Peter* is so close that I have cross-listed the tune as "newly identified" tune 201 and Popular Song number 130-a.

Finally, there are those tunes that continue to defy identification. In many cases, they are probably original with Ives; in a few instances, they may well belong to some now-forgotten source.

I have retained all of the tunes that originally appeared in the "Unknown" section of the first *Tunebook,* but have cross-listed, with their titles, the tunes that have been identified. Those tunes now bear two numbers: the original number from the first *Tunebook* and a new number, placing the source in one of the six categories: hymns; patriotic and military music; popular music; college music; popular instrumental tunes; and "classical" music.[2]

My close re-reading of the printed scores and manuscript sources for this revision has resulted in an additional six unidentified tunes. Certainly more await their discovery. I invite readers to send me their suggestions as to the identity of these slippery subjects and/or their suggested additions to the list of unidentified tunes, together with their locations.

192 = 177-a
BRAHMS, *SYMPHONY NO. 3, OP. 90*
first movement

mm. 47–48

002 ii (126—violin I)   Allegro [from] *Symphony No. 2*

193 = Unidentified

005 iv (39—flute)   *Thanksgiving and Forefathers' Day* [from]
A Symphony: New England Holidays

194 = 130-b
Push Dem Clouds Away

020 ii (86—violin)   *In the Inn* [from] *Set for Theatre Orchestra*

195 = 130-b

from the refrain to

Push Dem Clouds Away

020 ii (117—violin)   *In the Inn* [from] *Set for Theatre Orchestra*

196 = Unidentified

Note: The tune given below is a variant of the
tune originally given as Unknown 196; this version
occurs earlier in *Central Park in the Dark* than
I indicated in the original version
of the *Tunebook*

034 (28—flute)   *Central Park in the Dark*

197 = Unidentified

Ives original?

005 i (60—violin II)

Washington's Birthday [from] *A Symphony:*
New England Holidays

198 = Unidentified

Ives original?

[four measures have been added to

the beginning of this tune: see

All Made of Tunes, p. 498, note 43]

005 i (163—violin I)

Washington's Birthday [from] *A Symphony:*
New England Holidays

199 =

Ives, *Old Home Day*

mm. 9–13

Flute

005 iii (44—flute)   *The Fourth of July* [from] *A Symphony:*
                       New England Holidays

200 = 24

God Be with You

Violins I (2 only)

004 ii (17—violins I [2 only])   Allegretto [from] *Symphony No. 4*

201 = 130-a

Peter, Peter Pumpkin Eater

Orchestra Piano Primo

004 ii (72—Orchestra Piano Primo)   Allegretto [from] *Symphony No. 4*
116 (f4846, staff 14)   *The Celestial Railroad*

202 = 59

Throw Out the Life-Line

[the first two measures of the
earlier version have been excised here]

High Bells

004 ii (108—High Bells)   Allegretto [from] *Symphony No. 4*

203 =

Ives, *The Alcotts* [from] *Sonata No. 2 for Piano:*
Concord, Mass., 1840–60

Solo Piano

004 ii (170—Solo Piano)   Allegretto [from] *Symphony No. 4*

204 = Unidentified

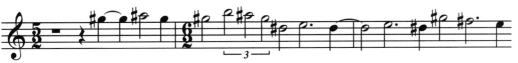

Flute I

004 iv (17—flute I)   Largo [from] *Symphony No. 4*

205 = Unidentified

Violins - Distant Choir

004 iv (27—Violins—Distant Choir)   Largo [from] *Symphony No. 4*

206 = possibly from 173-a
Beethoven,
Sonata in F Minor for Piano, Op. 2, no. 1
second movement
mm. 1–2 and
Bringing in the Sheaves 10

Violin I

057 ii (0—Violin I)   Prelude [from] *String Quartet No. 1: From the Salvation Army*

207 = 54
Shining Shore

Violin I

057 ii (32—Violin I)   Prelude [from] *String Quartet No. 1: From the Salvation Army*

208

last two measures from

Shining Shore 54

057 ii (54—Violin I)

Prelude [from] *String Quartet No. 1: From the Salvation Army*

209 = Unidentified

[possibly development of *Shining Shore 54*]

057 ii (73—Violin I)

Prelude [from] *String Quartet No. 1: From the Salvation Army*

210 =

Shining Shore 54

Nettleton 42

Beulah Land 8

Violin I   *p*   *cantabile*

057 iii (35—Violin I)

Offertory [from] *String Quartet No. 1: From the Salvation Army*

211 = Unidentified

Ives original?

Violin I   *mf*   *animando*

057 iii (49—Violin I)

Offertory [from] *String Quartet No. 1: From the Salvation Army*

212 = 13

Coronation

Violin I   *f*

057 iv (1—Violin I)

Postlude [from] *String Quartet No. 1: From the Salvation Army*

213 = 54

Shining Shore

[development of 207]

Violin II

057 iv (60—Violin II)

Postlude [from] *String Quartet No. 1: From the Salvation Army*

214 = Unidentified

possibly a fraternity tune?

[two measures have been added to the beginning

of the earlier version]

Violin

086 ii (91—violin)

Presto ("TSIAJ" or Medley on the Fence [or] on the Campus!) [from] *Trio for Violin, Violoncello, and Piano*

215 = Unidentified

possibly a fraternity tune?

Piano

086 ii (163—piano)

Presto ("TSIAJ" or Medley on the Fence [or] on the Campus!) [from] *Trio for Violin, Violoncello, and Piano*

216 = 103-a

The Gods of Egypt Bid Us Hail!

086 ii (178—Piano)

Presto ("TSIAJ" or Medley on the Fence [or] on the Campus!) [from] *Trio for Violin, Violoncello, and Piano*

217 = Unidentified

Ives original?

Piano

086 ii (46—piano)

Presto ("TSIAJ" or Medley on the Fence [or] on the Campus!) [from] *Trio for Violin, Violoncello, and Piano*

218 =

Ives, *The All-Enduring*

mm. 55–58

Violin

086 ii (100—violin)

Presto ("TSIAJ" or Medley on the Fence [or] on the Campus!) [from] *Trio for Violin, Violoncello, and Piano*

219 =

Kathleen Mavourneen 112 or

David 13-b or

Hexham 28-a

Solo Cello

267 (15—voice)   *Hymn*
332 (1—voice)   *Remembrance*
Possible borrowing:
   084 i (21—solo cello)   Largo cantabile *Hymn* [from] *A Set of Three Short Pieces*

220 = possibly 14-a

Dies Irae

Violin

005 ii (4—violin)

064 (f0712, m. 4—violin)

Decoration Day [from] *A Symphony:*
New England Holidays

Decoration Day for Violin and Piano

221 = Unidentified

Ives original?

Voice

315 (20—voice)

Old Home Day

222 = Unidentified

Voice

236 (8—voice)

Down East

223 = paraphrase of

Fountain 23

Voice

388 (12—voice)   *West London*

224 = paraphrase of

Fountain 23

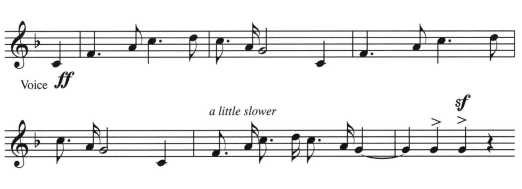

Voice *ff*

a little slower   *sf*

388 (36—voice)   *West London*

225 = Unidentified

Adagio

Flute

009 ii (p. 16: n3001, section 7, staff 8,   *An Afternoon or During Camp Meetin'*
    flute; clarinet)   *Week—One Secular Afternoon (In Bethel)*
                                [from] *Orchestral Set No. 3* [incomplete]

226 = Unidentified

009 ii (p. 20: n3005, staff 15)

An Afternoon or During Camp Meetin' Week—
One Secular Afternoon (In Bethel) [from]
Orchestral Set No. 3 [incomplete]

227 = Unidentified

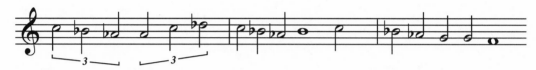

No instrument identified

009 iii (p. 33: n3058, staff 3)

[no tempo heading] [from] *Orchestral Set No. 3*
[incomplete]

228 = Unidentified

No instrument identified

427 (f7443, m. 1)

Burlesque Harmonization in F over E-flat

[8]

Musical Models

I have not given the music for these models since they technically do not constitute borrowing on Ives's part. Additionally, providing the models in their entirety, with melody, harmony, and rhythm—in order to compare them with Ives's re-casting of them—is beyond the scope of this book. Most of the models are readily available to anyone interested in pursuing this part of Ives's work.

Ludwig von Beethoven, *Sonata No. 1 in F minor for Piano,* Op. 2, no. 1 second movement = model for Ives's string quartet arrangement of this movement (Sinclair no. 439); probably 1896–97.

Ludwig van Beethoven, *Symphony No. 9,* 2nd movement = model for *Symphony No. 1,* 3rd movement; symphony composed mostly ca. 1898–1902.

Johannes Brahms, "Feldeinsamkeit," Op. 86, no. 2 = model for *Feldsamkeit/In Summer Fields;* 1898.

Johannes Brahms, *Symphony No. 1* = model for *Symphony No. 2;* 4th movement of Brahms = specific model for 4th and 5th movements; symphony composed mostly ca. 1900–1902.

Johannes Brahms, "Wiegenlied," Op. 49, no. 4 = model for *Wiegenlied;* possibly 1900; see also *Berceuse.*

Johannes Brahms, "Wie Melodien zieht es mir," Op. 105, no. 1 = model for *Wie Melodien zieht es mir;* 1900; see also *Evidence.*

Henry Carey, "Sally in Our Alley" = possible model for *In the Alley;* 1896.

Peter Cornelius, *Ein Ton* = model for *Ein Ton;* possibly 1898; and *Night of Frost in May;* possibly 1898.

Gaetano Donizetti, *Lucia di Lammermoor,* Act II, sextet = model for incomplete *Polonaise;* possibly 1887.

Antonin Dvořák, *Symphony No. 9* = model for *Symphony No. 2;* symphony composed mostly ca. 1900–1902.

Antonin Dvořák, *Symphony No. 9,* 1st movement = model for *Symphony No. 1;* specific modeling: Dvořák 1st movement in Ives's 1st movement; Dvořák 2nd movement in Ives's 2nd movement; Dvořák 4th movement in Ives's 4th movement; symphony composed mostly ca. 1898–1902.

Robert Franz, *Bitte* = model for *Weil' auf mir/Eyes So Dark;* possibly 1902.

Robert Franz, *Die blaue Frühlingsaugen* = possible model for *Frühlingslied;* Nov. 1896.

Robert Franz, "Marie," Op. 18, no. 1 = model for *Marie;* 1896.

Robert Franz, "Widmung," Op. 14, no. 1 = possible model for *Widmung;* possibly 1898; see also *There Is a Lane.*

Benjamin Godard, *Chanson de Florian* = model for *Chanson de Florian;* possibly 1901.

Edvard Grieg, *Gamle mor,* Op. 33, no. 7 = model for *The Old Mother;* 1897 or '98.

Halfdan Kjerulf, "Laengsel," Op. 1, no. 4 = model for *Sehnsucht;* possibly 1899; see also *Rosenzweige.*

Jules Massenet, *Élégie* = model for *Élégie;* 1901.

Felix Mendelssohn, *Gruss,* Op. 19a, no. 5 = model for *Gruss;* possibly 1898.

William Monk, *Eventide* = possible model for *Abide with Me;* ca. 1897; earlier version possibly 1890.

Horatio Parker, *Hora novissima* = model for *The Celestial Country;* 1898–99, with revisions through 1901; see Sinclair, pp. 250–57 for more detail.

David Wallis Reeves, *Second Regiment Connecticut National Guard March* = model for *Holiday Quickstep;* 1887.

Franz Schubert, *Impromptu in C Minor,* Op. 90, no. 1; arranged by Ives as the incomplete *Schubert: Impromptu in C Minor;* probably 1896–97.

Franz Schubert, *Impromptu in B♭,* Op. 142, no. 3; arranged by Ives as the incomplete *Schubert: Impromptu in B♭;* probably 1896–97.

Franz Schubert, *Marche Militaire in D,* Op. 51, no. 1; arranged by Ives as *Schubert: Marche Militaire in D;* 1896–97.

Franz Schubert, "Romanze," No. 3b from *Rosamunde,* Op. 26, D. 797 = model for *Rosamunde;* possibly 1898.

Franz Schubert, *Symphony No. 8,* 1st movement = model for *Symphony No. 1,* 1st movement; symphony composed mostly ca. 1898–1902.

Franz Schubert, "Wandrers Nachtlied," Op. 96, no. 3, D. 768 = model for *Ilmenau/Over all the treetops;* 1901.

Robert Schumann, "Die Lotosblume," Op. 25, no. 7 = model for incomplete *Die Lotosblume/The Lotus Flower;* possibly 1899; and *The South Wind/Die Lotosblume;* adapted 1908 from music composed possibly 1899.

Robert Schumann, "Du bist wie eine Blume" = possible model for *Du bist wie eine Blume;* possibly 1897; see also *Country Celestial* and *When Stars Are in the Quiet Skies.*

Robert Schumann, "Ich grolle nicht," from *Dichterliebe* = model for *Ich grolle nicht/I'll not complain;* probably 1898.

Robert Schumann, "Préambule" and "Valse noble" from *Carnaval;* arranged by Ives probably 1896–97.

Oley Speaks, "On the Road to Mandalay" = model for *The One Way;* possibly 1923.

Peter Tchaikovsky, *Symphony No. 4* = model for *Symphony No. 2;* symphony composed mostly ca. 1900–1902.

Peter Tchaikovsky, *Symphony No. 6,* 3rd movement = model for *Symphony No. 1,* 4th movement; symphony composed mostly ca. 1898–1902.

John Greenleaf Whittier, *Whittier* = model for *Serenity* (mostly lost choral work); possibly 1909; see also the song *Serenity.*

[9]

Compositions with Borrowings

Compositions appear here in the order in which they are found in Sinclair's *A Descriptive Catalogue of the Music of Charles Ives*. Given here are: Sinclair's number for each work; title and date of Ives's composition; the title of the music borrowed; the discrete entry number for that music; the number of the measure in Ives in which the borrowed melody is first heard and the instrument playing it (except when the work is for piano or organ). Borrowings are presented in the order in which they appear in a composition. When two or more different borrowings begin at the same time, they are listed in alphabetical order.

I. WORKS FOR ORCHESTRA

A. Symphonies

001 *Symphony No. 1* (mostly ca. 1898–1902)

  i. Allegro

   Shining Shore 54 (10—violin II)
   Beulah Land 8 (12—flute)

  ii. Adagio molto

   Dvořák, *Symphony No. 9* ii 179-b (3—English horn)

  iv. Allegro molto

   Tchaikovsky, *Symphony No. 6* iii 188-a (329—winds)

002 *Symphony No. 2* (mostly ca. 1900–1902; revisions made ca. 1909–10)

i. Andante moderato

Massa's in de Cold Ground 121 (7—violin I)
Nettleton 42 (10—violin I)
Pig Town Fling 167 (23—violin I)
Columbia, the Gem of the Ocean 75 (66—horns)
Brahms, *Symphony No. 1* iv 175-c (76—violin I)
J. S. Bach, *Sinfonia in F Minor, BWV 795* 172-a (93—violin I)

ii. Allegro

Wake Nicodemus 144 (1—flute)
Bringing in the Sheaves 10 (42—violin)
Where, O Where 157 (72—flute)
Brahms, *Symphony No. 3* i 177-a [formerly = 192] (126—violin I)
Hamburg 26 (137—trombone I)
Naomi 40 (145—trombone I)
Brahms, *Symphony No. 3* i 177 (149—violin)
Brahms, *Symphony No. 1* i 175-a (186—violin II and lower strings)

Possible borrowing:

Massa's in de Cold Ground 121 (84—violin I)

iii. Adagio cantabile

Beulah Land 8 (11—violin I)
Materna 36 (14—violin I)
There Is a Happy Land 57 (15—violin II)
Brahms, *Symphony No. 1* ii 175 (16—flute I)
Wagner, *Tristan und Isolde: Prelude* (3) 191 (25—flute)
J. S. Bach, *Sinfonia in F Minor, BWV 795* 172-a (34—oboe I)
Wagner, *Tristan und Isolde: Prelude* (2) 190 (44—violin I)
Missionary Chant 37 (45—horns I and II)
Nettleton 42 (49—horns I and II)
Massa's in de Cold Ground 121 (59—flute)
America 69 (72—flute)

Possible borrowing:

Cleansing Stream 12-b (16—flute I)

iv. Lento maestoso

Brahms, *Symphony No. 1* iv 175-b (1—horn)
Massa's in de Cold Ground 121 (10—flute)
Columbia, the Gem of the Ocean 75 (16—trombone)
Pig Town Fling 167 (17—flute)
Brahms, *Symphony No. 1* iv 175-c (26—violins)
Brahms, *Vier ernste Gesänge,* iii 177-b (29–30—voice)
J. S. Bach, *Sinfonia in F Minor, BWV 795* 172-a (34—oboe)
Brahms, *Symphony No. 1* iv 175-d (37—trombone)

v. Allegro molto vivace

Tchaikovsky, *Symphony No. 4* iii 186-j (1—violins)
De Camptown Races 100 (7—violin)
Columbia, the Gem of the Ocean 75 (11—bassoon I)
J. S. Bach, *Sinfonia in F Minor*, BWV 795 172-a (25—violin I)
Street beat 86-a (27—snare drum)
Turkey in the Straw 169 (37—violin)
Pig Town Fling 167 (52—violin II)
Antioch 3 (69—horn I)
Long, Long Ago 119 (70—flute I)
J. S. Bach, *Fugue in E Minor* [from] *Well-Tempered Clavier*, Book I 172-b (147—violin I)
Where, O Where 157 (181—violin I)
Wake Nicodemus 144 (181—violin I)
Massa's in de Cold Ground 121 (228—flute)
Missionary Chant 37 (228—trumpet II)
Brahms, *Symphony No. 1* iv 175-d (246—bassoon)
Reveille 83 (250—trumpet I)

Possible borrowing:

The Kerry Dance 165 (11—violin II)
Dvořák, *Symphony No. 9* i (60—flute)
Old Black Joe 128 (65—horn I)

003 *Symphony No. 3: The Camp Meeting* (Assembled/recomposed 1904 from material composed mostly ca. 1901; revised and completed ca. 1909–11)

i. *Old Folks Gatherin'* (Andante maestoso)

Erie 17 (2—violin I)
Azmon 5 (6—violin I)
Woodworth 67 (55—horns)

ii. *Children's Day* (Allegro)

Naomi 40 (2—horn)
Fountain 23 (2—violin I)
There Is a Happy Land 57 (50—flute)
There's Music in the Air 142 (64—flute)

Possible borrowing:

Blessed Assurance 9 (70—violin I)

iii. *Communion* (Largo)

Woodworth 67 (1—cello)
Azmon 5 (13—violin I)

Possible borrowing:

Erie 17 (45—flute)

iv. rejected 4th movement (Allegro)

The Beautiful River 6 (f0657, m. 1)

004   *Symphony No. 4* (Assembled/recomposed ca. 1910–16, possibly as late as 1919, from material composed 1898–1911)

i. *Prelude*

Bethany 7 (2—2 violins)
In the Sweet Bye and Bye 29 (5—cello)
Proprior Deo 49 (17—flute)
Watchman 61 (17—voices)
Something for Thee 55 (19—flute)
Westminster Chimes 170 (21—cello)
Welcome Voice 63 (23—flute)
Crusader's Hymn 13-a (25—flute)

ii. Allegretto

Beulah Land 8 (1—bass)
God Be with You 24 (1—bassoon) [= formerly Unknown 200]
Martyn 35 (6—solo piano)
Home! Sweet Home! 108 (11—violin I/others)
Nettleton 42 (13—violins I [2 only])
Tramp, Tramp, Tramp 89 (35—trombone)
Throw Out the Life-Line 59 (35—cello)
In the Sweet Bye and Bye 29 (38—violin I/others)
Marching Through Georgia 79 (39—bassoon)
The Beautiful River 6 (48—solo piano)
Washington Post March 90 (56—tuba)
Blow the Man Down 159 (72—piccolo)
Turkey in the Straw 169 (72—violin)
Peter, Peter Pumpkin Eater 130-a (72—orchestra piano primo) [= formerly Unknown 201]
De Camptown Races 100 (75—clarinet)
Massa's in de Cold Ground 121 (96—flute)
Hail! Columbia 77 (110—trumpet)
Old Black Joe 128 (112—solo piano)
There Is a Happy Land 57 (115—flute)
Westminster Chimes 170 (116—celesta)
Columbia, the Gem of the Ocean 75 (123—trumpet)
Street beat 86-a (123—orchestra piano I)
Reveille 83 (132—trumpet III)
Pig Town Fling 167 (175—bassoon)
Long, Long Ago 119 (178—orchestra piano I)
Yankee Doodle 92 (232—piccolo)
Saint Patrick's Day 168 (248—bassoon)
Garryowen 163 (252—violin I)
Irish Washerwoman 164 (257—violin I)
Bugle Call Derivative 74 (259—piccolo)

iii. Fugue

Missionary Hymn 38 (1—cello)
Christmas 12 (14—violin II)
Coronation 13 (21—flute)
Bach, *Toccata and Fugue in D Minor,* BWV 538 172-c (52—violin I)
Welcome Voice 63 (111—clarinet)
Antioch 3 (116—trombone)

Possible borrowing:

Brown 10-a (or) *Lischer* 33-a (89—flute)
Church Triumphant 12-a (89—clarinet)

iv. Largo

Street beat 86-a (1—battery unit)
Bethany 7 (6—5 violins)
Dorrnance 15 (11—violin I)
Unidentified 204 (17—flute)
Martyn 35 (24—clarinet)
Unidentified 205 (27—violins, 1 or 2 only)
Missionary Chant 37 (36—flute)
Westminster Chimes 170 (45—bell)
Antioch 3 (50—bassoon)
Nettleton 42 (52—celesta)
Azmon 5 (53—horn)
St. Hilda 51 (65—horn)
There Is a Happy Land 57 (65—oboe)
Proprior Deo 49 (72—oboe)
Something for Thee 55 (74—oboe)

005   *A Symphony: New England Holidays* (assembled perhaps ca. 1917)

i. *Washington's Birthday* (ca. 1909–13)

Home! Sweet Home! 108 (1—violin I)
Old Folks at Home 129 (7—horn)
Turkey in the Straw 169 (51—flute)
Unidentified 197 (60—violin II)
College Hornpipe 161 (81—flute)
De Camptown Races 100 (86—horn)
For He's a Jolly Good Fellow 101 (99—flute)
The White Cockade 171 (109—violin I)
Massa's in de Cold Ground 121 (116—flute)
Irish Washerwoman 164 (127—horn)
The Campbells Are Comin' 160 (135—horn)
Garryowen 163 (141—horn)
Fisher's Hornpipe 162 (145—piccolo)
Saint Patrick's Day 168 (145—horn)
Money Musk 166 (156—piccolo)

Pig Town Fling 167 (163—violin I)
Unidentified 198 (167—violin I)
Goodnight, Ladies 104 (178—flute)

ii. *Decoration Day* (ca. 1912–13)

Adeste Fideles 1 (1—violin I)
Over There 82 (22—trumpet I)
Marching Through Georgia 79 (37—flute)
Tenting on the Old Camp Ground 88 (61—violin I)
Taps 87 (74—trumpet)
Bethany 7 (75—violins Ia)
Second Regiment Connecticut National Guard March 84 (89—piccolo)
Battle Hymn of the Republic 72 (132—E♭ clarinet)

Possible borrowing:

Dies irae 14-a (5—English horn) [= formerly Unknown 220]
Lambeth 32 (20—violins Ia, b)
Yankee Doodle 92 (46—violin I)

iii. *The Fourth of July* (ca. 1911–13)

Columbia, the Gem of the Ocean 75 (1—violin)
Cuckoo's Call 161-a (16—piccolo)
Assembly 70 (27—horn)
The Battle Cry of Freedom 71 (27—cello)
Marching Through Georgia 79 (34—trumpet)
College Hornpipe 161 (45—oboe)
Fisher's Hornpipe 162 (49—piccolo)
Battle Hymn of the Republic 71 (49—violin)
Reveille 83 (57—horn)
Hail! Columbia 77 (64—clarinet)
Street beat 86-a (66-a—drums; piano)
Tramp, Tramp, Tramp 89 (69—piccolo)
The Girl I Left Behind Me 102 (71—piccolo)
London Bridge 118 (74—piccolo)
Garryowen 163 (82—piano)
Saint Patrick's Day 168 (88—piano)
Katy Darling 113 (99—piccolo)
Yankee Doodle 92 (99—xylophone)
Dixie's Land 76 (109—piccolo)
Kingdom Coming 114 (110—piccolo)
The Star Spangled Banner 86 (114—trumpet)

Possible borrowing:

The White Cockade 171 (66-a—piccolo)
Irish Washerwoman 164 (97—horn)

iv. *Thanksgiving and Forefathers' Day* (ca. 1904 version probably lost; ?recomposed ca. 1919)

Federal Street 22 (4—flute)
Shining Shore 54 (9—flute)
Laban 31 (29—violin I)
Nettleton 42 (36—flute)
Unidentified 193 (39—flute)
Valentia 60-a (43—oboe)
Arlington 3-a (50—viola I)
Duke Street 16 (51—horns III and IV)
Azmon 5 (169—oboe I)
In the Sweet Bye and Bye 29 (172—flute)

006   *Universe Symphony* (1911–28)

Section A: *Bethany* 7 (f1831, 7 staves from top of page)

Section C: *Bethany* 7 (f1845, staff 1)

Possible borrowing:

Massa's in de Cold Ground 121 (Section A: f1835, 5 staves from bottom of page)
Erie 17 (Section A: f1832, staff 1)

B. Sets

i. Orchestral Sets

007   *Orchestral Set No. 1: Three Places in New England* (Version 1 assembled/reworked ca. 1913–14, from material composed ca. 1903–12; revised as version 2 for chamber orchestra, 1929)

i. *The "Saint Gaudens" in Boston Common (Col. Shaw and his Colored Regiment)*

Old Black Joe 128 (1—flute); also see *Jesus Loves Me* 30
The Battle Cry of Freedom 71 (27—flute)
Marching Through Georgia 79 (38—violin I)
Reveille 83 (54—horn)
Deep River 14 (56—horn)
Massa's in de Cold Ground 121 (72—violin I)

Possible borrowing:

Jesus Loves Me 30 (2—bass) or *Old Black Joe* 128

ii. *Putnam's Camp, Redding, Connecticut*

Happy Day 27 (8—bassoon)
The British Grenadiers 73 (14—flute)
Reveille 83 (18—bassoon)
Street beat 86-a (25—drums)
Arkansas Traveler 158 (27—clarinet)
Liberty Bell March 78 (27—piano)
Semper Fideles 85 (27—trombone)

Massa's in de Cold Ground 121 (27—flute)
Marching Through Georgia 79 (30—piano)
The Battle Cry of Freedom 71 (32—trumpet)
Yankee Doodle 92 (35—violin I)
Hail! Columbia 77 (74—violin I)
The Star Spangled Banner 86 (162—oboe)

iii. *The Housatonic at Stockbridge*

Dorrnance 15 (3—cello)
Missionary Chant 37 (6—horn)

008   *Orchestral Set No. 2* (Assembled/reworked ca. 1919 from material composed ca. 1909–19; revised ca. 1925)

i. *An Elegy to Our Forefathers*

Old Black Joe 128 (3—zither)
Oh, Nobody Knows de Trouble I've Seen 43 (15—trumpet II)
Reveille 83 (19—flute)
Jesus Loves Me 30 (21—trumpet)
Nettleton 42 (23—zither)
Massa's in de Cold Ground 121 (24—flute)

ii. *The Rockstrewn Hills Join in the People's Outdoor Meeting*

Turkey in the Straw 169 (23—bassoon I)
Happy Day 27 (28—piano)
Bringing in the Sheaves 10 (38—violin I)
Welcome Voice 63 (39—violin I)
Yankee Doodle 92 (43—flute)
The Girl I Left Behind Me 102 (78—trumpet)
Rock-a-bye Baby 132 (127—flute)
Massa's in de Cold Ground 121 (153—trumpet)

iii. *From Hanover Square North, at the End of a Tragic Day, the Voice of the People Again Arose*

Te Deum 56-a (1—voice)
In the Sweet Bye and Bye 29 (23—clarinet)
Massa's in de Cold Ground 121 (83—viola)
Ewing 20 (102—organ)
My Old Kentucky Home 123 (108—upper cello)

009   *Orchestral Set No. 3* (composed 1919–26)

i. [Andante moderato]: except where noted, measure numbers follow David Porter's unpublished performance score of this movement. I have included what I believe to be three borrowings that Porter did not mention. I have given their sources in the Ives manuscripts in which they appear.

Old Hundredth 44 (2—bass)
Dorrnance 15 (13—piano)

Hebron 28 (q2998—no. 1789—section C of sketch, staff 10); does not appear in Porter's performance score

Street beat 86-a (19—strings); while this is not in the same pattern as typical *Street beat* borrowings, Ives indicates that all pizzicato strings here are "used as drums"

Shining Shore 54 (22—trombone)

Beethoven, *Andante favori in F* (26—flute)

Woodworth 67 (28—woodwinds)

Nettleton 42 (33—celesta)

The Beautiful River 6 (52—flute and trumpet)

Materna 36 (p. 9: q2998; section C of sketch; staff 15); does not appear in Porter's performance score

Battle Hymn of the Republic 72 (p. 11: q2999; section D of sketch; staff 6); does not appear in Porter's performance score

Dies irae 14-a (p. 13: q3000, section E of sketch; staff 14; distant piano; celesta); does not appear in Porter's performance score

Possible borrowing:

Watchman 61 (n1058, staff 10—trombone); does not appear in Porter's performance score

ii. *An Afternoon or During Camp Meetin' Week—One Secular Afternoon (In Bethel)*

Note: photostat numbering taken from David Porter's thesis; page numbers correspond to Porter: "Part II: Transcript of Ives' MSS." Porter does not give page numbers in this section; these have been added here.

In the Sweet Bye and Bye 29 (p. 15: n3002, staff 2)

Shining Shore 54 (p. 15: n3002, staff 5)

Has Anybody Here Seen Kelly? 106 (p. 15: n3002, staff 9, upside down)

Columbia, the Gem of the Ocean 75 (p. 15: n3002, staff 10, upside down; trumpet)

Battle Hymn of the Republic 72 (p. 15: n3002, staff 11, upside down; cornets)

Unidentified 225 (p. 16: n3001, staff 8, flute-clarinet)

Azmon 5 (p. 16: n3002, section 2, staff 1, violin II)

Materna 36 (p. 16: n3002, section 2, staff 1, violin II)

Kingdom Coming 114 (p. 16: n3002, section 6, staff 8, solo trombone)

Grandfather's Clock 105 (p. 16: n3002, section 6, staff 8, trombone)

Little Brown Jug 116 (p. 16: n3002, section 7, staff 10)

Silver Threads Among the Gold 134 (p. 16: n3002, section 7, staff 11)

Nancy Lee 123-a (p. 17: n3003, staff 1, trumpet-cornet)

Alexander 94 (p. 17: n3003, section 8, staff 2)

Reveille 83 (p. 19: n3004, staff 3, fife)

Street beat 86-a (p. 19: n3004, staff 4, snare drum)

The Girl I Left Behind Me 102 (p. 19, n3004, staff 7, fife)

Turkey in the Straw 169 (p. 19: n3004, staff 7, fife)

Windsor 66 (p. 19, n3004, staff 9)

Greenwood 25 (p. 19, n3004, staff 13)

Tramp, Tramp, Tramp 89 (p. 20: n3005, staff 8)

I've Been Working on the Railroad 109 (p. 20: n3005, staff 10, male chorus or trombones)

Where Did You Get That Hat? 144-a (p. 20: n3005, staff 14)

Unidentified 226 (p. 20: n3005, staff 15; horn, cello, trombone)

Jingle, Bells 110 (p. 21: n3144, staff 9)

My Old Kentucky Home 123 (p. 21: n3144, staff 16)

Ives also mentions *Throw Out the Life-Line* (59), but he does not quote from it.

iii. —[no tempo heading]

Woodworth 67 (p. 28: n3057, staff 1, harp)

Nettleton 42 (p. 28: n3057, staff 3)

Azmon 5 (p. 28: n3057, staff 4)

Shining Shore 54 (p. 28: n3057, staff 10)

Home! Sweet Home! 108 (p. 29: n3063, staff 1)

Unidentified 227 (p. 33: n3058, staff 3)

Even Me 18 (p. 33: n3058, staff 9, trumpet)

Dorrnance 15 (p. 35: n3008-a, staff 6)

Old Hundredth 44 (p. 36: n3244, staff 6)

Retreat 50 (p. 37: n3056, staff 6)

ii. Sets for Chamber Orchestra

010   Set No. 1 (assembled probably in 1913 from music composed 1907–11)

iii. *The Ruined River* (Allegro) (1912)

Tammany 139 (7—piccolo)

Ta-ra-ra Boom-de-ay! 140 (13—cornet)

v. *Calcium Light Night* (Slow March time) (1898–1907)

Few Days 150 (4—trombone)

Jolly Dogs 154 (8—piccolo)

A Band of Brothers in DKE 146 (12—clarinet)

Tramp, Tramp, Tramp 89 (22—clarinet)

Marching Through Georgia 79 (26—clarinet)

011   Set No. 2 (assembled possibly in 1913–14 from music composed 1911–12)

iii. *Andante: The Last Reader* (1911)

Cherith 11 (1—cornet)

Manoah 34 (8—cornet)

Possible borrowing:

Araby's Daughter 96 (f2698, staff 3, last measure)

St. Peter 52 (f2699, m. 17)

012   Set No. 3 (assembled possibly in 1918–19 from music composed in 1912–18)

i. *Adagio sostenuto: At Sea* (no date; sometime before 1914)

Possible borrowing:

> *Consolation* 12-c (f2743, staff 1, m. 1)
> *Azmon* 5 (f2743, m. 6—solo English horn)
> *Missionary Chant* 37 (f2743, m. 8—English horn)
> *Bethany* 7 or *Nettleton* 42 (f2777, staff 1, m. 1)

 ii. *Luck and Work* (1916)

Possible borrowing:

> *Bethany* 7 or *Nettleton* 42 (f2777, staff 1, m. 1)

013 *Set No. 4: Three Poets and Human Nature* (planned after 1922 printing of *114 Songs*; probably between 1925 and 1930)

 iii. Matthew Arnold (Moderato)

> *Fountain* 23 (f8148, last 3 measures)

014 *Set No. 5: The Other Side of Pioneering, or Side Lights on American Enterprise* (planned after 1922 printing of *114 Songs*; probably after 1925)

 i. *The New River*

Possible borrowing:

> *Tammany* 139 (f6157, staff 1, m. 3—piano)
> *Ta-ra-ra 'Boom-de-ay!* 140 (f6158, m. 1—voice)

 iii. *Charlie Rutlage* (in moderate time)

> *Get Along Little Dogies* 103 (f6164, staff 1, m. 1—piano)

015 *Set No. 6: From the Side Hill* (planned after 1922 printing of *114 Songs*; probably between 1925 and 1930)

 ii. *The Rainbow*

> *Serenity* 53 (f6161, staff 2, m. 1—voice)

 iii. *Afterglow*

Possible borrowing:

> *Erie* 17 (f6180, staff 4, last portion—voice)

 iv. *Evening*

> *Bethany* 7 (f6153, staff 3, last notes of voice)

016 *Set No. 7: Water Colors* (planned after the Jan. 1925 completion of the original song version of movement iv (*A Sea Dirge*; probably before 1930)

 i. *At Sea*

> *Bethany* 7 (f6156, m. 5—voice)
> *Missionary Chant* 37 (f6156, m. 8—voice)

Possible borrowing:

> *Consolation* 12-c (f6156, m. 2—voice)
> *Azmon* 5 (f6156, m. 6—voice)

iii. *The Pond*

    Kathleen Mavourneen 112 or *David* 13-b, or *Hexham* 28-a (1—horn)
    Taps 87 (8—flute])

017   *Set No. 8: Songs Without Voices* (planned after 1922 printing of *114 Songs;* perhaps in early 1930)

    i. *The New River*

        Ta-ra-ra Boom-de-ay! 140 (f2282, score 2, voice)

    Possible borrowing:

        Tammany 139 (f2781, score 1, m. 3—piano)

018   *Set No. 9 of Three Pieces* (assembled possibly in 1934)

    i. *Andante con moto: The Last Reader*

        Cherith 11 (f2746, m. 1—English horn)
        Manoah 34 (f2747, m. 7—English horn)
        Bethany 7 (f2749, m. 14—English horn)
        St. Peter 52 (f2750, m. 17—English horn)

    Possible borrowing:

        Araby's Daughter 96 (f2747, m. 6—English horn)

019   *Set No. 10 of Three Pieces* (assembled probably in May–June 1934)

    ii. *Allegro-Andante: Luck and Work*

    Possible borrowing:

        Nettleton 42 (f2770, m. 5—Basset horn)

020   *Set for Theatre Orchestra* (assembled/reworked ca. 1914, based on material composed between 1899 and, according to Ives, 1906)

    ii. *In the Inn*
        After the Ball 93 (29—violin)
        Reuben and Rachel 131 (34—violin)
        Bringing in the Sheaves 10 (41—piano)
        Ta-ra-ra Boom-de-ay! 140 (74—violin)
        Push Dem Clouds Away 130 (86—violin) [= former Unknown 194]
        The Girl I Left Behind Me 102 (101—clarinet)
        Welcome Voice 63 (125—violin)

    iii. *In the Night*
        De Little Cabins All Am Empty Now 117 (3—horn)
        Massa's in de Cold Ground 121 (10—high bells)
        Eventide 19 (11—solo cello)

C. Overtures

021 *Alcott Overture* [mostly lost]
    Massa's in de Cold Ground 121 (f2488)
    Bethany 7 (f2488)
    Missionary Chant 37 (f2488)

022 *Emerson Overture for Piano and Orchestra* [incomplete] (sketched ca. 1910–11 and revised in 1919 or later)
    Beethoven, *Symphony No. 5 i* 173 (No. 2214, brace 3); similarities among parts of Beethoven, *Symphony No. 5 i* 173, *Missionary Chant* 37, and *Parah* 48 make unequivocal identification difficult

023 *Matthew Arnold Overture* [incomplete] (Dec. 1912)
    Fountain 23 (f2335, score 2, m. 6)

024 *Overture and March "1776"* (Dec. 1903; revised ca. 1907)
    Hail! Columbia 77 (5—oboe)
    The British Grenadiers 73 (16—flute)
    Bugle Call Derivatives 74 (34—flute)
    Battle Hymn of the Republic 72 (42—clarinet)
    Columbia, the Gem of the Ocean 75 (42—cornet)
    Saint Patrick's Day 168 (44—violin)
    Tramp, Tramp, Tramp 89 (53—flute)
    Yankee Doodle 92 (67—oboe)
    The Star Spangled Banner 86 (75—violin I)
    Street beat 86-a (41—drum)

027 *Robert Browning Overture* (ca. 1908–12; partly revised ca. 1936–42 with Henry Cowell's assistance
    Adeste Fideles 1 (50—trumpet)
    Christmas 12 (371—horn)

D. Marches

028 *Holiday Quickstep* (1887)
    Reeves, *Second Regiment Connecticut National Guard March* 84 (60—cornets)

029 *March No. 2, with "Son of a Gambolier"* (1892)
    The Son of a Gambolier 135 (25—E-flat cornet)

031 *March No. 3, with "My Old Kentucky Home"* (ca. 1892)
    My Old Kentucky Home 123 (41—cornet I)

033 *March: The Circus Band* (version 1: probably 1899; version 2: probably in mid to late 1920s; version 3: arranged probably in mid to late 1930s); the following quotations appear in version 3
    Street beat 86-a (41—drums)

Jolly Dogs 154 (89—voices)
Marching Through Georgia 79 (81—horn)
Riding Down from Bangor 131-a (81—voice)
Reuben and Rachel 131 (89—voices)

E. Other Works

034   *Central Park in the Dark* (July–Dec. 1906)
        Ben Bolt 99 (12—clarinet)
        Violets 143 (44—solo violin)
        Unknown 196 (65—oboe)
        Hello! Ma Baby 107 (67—piano I)
        Street beat 86-a (91—piano II)
        The Campbells Are Comin' 160 (93—flute)
        Freshmen in the Park 150-a (95—piano II)
        Washington Post March 90 (103—piano II)

036   *"Country Band" March* [incomplete] (no earlier than 1905; revised ca. 1914)
        London Bridge 118 (24—flute)
        The Girl I Left Behind Me 102 (26—flute)
        Arkansas Traveller 158 (44—cornet I)
        Massa's in de Cold Ground 121 (44—flute)
        Marching Through Georgia 79 (50—flute)
        Semper Fideles 85 (53—clarinet)
        The Battle Cry of Freedom 71 (55—cornet)
        Yankee Doodle 92 (59—cornet)
        Violets 143 (76—cornet I)
        My Old Kentucky Home 123 (105—violin)
        The British Grenadiers 73 (160—violin I)
        Street beat 86-a (45—drums)
        Unidentified 230 (64—violins)

037   *The General Slocum* [incomplete] (sketched probably in 1906)
        Quotations are given in alphabetical order
        Bethany 7 (no. 2211, brace 2)
        Little Annie Rooney 115 (no. 2210, brace 2)
        Ma Blushin' Rosie 120 (no. 2210, brace 3)
        The Sidewalks of New York 133 (no. 2210, brace 2)
        Throw Out the Life-Line 59 (no. 2211, brace 2)
        Violets 143 (no. 2210, brace 3)

038   *The Gong on the Hook and Ladder or Firemen's Parade on Main Street* (arranged perhaps in 1934 from music composed possibly ca. 1911 or as early as 1905); cf. 070
        Oh, My Darling Clementine 126 (13—flute)
        Few Days 150 (20—trumpet)
        Marching Through Georgia 79 (27—trumpet)

039 *Piece for Small Orchestra and Organ* [mostly lost] (perhaps ca. 1905)
　　Quotations are given in alphabetical order
　　The Battle Cry of Freedom 71 (no. 2490)
　　Dixie's Land 76 (no. 2490)
　　Home! Sweet Home! 108 (no. 2489)
　　In the Sweet Bye and Bye 29 (no. 2490)
　　My Old Kentucky Home 123 (no. 2490)
　　Nettleton 42 (no. 2490)
　　On the Banks of the Wabash, Far Away 130 (no. 2490)

040 *The Pond* (ca. 1906; revised 1912 or later)
　　Kathleen Mavourneen 112 (3—voice or trumpet); this may be *David* (13-b) or
　　　Hexham (28-a)
　　Taps 87 (10—flute)

042 *Three Ragtime Dances* [mostly lost] (1911)

　　ii. [2nd Ragtime Dance]

　　　Happy Day 27 (f2481, staff 1, m. 1)
　　　Pig Town Fling 167 (f2481, score 1, m. 3)
　　　Welcome Voice 63 (f2481, staff 1, m. 3)

043 *Four Ragtime Dances* (earlier materials sketched ca. 1899–1902; ink score ca. 1919)
Ragtime Dance No. 1

　　　Bringing in the Sheaves 10 (20—clarinet)
　　　Happy Day 27 (49—violin)
　　　Welcome Voice 63 (96—violin)

Ragtime Dance No. 2

　　　Happy Day 27 (5—violin)
　　　Bringing in the Sheaves 10 (14—clarinet)
　　　Welcome Voice 63 (63—violin)

Ragtime Dance No. 3

　　　Bringing in the Sheaves 10 (15—clarinet)
　　　Welcome Voice 63 (104—violin)

Ragtime Dance No. 4

　　　Bringing in the Sheaves 10 (13—violin)
　　　Happy Day 27 (53—trombone)
　　　Melodic similarities between "Happy Day" and "Bringing in the Sheaves" make
　　　　absolute determination somewhat equivocal.
　　　Welcome Voice 63 (104—flute)

045 *The Rainbow* (1914)

Serenity 53 (12—English/basset horn)

046 *Skit for Danbury Fair* [incomplete] (1902)

    Happy Day 27 (f2428, score 1, m. 8)

    Bringing in the Sheaves 10 (f2428, score 2, m. 1)

047 *Take-Off No. 7: Mike Donlin–Johnny Evers* [incomplete] (1907)

    Ta-ra-ra Boom-de-ay! 140 (1—winds)

    When Johnny Comes Marching Home 91 (2—winds)

049 *Tone Roads et al.* (assembled as a set possibly in 1915 from pieces composed 1911–15)

    On the Banks of the Wabash, Far Away 130 (a setting of this superscription to *Slow and fast "Rondo rapid transit"* appears in f2724). The quotation, however, does not appear in the actual score of this piece

051 *Yale-Princeton Football Game* [incomplete?] (sketched in orchestral version ca. 1898–99

    Dear Old Yale 149 (f2203, bottom staff)

    Harvard Has Blue Stocking Girls 151 (f2203, 3 staves from bottom of page)

    Hold the Fort 152 (f2203, bottom staff)

    Hy-can nuck a no 153 (f2203, 2 staves from bottom of page)

    Old Nassau 155 (f2203, 4 staves from bottom of page)

    Second Regiment Connecticut National Guard March 84 (f2203)

    Brekeke-kek, ko-ax, ko-ax 148-a (f2203, m. 6)

    Yale's Short Cheer (9 "Rah"/3 "Yale") 157-a (f2203, m. 5)

II. WORKS FOR BAND

052 *Fantasia on "Jerusalem the Golden"* (1888 or 1889) *Ewing* 20 (1—cornet)

053 *March in F and C, with "Omega Lambda Chi"* (arranged in 1896 from music composed in 1892 or 1895/96)

    Omega Lambda Chi 156 (9—E-flat basses)

054 *March "Intercollegiate," with "Annie Lisle"* (composed or arranged 1892)

    Annie Lisle 95 (27—trombone)

III. WORKS FOR CHAMBER ENSEMBLE

A. String Quartets

057 *String Quartet No. 1: From the Salvation Army* (1898–1902, based on organ pieces from 1896–98)

    i. *Chorale* (Andante con moto)

        Missionary Hymn 38 (1—cello)
        *Christma*s 12 (12—viola)
        Coronation 13 (16—violins)
        J. S. Bach, *Fugue in D Minor* [from] *Toccata and Fugue in D Minor,* BWV 538 172-c (21—violin II)

    ii. Prelude (Allegro)

        Beulah Land 8 (8—violin I)
        Shining Shore 54 (12—violin I)
        Bringing in the Sheaves 10 (18—cello)

    Possible borrowing:

        Beethoven, *Sonata in F Minor for Piano,* Op. 2, no. 1/ii 173-a (1—violin I)

    iii. *Offertory*

        Nettleton 42 (1—violin I)
        Unidentified 210 (35—violin I)
        Beulah Land 8 (39—violin I)
        Unidentified 211 (49—violin I)
        Shining Shore 54 (58—cello)

    iv. *Postlude*

        Coronation 13 (1—violin I) = formerly Unknown 212
        Webb 62 (2—violin I)
        Unidentified 213 (60—violin II)
        Shining Shore 54 (147—violin II)

058 *String Quartet No. 2* (composed/assembled 1911–13; movement ii material dating from 1907)

    i. *Discussions*

        Wagner, *Tristan und Isolde: Prelude* [1] 189 (1—viola)
        Columbia, the Gem of the Ocean 75 (7—violin II)
        Dixie's Land 76 (60—viola)
        Marching Through Georgia 79 (62—violin II)
        Turkey in the Straw 169 (62—viola)
        Hail! Columbia 77 (64—violin I)
        Taps 87 (81—violin I)

ii. *Arguments*

Columbia, the Gem of the Ocean 75 (48—viola)
Hail! Columbia 77 (87—violin I)
Tchaikovsky, *Symphony No. 6* iii 188 (87—cello)
Brahms, *Symphony No. 2* i 176 (92—violin I)
Beethoven, *Symphony No. 9* iv 174 (96—violin II)
Marching Through Georgia 79 (97—violin I)
Massa's in de Cold Ground 121 (101—violin I)

iii. *The Call of the Mountains*

Nettleton 42 (13—violins)
Bethany 7 (49—violin I)
Westminster Chimes 170 (78—viola)

B. Violin Sonatas

059 *Pre-First Sonata for Violin and Piano* (ca. 1902–1907; based in part on material composed possibly as early as 1897; revised 1907)

i. Allegretto moderato

God Be with You 24 (f3236, m. 11—violin)
Beethoven, *Andante favori* 173-c (f3237, m. 15—violin)
The Battle Cry of Freedom 71 (f3240, m. 57—violin)
Tenting on the Old Camp Ground 88 (f3246, m. 126—violin)

ii. Largo

Araby's Daughter 96 (f3247, m. 1—violin)
Tramp, Tramp, Tramp 89 (30—piano)

rejected third movement: Scherzo

College Hornpipe 161 (15—violin)
Money Musk 166 (34—violin)
The White Cockade 171 (no. 3213, staff 3, piano)

iii. Largo-Allegro

Autumn 4 (1—violin)

060 *Sonata No. 1 for Violin and Piano* (assembled/recomposed ca. 1914 from movements composed 1901–1908)

i. Andante-Allegro vivace

Shining Shore 54 (17—piano)
Bringing in the Sheaves 10 (65—violin)
Araby's Daughter 96 (146—violin)

ii. Largo cantabile

Araby's Daughter 96 (1—violin)

Tramp, Tramp, Tramp 89 (30—piano)
Work Song 68 (82—violin)

iii. Allegro

Work Song 68 (1—piano)
Watchman 61 (41—violin)

061 *Sonata No. 2 for Violin and Piano* (assembled/recomposed ca. 1914 from movements composed 1901, 1903, and 1907–10; revised 1919)

i. *Autumn*

Autumn 4 (4—piano)
Oh! Susanna 127 (19—violin)

ii. *In the Barn*

College Hornpipe 161 (14—violin)
Money Musk 166 (35—violin)
Happy Day 27 (40—piano)
The White Cockade 171 (64—piano)
Turkey in the Straw 169 (73—violin)
The Battle Cry of Freedom 71 (108—violin)

iii. *The Revival*

Nettleton 42 (1—violin)

062 *Sonata No. 3 for Violin and Piano* (assembled/recomposed in 1914 from movements composed 1901–1904)

i. Adagio

Need 41 (4—violin)
Beulah Land 8 (114—violin)

ii. Allegro

There'll Be No Dark Valley 58 (15—violin)
The Beautiful River 6 (53—violin)

iii. Adagio cantabile

Need 41 (1—piano)
Happy Day 27 (8—piano)

063 *Sonata No. 4 for Violin and Piano: Children's Day at the Camp Meeting* (assembled ca. 1916 from movements composed 1900–16)

i. Allegro

Old Old Story 45 (8—violin)
Ives, *Fourth Fugue in B-flat* 184 (16—piano)

ii. Largo-Allegro (conslugarocko)-Andante con spirito-Adagio cantabile-Largo cantabile)

Jesus Loves Me 30 (1—piano)

iii. Allegro

The Beautiful River 6 (1—piano)

rejected iv (Adagio-Faster)

torn out of score of *Fourth Violin Sonata* and developed into *Second Violin Sonata*

Nettleton 42 (f3278, staff 1, violin)

C. Other Works

064 *Decoration Day* for Violin and Piano (arranged after 1919 from music composed in Sept 1912

Adeste Fideles 1 (f0712, m. 1—piano)

Marching Through Georgia 79 (f0714, m. 37—violin)

The Battle Cry of Freedom 71 (f0715, m. 65—violin)

Bethany 7 (f0716, m. 75—piano)

Tenting on the Old Camp Ground 88 (f0715, m. 68—violin)

Taps 87 (f0716, m. 75)

Street beat 86-a (f0716, m. 81—piano)

Reeves, *Second Regiment Connecticut National Guard March* 84 (f0716, m. 89—piano)

Possible borrowing:

   Dies irae 14-a (f0712, m. 4—violin)
   Lambeth 32 (f0713, m. 20)
   Yankee Doodle 92 (f0714, m. 46—piano)
   Battle Hymn of the Republic 72 (f0715, m. 60—piano)

065 *From the Steeples and the Mountains* (1901)

Wild Bells 65 (f2421, m. 1—high bells I)

Possible borrowing:

   Taps 87 (f2421, m. 6—trumpets/trombones)

069 *Fugue in Four Keys on "The Shining Shore"* [incomplete] (possibly ca. 1902)

Shining Shore 54 (f3036, m. 1—cello)

Azmon 5 (f5563, staff 3)

070 *The Gong on the Hook and Ladder or Firemen's Parade on Main Street* (perhaps ca. 1911 or as early as 1905)

Oh, My Darling Clementine 126 (13—flute)

Few Days 150 (20—flute)

Marching Through Georgia 79 (27—trumpet)

080 *Prelude on "Eventide"* (possibly 1899)

    Eventide 19 (3—trombone)

083 *Scherzo for String Quartet* (Dec. 1904)

    Bringing in the Sheaves 10 (2—cello)

    Massa's in de Cold Ground 121 (5—cello)

    My Old Kentucky Home 123 (10—cello)

    College Hornpipe 161 (14—violin I)

    Streets of Cairo 137 (17—violins)

084 *A Set of Three Short Pieces* (assembled probably in 1935—possibly in 1914—from movements composed 1903–1908)

    i. *Largo cantabile: Hymn*

        More Love to Thee 39 (4—violin I)
        Olivet 46 (27—cello)

    Possible borrowing:

        Kathleen Mavourneen 112, or *David* 13-b, or *Hexham* 28-a (21—cello)

    ii. *Scherzo: Holding Your Own!*

        Bringing in the Sheaves 10 (2—cello)
        Massa's in de Cold Ground 121 (5—cello)
        My Old Kentucky Home 123 (10—cello)
        College Hornpipe 161 (14—violin I)
        Streets of Cairo 137 (17—violins)

    iii. *Adagio cantabile: The Innate*

        The Beautiful River 6 (1—violin)
        Nettleton 42 (3—piano)

086 *Trio for Violin, Violoncello, and Piano* (revised probably in 1911 and again ca. 1914 from music composed possibly in 1896 and 1904–1907)

    ii. Presto ("TSIAJ" or Medley on the Fence [or] on the Campus!)

        A Band of Brothers in DKE 146 (16—violin)
        Marching Through Georgia 79 (43—violin)
        Few Days 150 (47—violin)
        Jingle, Bells 110 (50—violin)
        Freshmen in the Park 157-a (65—violin)
        My Old Kentucky Home 123 (68—piano)
        That Old Cabin Home upon the Hill 141 (68—cello)
        In the Sweet Bye and Bye 29 (84—cello)
        Second Regiment Connecticut National Guard March 84 (88–cello)
        College Hornpipe 161 (89—violin)
        Unidentified 214 (93—violin)
        Turkey in the Straw 169 (108—violin)

Pig Town Fling 167 (118—violin)
The Campbells Are Comin' 160 (119—cello)
Long, Long Ago 119 (120—violin)
Happy Day 27 (125—violin)
Ta-ra-ra Boom-de-ay! 140 (130—violin)
Dixie's Land 76 (145—violin)
Unidentified 215 (163—piano)
Hold the Fort 152 (169—piano)
Saint Patrick's Day 168 (170—violin)
Reuben and Rachel 131 (173—cello)
The Gods of Egypt Bid Us Hail! 150-b (178—piano) [= former Unknown 216]
Fountain 23 (187—piano)

iii. Moderato con moto

Toplady 60 (130—cello)

IV. WORKS FOR PIANO

A. Sonatas

087   *Sonata No. 1 for Piano* (assembled or revised perhaps as late as 1919, incorporating music composed 1901–1909)

i. Adagio con moto-Andante con moto-Allegro risoluto-Adagio cantabile

Lebanon 33 (12)
Where Is My Wandering Boy? 64 (35)

ii-a Allegro moderato-Andante

Happy Day 27 (1)
Bringing in the Sheaves 10 (4)
Welcome Voice 63 (51)

ii-b Allegro-Meno mosso con moto: *"In the Inn"*

Bringing in the Sheaves 10 (100)
Happy Day 27 (132)
Welcome Voice 63 (184)

iii. Largo-Allegro-Largo

Erie 17 (2)
Possible borrowing:
Lebanon 33 (69)

iv-a [no tempo heading]

Welcome Voice 63 (149)

iv-b Allegro-Presto-Slow

Bringing in the Sheaves 10 (8)
Happy Day 27 (45)
Welcome Voice 63 (98)

v. Andante maestoso-Adagio cantabile-Allegro-Andante

Lebanon 33 (5)
Happy Day 27 (129)
There Is a Happy Land 57 (143)

088 *Sonata No. 2 for Piano: Concord, Mass., 1840–60* (assembled/recomposed ca. 1915 from music composed 1904–15; revised ca. 1919; revised in 1920s–40s for second edition)

i. *Emerson*

Beethoven, *Symphony No. 5* i 173 (p. 1, staff 1)
Possible borrowing:
  Crusader's Hymn 13-a (p. 3, staff 3)
  Wagner, Prelude to *Tristan und Isolde* [1] 189 (p. 13, staff 4, m. 1)
  Martyn 35 (p. 19, staff 3, right hand)

ii. *Hawthorne*

Beethoven, *Symphony No. 5* i 173 (p. 31, staff 2)
Beethoven, *Sonata in B-flat for Piano,* Op. 106 i ("Hammerklavier") 173-b (p. 31, staff 4)
Martyn 35 (p. 33, staff 1)
Columbia, the Gem of the Ocean 75 (p. 43, staff 3)
Debussy, "Golliwog's Cakewalk" from *Children's Corner* 178-a (p. 37, staff 3, right hand)
Peter, Peter Pumpkin Eater 130-a (p. 23, staff 2, right hand)

iii. *The Alcotts*

Missionary Chant 37 (p. 53, staff 1)
Beethoven, *Symphony No. 5* i 173 (p. 53, staff 3)
Martyn 35 (p. 53, staff 3)
Beethoven, *Sonata for Piano in B-flat,* Op. 106 i ("Hammerklavier") 173-b (p. 55, staff 2)
Wagner, *Wedding March* [from] *Lohengrin* 191-a (p. 55, staff 3)
Loch Lomond 117-a (p. 55, staff 4, m. 2)
Stop That Knocking at My Door 136 (p. 56, staff 1)

iv. *Thoreau*

Massa's in de Cold Ground 121 (p. 62, staff 1)
Beethoven, *Symphony No. 5,* i, 173 (p. 63, staff 4)
Beethoven, *Sonata for Piano in B-flat,* Op. 106 i ("Hammerklavier") 173-b (p. 68, staff 1)
Possible borrowing:
  Martyn 35 (p. 67, staff 1)

089   *Three-Page Sonata* (Sept 1905; revised 1925 or later)
       Proprior Deo 49 (31)
       Westminster Chimes 170 (49)

    Possible borrowing:

      Need 41 (37)
      Carl Foeppl, *Cornet Fantasy on Ever of Thee* 100-a (41)

B. Studies

094   *Study No. 6: Andante* (probably 1907–1908)
     Bethany 7 (f4791, staff 4, m. 1)

097   *Study No. 9: The Anti-Abolitionist Riots in the 1830s and 1840s* (probably 1908)
     Beethoven, *Symphony No. 5*, i 173 (p. 4, staff 2)

101   *Study No. 16: Andante cantabile* [incomplete] (possibly 1908, but more likely in the late 1920s)
     Home! Sweet Home! 108 (f4802, staff 6)

103   *Study No. 19* [incomplete] (mid-1920s)
     Even Me 18 (f4803, bottom staff, m. 1)

104   *Study No. 20: March* (Slow Allegro or Fast Andante) (mid-1920s)
     Battle Hymn of the Republic 72 (71)
     I've Been Working on the Railroad 109 (75)
     The Girl I Left Behind Me 102 (77)
     Turkey in the Straw 169 (80)
     Alexander 94 (83)

105   *Study No. 21: Some Southpaw Pitching* (ca. 1914)
     Massa's in de Cold Ground 121 (p. 3, staff 4)
     Antioch 3 (p. 5, staff 1)
     J. S. Bach, *Sinfonia in F Minor*, BWV795 172-a (p. 6, staff 1)

107   *Study No. 23: Allegro* (ca. 1912–14)
     Hello! Ma Baby 107 (22)
    Possible borrowing:
     Throw Out the Life-Line 59 (53)

C. Marches

109 *March No. 1 for Piano, with "Year of Jubilee"* (ca. 1890–92)

Year of Jubilee 145 (17)

That Old Cabin Home upon the Hill 141 (65)

110 *March No. 2 for Piano, with "Son of a Gambolier"* [incomplete] (probably 1892)

The Son of a Gambolier 135 (22)

111 *March No. 3 for Piano, with "Omega Lambda Chi"* (possibly 1892, but 1895–96 more likely)

Omega Lambda Chi 156 (3)

112 *March No. 5 for Piano, with "Annie Lisle"* (probably 1892)

Annie Lisle 95 (28)

113 *March No. 6 for Piano, with "Here's to Good Old Yale"* (sometime between 1892 and 1897)

Bingo 148 (41)

114 *March in G and C for Piano, with "See the Conquering Hero Comes"* (possibly early 1893)

Handel, *See the Conquering Hero Comes* [from] *Judas Maccabeus* 18 (1)

115 *March for Piano: The Circus Band* (no earlier than 1899)

Street beat 86-a (f6411, m. 41)

D. Other Works

116 *The Celestial Railroad* (adapted probably summer 1925 from music composed 1910–13); measure numbers given here are those from unpublished edition of *The Celestial Railroad*, made by Thomas M. Brodhead; other designations are from Ives's manuscripts (f4833–4863)

Old Black Joe 128 (7)

God Be With You 24 (16)

Street beat 86-a (22)

Tramp, Tramp, Tramp 89 (36)

Peter, Peter Pumpkin Eater 130-a (43)

De Camptown Races 100 (48)

Old Black Joe 128 (65)

Columbia, the Gem of the Ocean 75 (76)

Marching Through Georgia 79 (87)

Ives, *Sonata No. 2 for Piano: Concord, Mass.;* "Human Faith" motive from third movement (111)

Beethoven, *Symphony No. 5* i 173 (136)

Ives, *Sonata No. 2 for Piano: Concord, Mass.;* "Alcott" theme from third movement (139)

Martyn 35 (147)

Yankee Doodle 92 (203)

Massa's in de Cold Ground 121 (f4848, staff 9)

Hello! Ma Baby 107 (f4857, staff 1)

Beulah Land 8 (f4860, staff 1)

Ives, *"Country Band" March* 183-a (175)

The Battle Cry of Freedom 71 (f4846, staff 4, bass clef)

Beethoven, *Sonata in B-flat for Piano,* Op. 106 i ("Hammerklavier") 173-b (f4856, staff 11)

Possible borrowing:

> *Throw Out the Life-Line* 59 (43)
> *Long, Long Ago* 119 (43)
> *In the Sweet Bye and Bye* 29 (f4844, staff 11)

118 *Invention in D* (ca. 1897)

J. S. Bach, *Sinfonia in A Minor,* BWV 799 172 (20)

122 Set of Five Take-Offs (possibly between 22 Dec. 1906 and 1 Jan. 1907)

iv. *Scene-Episode*

> *Happy Day* 27 (2)

123 *Four Transcriptions from "Emerson"*

i. Slowly (adapted possibly 1917 from music of 1910–11)

Beethoven, *Symphony No. 5* i 173 (f4907, staff 3, m. 2, right hand)
Wagner, *Tristan und Isolde: Prelude* [1] 189 (f4907, staff 4, m. 1, right hand)
Martyn 35 (f4908, staff 1, m. 2, right hand)
Beethoven, *Sonata for Piano in B-flat,* Op. 106 i ("Hammerklavier") 173-b (f4908, staff 4, left hand)

ii. Moderato (adapted possibly 1922 from music of 1910–11)

Beethoven, *Symphony No. 5* i 173 (f4910, staff 2, right hand)
Beethoven, *Sonata for Piano in B-flat,* Op. 106 i ("Hammerklavier") 173-b (f4910, staff 2, right hand)
Martyn 35 (f4910, staff 3, right hand)

iii. Largo (adapted possibly 1922 from music of 1910–11)

Wagner, *Tristan und Isolde: Prelude* [1] 189 (f4917, staff 1, right hand)

iv. Allegro agitato-Broadly (adapted possibly 1922 from music of 1910–11)

Wagner, *Tristan und Isolde: Prelude* [1] 189 (f4918, staff 1, right hand)
Beethoven, *Symphony No. 5* i 173 (f4919, staff 1, right hand)
Martyn 35 (f4919, staff 2, right hand)
Beethoven, *Sonata for Piano in B-flat*, Op. 106 i ("Hammerklavier") 173-b (f4920, staff 2, right hand)

125   *Waltz-Rondo* (1911)

Columbia, the Gem of the Ocean 75 (138)

Turkey in the Straw 169 (140)

College Hornpipe 161 (145)

The White Cockade 171 (148)

Fisher's Hornpipe 162 (193)

Marching Through Georgia 79 (196)

E. Duets

127   *Drum Corps or Scuffle* [mostly lost] (before 1 Sept. 1902)

Happy Day 27 (f4968, staff 1, m. 2); [this citation might also be *Bringing in the Sheaves* 10]

128   *Three Quarter-Tone Pieces* (adapted 1923–24 from music probably dating 1904–14)

ii. Allegro

The Battle Cry of Freedom 71 (47—piano I)
Happy Day 27 (66—piano I)

iii. *Chorale*

America 69 (6—piano I)
La Marseillaise 80 (55—piano II)

V. WORKS FOR ORGAN

131   *"Adeste Fideles" in an Organ Prelude* (perhaps Dec. 1898; revised ca. 1899)

Adeste Fideles 1 (2)

137   *Interludes for Hymns* (possibly ca. 1898)

i. *Interlude for "Nettleton"*
Nettleton 42 (f5067, m. 1)

 ii. *Interlude for "Bethany"*
  Bethany 7 (f5068, brace 1)

 iv. *Interlude for "Woodworth"*
  Woodworth 67 (no. 2352)

139 *Postlude for Thanksgiving Service* [mostly lost] (possibly 1897)

 Federal Street 22 (f0888, m. 17)

 Shining Shore 54 (f0888)

140 *Variations on "America"* (ca. 1891–92)

 America 69 (1)

VI. WORKS FOR CHORAL ENSEMBLE

A. Sacred Works

i. Multi-Movement Works

ii. Psalms

152 *Psalm 90* (possibly summer 1894; revised ca. 1897–98)

 The Last Hope 180 (46—tenor); also known as the hymn, *Mercy,* as arranged by Edwin Pond Parker

iii. Other Works for Choral Ensemble

168 *Hymn, Op. 2, No. 1* [incomplete] (July 1887)

 Crusader's Hymn 13-a (f5837, m. 1—soprano)

177 *Serenity* [mostly lost] (possibly 1909)

 Serenity 53 (f5593)

178 *Turn Ye, Turn Ye* (possibly 1896)

 Expostulation 21 (2—soprano)

B. Secular Works

i. Chorus with Instrumental Ensemble

180 *An Election* (probably Nov. 1920)

 Over There 82 (8—voices)

 The Star Spangled Banner 86 (49—violin)

 It's Raining, It's Pouring 108-a (f5794, staff 12, last measure)

181   *General William Booth Enters into Heaven* (arr. summer 1934 from song version)
     Street beat 86-a (1—piano)
     Fountain 23 (4—voice)
     Oh, Dem Golden Slippers 125 (51—piano)
     Reveille 83 (70—voice)
     Onward, Upward 47 (73—voice)

182   *He Is There!* (arr. possibly 1918)
     Columbia, the Gem of the Ocean 75 (19—chorus)
     Dixie's Land 76 (21—piccolo)
     Battle Hymn of the Republic 72 (22—trombone)
     Marching Through Georgia 79 (23—chorus)
     Tramp, Tramp, Tramp 89 (23—chorus)
     Yankee Doodle 92 (24—piccolo)
     Over There 82 (28—piccolo)
     Maryland, My Maryland 81 (29—piccolo)
     La Marseillaise 80 (31—piccolo)
     Tenting on the Old Camp Ground 88 (35—chorus)
     The Battle Cry of Freedom 71 (43—piccolo)
     The Star Spangled Banner 86 (48—piccolo)
     Reveille 83 (51—piccolo)
     Just Before the Battle, Mother 111 (28—piccolo—in sketches only; replaced in final
       version by *Over There* 82)

183   *Johnny Poe* [incomplete] (possibly 1927)
     Old Nassau 155 (44—bass voice)

184   *Lincoln, the Great Commoner* (possibly 1920)
     Battle Hymn of the Republic 72 (5—bassoon)
     Hail! Columbia 77 (12—oboe)
     Columbia, the Gem of the Ocean 75 (12—clarinet)
     The Star Spangled Banner 86 (14—flute)
     America 69 (16—trumpet)

186   *The New River* (adapted possibly 1915 from music of probably June 1911)
     Tammany 139 (7—piccolo)
     Ta-ra-ra Boom-de-ay! 140 (13—voices)

187 *Sneak Thief* [incomplete] (probably Oct. 1914)

    Assembly 70 (f5756, m. 15—piano)

    Marching Through Georgia 79 (18—piano)

    America 69 (19—piano)

    The Star Spangled Banner 86 (20—chorus)

    Columbia, the Gem of the Ocean 75 (21—trumpet)

    The Battle Cry of Freedom 71 (22—trumpet)

188 *They Are There! (A War Song March)* (Ives's orchestral sketch: 1918?)

    Columbia, the Gem of the Ocean 75 (19—chorus)

    Dixie's Land 76 (21—flute)

    Battle Hymn of the Republic 72 (22—trombone)

    Marching Through Georgia 79 (23—flute)

    Tramp, Tramp, Tramp 89 (23—chorus)

    Yankee Doodle 92 (24—flute)

    Over There 82 (28—flute)

    Maryland, My Maryland 81 (29—flute)

    La Marseillaise 80 (31—flute)

    Tenting on the Old Camp Ground 88 (34—chorus)

    The Battle Cry of Freedom 71 (43—flute)

    The Star Spangled Banner 86 (48—flute)

    Reveille 83 (51—flute)

    ii. Partsongs

192 *The Bells of Yale* (fall 1897; revised ca. 1900)

    Battell Chimes 147 (24—piano)

193 *The Boys in Blue* (possibly 1896)

    Yale's Short Cheer (9 "Rah"/3 "Yale") 157-b (f6045, brace 5)

VIII. SONGS

Unless otherwise noted measure numbers are from *Charles Ives: 129 Songs,* edited by H. Wiley Hitchcock. Exceptions are Sinclair numbers 234, 318, and 357, taken from *Forty Earlier Songs,* edited by John Kirkpatrick; Sinclair numbers 335, 440, and 441, taken from *Eleven Songs and Two Harmonizations,* edited by John Kirkpatrick; and Sinclair number 282, taken from Ives's manuscript.

207 *Afterglow* (1919)

Erie 17 (133—voice)

213 *At Sea* (arr. 1921 from music of possibly 1912)

Possible borrowing:

> *Bethany* 7 or *Consolation* 12-c (2—voice)
> *Azmon* 5 (6—voice)
> *Missionary Chant* 37 (8—voice)

214 *At the River* (arr. 1916 from music of ca. 1914–16)

The Beautiful River 6 (5—voice)

222 *The Camp Meeting* (arr. 1912 from music of 1901)

Azmon 5 (5—piano)

Woodworth 67 (11—voice)

226 *Charlie Rutlage* (1920 or '21 from music of ca. 1905 and arr. 1909)

Git Along Little Dogies 103 (24—piano)

229 *The Circus Band* (adapted 1899 or later from music of 1894)

Street beat 86-a (41—piano)

230 *The Collection* (composed or adapted 1920)

Tappan 56 (8—voice)

235 *Disclosure* (1921)

Possible borrowing:

> *Olivet* 46 (2—voice)
> *Antioch* 3 (12—voice) (or) *Olivet* 46

236 *Down East* (1919)

Unidentified 222 (8—voice)

Bethany 7 (35—voice)

243 *The Ending Year* (adapted Oct. 1902 from music of possibly 1898)

> Note: measure number from *Forty Earlier Songs*

Franck, *Symphony in D Minor* i 179-c (6—voice and piano)

244 *Evening* (1921)

Bethany 7 (16—voice)

255 *General William Booth Enters into Heaven* (arr. Sept. 1914 from version for chorus and band)

Street beat 86-a (1—piano)

Fountain 23 (4—voice)

Oh, Dem Golden Slippers 125 (51—piano)

Reveille 83 (70—voice)

Onward, Upward 47 (72—voice)

Possible borrowing:

    Handel, *Hallelujah* [from] *Messiah* 182-a (61—voice)

259   *The Greatest Man* (1921)

On the Banks of the Wabash, Far Away 130 (9—voice)

I've Been Working on the Railroad 109 (16—voice)

Rossini, *Overture* [to] *William Tell* 186 (21—voice)

262   *He Is There!* (May 1917; some of music from 1914)

Marching Through Georgia 79 (11—voice)

Columbia, the Gem of the Ocean 75 (19—voice)

Dixie's Land 76 (21—obligato)

Tramp, Tramp, Tramp 89 (23—voice)

Yankee Doodle 92 (24—obligato)

Over There 82 (25—voice)

Reveille 83 (28—obligato)

Maryland, My Maryland 81 (29—obligato)

La Marseillaise 80 (31—obligato)

The Battle Cry of Freedom 71 (31—voice)

Tenting on the Old Camp Ground 88 (34—piano)

The Star Spangled Banner 86 (48—obligato)

Just Before the Battle, Mother 111 (28—obligato—in sketches only; replaced in final
    version by *Over There* 82)

265   *His Exaltation* (arr. 1913 from music of Oct. 1907 or 1909)

Autumn 4 (12—voice)

266   *The Housatonic at Stockbridge* (arr. possibly 1908)

Missionary Chant 37 (6—voice)

Dorrnance 15 (8—voice)

267   *Hymn* (arr. 1921 from music of Aug. 1904)

More Love to Thee 39 (6—piano)

Olivet 46 (21—voice)

Possible borrowing:

    Kathleen Mavourneen 112, *David* 13-b, or *Hexham* 28-a (15—voice)

273   *Immortality* (possibly Mar. 1921)

St. Peter 52 (13—voice)

277 *In Flanders Fields* (probably Apr. 1917; revised 1919)

  Columbia, the Gem of the Ocean 75 (2—piano)

  The Battle Cry of Freedom 71 (6—piano)

  America 69 (14—voice)

  Taps 87 (14—piano)

  Reveille 83 (20—piano)

  All Saints New 2 (21—voice)

  Street beat 86-a (28—piano)

  La Marseillaise 80 (29—voice)

282 Incomplete Song [II] (composed possibly 1899)

  In the Sweet Bye and Bye 29 (f6766, brace 2)

284 *The Innate* (arr. 1916 from music of Nov. 1908)

  The Beautiful River 6 (1—piano)

  Nettleton 42 (27—voice)

286 *The Last Reader* (arr. 1921 from music of June 1911)

  Cherith 11 (1—voice)

  St. Peter 52 (2—voice)

  Bethany 7 (6—voice)

  Araby's Daughter 96 (7—voice)

  Manoah 34 (7—voice)

  Possible borrowing:

    Jesus Loves Me 30 or *Watchman* 61 (20—voice)

289 *Lincoln, the Great Commoner* (arr. possibly 1919 from music of 1912)

  Battle Hymn of the Republic 71 (5—piano)

  Hail! Columbia 77 (12—voice)

  Columbia, the Gem of the Ocean 75 (28—piano)

  America 69 (32—voice)

  The Star Spangled Banner 86 (44—piano/voice)

293 *Luck and Work* (arr. 1920 from music of possibly 1917)

  Possible borrowing:

    Nettleton 42 (5—voice)

313 *Nov. 2, 1920 (An Election)* (arr. 1921 from music probably of Nov. 1920)

  Over There 82 (8—voice)

  It's Raining, It's Pouring 108-a (22—voice)

  The Star Spangled Banner 86 (49—voice)

315 *Old Home Day* (possibly ca. 1914; revised 1920)

    Battle Hymn of the Republic 72 (20—voice)

    Unidentified 221 (20—voice)

    Street beat 86-a (23—piano)

    Arkansas Traveller 158 (25—obligato)

    The Girl I Left Behind Me 102 (25—obligato)

    Garryowen 163 (32—obligato)

    Saint Patrick's Day 168 (35—obligato)

    Annie Lisle 95 (37—voice)

    Auld Lang Syne 98 (37—obligato)

    Assembly 70 (44—obligato)

318 *On Judges' Walk* (possibly 1895 or spring 1898; revised probably between 1899 and 1902)

    The Shining Shore 54 (11—voice)

320 *On the Counter* (1920)

    Nevin, *Narcissus* [from] *Water Scenes*, Op. 13, no. 4 185 (18—voice)

    Auld Lang Syne 98 (20—piano)

330 *The Rainbow (So May It Be!)* (arr. 1921 from music of 1914)

    Serenity 53 (13—voice)

331 *Religion* (adapted possibly 1910 or 1914? from music of 1902)

    Shining Shore 54 (1—voice)

    Azmon 5 (8—piano)

    Bethany 7 (10—piano)

332 *Remembrance* (arr. 1921 from music of ca. 1906)

    Taps 87 (8—piano)

    Possible borrowing:

        Kathleen Mavourneen 112, *David* 13-b, or *Hexham* 28-a (1—voice)

333 *Requiem* (Nov. 1911; perhaps actually 1914?)

    Taps 87 (19—voice)

335 *Rock of Ages* (possibly ca. 1891–92)

    Rathbun 49-a (31—voice)

339 *Rough Wind* (adapted 1902 from music of 1895 or spring 1898)

    Shining Shore 54 (12—voice)

347 *Serenity* (arr. 1919 from music of possibly 1909)

    Serenity 53 (2—voice)

348 *The Side Show* (adapted 1921 from music of probably May 1896)

Are You the O'Reilly 97 (2—voice)

Tchaikovsky, *Symphony No. 6*, Op. 74, 2nd movement 187 (18—voice)

349 *Slow March* (possibly summer 1887)

Handel, *Dead March* [from] *Saul* 182 (1—piano)

353 *A Son of a Gambolier* (arr. 1895 [possibly 1919–21] from music of 1892)

A Son of a Gambolier 135 (1—piano)

357 *The Song of the Dead* [lost] (possibly 1898)

Franck, *Symphony in D Minor* i 179-c (6—voice and piano)

Note: John Kirkpatrick's conjecture is that this was probably the first song in a group of three Kipling songs that Ives composed. See *Forty Earlier Songs*, p. x and Sinclair's *Descriptive Catalogue*, p. 506 for more details

371 *They Are There!* (adapted fall 1942 from music of May 1917)

Marching Through Georgia 79 (11—voice)

Columbia, the Gem of the Ocean 75 (19—voice)

Dixie's Land 76 (21—obligato)

Battle Hymn of the Republic 72 (22—voice)

Tramp, Tramp, Tramp 89 (23—voice)

Yankee Doodle 92 (24—obligato)

Over There 82 (25—voice)

Reveille 83 (28—obligato)

Maryland, My Maryland 81 (29—obligato)

La Marseillaise 80 (31—obligato)

Tenting on the Old Camp Ground 88 (34—piano)

The Battle Cry of Freedom 71 (38—voice)

The Star Spangled Banner 86 (48—obligato)

Just Before the Battle, Mother 111 (28—obligato—in sketches only; replaced in final version by *Over There* 82)

372 *The Things Our Fathers Loved* (arr. 1917 from music of perhaps 1905)

My Old Kentucky Home 123 (4—voice)

On the Banks of the Wabash, Far Away 130 (6—voice)

Nettleton 42 (7—voice)

The Battle Cry of Freedom 71 (10—piano)

In the Sweet Bye and Bye 29 (15—voice)

Possible borrowing:

　　Dixie's Land 76 (1—voice)

373   *Thoreau* (arr. 1915 from music of 1910–15)

      Massa's in de Cold Ground 121 (53—piano)

378   *Tom Sails Away* (adapted Sept. 1917 from music of possibly 1914)

      Araby's Daughter 96 (2—voice)

      Taps 87 (10—voice)

      Columbia, the Gem of the Ocean 75 (20—voice)

      Over There 82 (22—voice)

      Possible borrowing:

         Deep River 14 (2—voice)

379   *Two Little Flowers* (1921)

      St. Peter 52 (2—voice)

382   *The Waiting Soul* (adapted 1908 from music possibly of 1898)

      Franck, *Symphony in D Minor* i 179-c (6—voice and piano)

385   *Waltz* (ca. 1894–95; revised 1921)

      Little Annie Rooney 115 (1—piano)

386   *Watchman! (II)* (adapted 1913 from music of 1906–?08)

      Watchman 61 (5—voice)

388   *West London* (1921; arr. in part from music of Dec. 1912)

      Fountain 23 (43—piano)

397   *The World's Highway* (probably 1906)

      Possible borrowing:

         Shining Shore 54 (13—voice)

IX. EXERCISES

426   *Burlesque Harmonization in C* (possibly 1892)

      Possible borrowing:

         Bingo 148 or *Lebanon* 33 (f7444, m. 1—piano)

427   *Burlesque Harmonization in F over E-flat* (possibly 1891)

      Unidentified 228 (f7433, m. 1)

428   *Burlesque Harmonizations of "London Bridge"* (possibly 1891)

      London Bridge 118 (no. 7440, staff 1, m. 1)

436   *Take-Off on "Surprise Symphony"* (1909)

      Haydn, *Symphony No. 94*, second movement 183 (f7457, m. 1)

X. ARRANGEMENTS OF WORKS BY OTHER COMPOSERS

440   *E. Ives: Christmas Carol* (arr. Nov. 1925)

     Battell Chapel Chimes 147 (16—bells)

441   *In the Mornin'* (arr. 1929)

     Give Me Jesus 23-a (1—voice)

446   *Search Me, O Lord* (arr. possibly ca. 1891–92) [may, or may not, be original with Ives; see Sinclair, p. 580 and Kirkpatrick in *American Grove*, p. 519]

     Search Me, O Lord 52-a (1—soprano)

XI. UNIDENTIFIED FRAGMENTS

447   Two chords, etc. headed "Sun Rise Chord [over East Rock] . . ."

     My Bonnie Lies Over the Ocean 122 (f0001, staff 4)

461   Four mm., 2/4 [on a manuscript for *Thanksgiving*]

     In the Sweet Bye and Bye 29 (f0901)

593   One line on 3 staves

     The Battle Cry of Freedom 71 (f2610)

     Eventide 19 (f2610)

600   Four mm., 4/4, possibly for *Overture: Nationals*

     Hail! Columbia 77 (f6293)

632   One line mostly on 2 staves

     Turkey in the Straw 169 (f7574)

[10]

Possible Borrowings

In *All Made of Tunes* and *A Descriptive Catalogue of the Music of Charles Ives,* Burkholder and Sinclair, respectively, include some tunes whose melodic profiles suggest borrowings, but whose contours are not unequivocal enough to allow those authors to mark them as definite borrowings. What one listener hears as a borrowed tune, another may hear as an Ives original or as being derived from a source different from that identified by the first hearer. I have added this category of "Possible Borrowings" so that the reader may decide for her/himself.

It can be difficult to determine that fine line that can exist between originality and borrowings. For example, *Azmon, Happy Day, Shining Shore,* and *Webb* all begin on the 5th scale degree below the tonic, ascend a perfect 4th to the tonic, and continue the ascent, peaking at the 3rd scale degree—a major 6th above the tune's starting pitch. Depending upon the context of that interval, any one of these sources might be the one from which Ives borrows *or* he might not be borrowing from any of them. That melodic contour—not all that uncommon—may have become part of his musical language consciously or unconsciously. One must be careful not to attribute too much to quotation, for there is, in fact, much originality in Ives.

I have arranged the following list in consecutive order, following Sinclair's numbering of Ives's compositions.

002 ii   Allegro [from] *Symphony No. 2*
                Massa's in de Cold Ground   **121**   (84—violin I)

002 iii   Adagio cantabile [from] *Symphony No. 2*
                Cleansing Stream   **12-b**   (16—flute)

002 v   Allegro molto vivace [from] *Symphony No. 2*
             The Kerry Dance   **165**   (11—violin II)
             Dvořák, *Symphony No. 9*   **i 179a**   (60—violin I)
             Old Black Joe   **125**   (65—horns III and IV)

003 ii   *Children's Day* [from] *Symphony No. 3: The Camp Meeting*
             Blessed Assurance   **9**   (70—violin I)

004 iii   Fugue [from] *Symphony No. 4*
             Brown   **10-a**   or *Lischer*   **33-a**   (89—flute)
             Church Triumphant   **12-a**   (89—clarinet)

005 ii   *Decoration Day* [from] *A Symphony: New England Holidays*
             Dies irae   **14-a**   (5—English horn)
             Lambeth   **32**   (20—violin I)
             Yankee Doodle   **92**   (46—violin I)

005 iii   *The Fourth of July* [from] *A Symphony: New England Holidays*
             The White Cockade   **171**   (66-a—piccolo)
             Irish Washerwoman   **164**   (97—horn)

006   *Universe Symphony*
             Erie   **17**   (Section A: f1832, staff 1)
             Massa's in de Cold Ground **121** (Section A: f1835, 5 staves from bottom
                 of page)

007 i   *The "St. Gaudens" in Boston Common (Col. Shaw and his Colored Regiment)*
                         [from] *Orchestral Set No. 1: Three Places in New England*
             Old Black Joe   **128**   or *Jesus Loves Me*   **30**   (2—bass)

009 i   Andante moderato [from] *Orchestral Set No. 3* [incomplete]
             Watchman   **61**   (n1058, staff 10—trombone)

302   THE CHARLES IVES TUNEBOOK

011 iii   *Andante: The Last Reader* [from] *Set No. 2*

           Araby's Daughter   **96**   (f2698, staff 3, last measure)

           St. Peter   **52**   (f2699, m. 17)

012 i   *Adagio sostenuto: At Sea* [from] *Set No. 3*

           Azmon   **5**   (f2743, 6—solo English horn)

           Missionary Chant   **37**   (f2743, 8—English horn)

           Consolation   **12-c**   (f2743, staff 1, m. 1)

           Bethany   **7**   or *Nettleton*   **42**   (f2777, staff 1, m. 1)

012 ii   *Luck and Work* [from] *Set No. 3*

           Bethany   **7**   or *Nettleton*   **42**   (f2777, staff 1, m. 1)

014 i   *The New River* [from] *Set No. 5: The Other Side of Pioneering or Side Lights on American Enterprise*

           Tammany   **139**   (f6157, staff 1, m. 3—piano)

           Ta-ra-ra Boom-de-ay!   **140**   (f6158, m. 1—voice)

015 iii   *Afterglow* [from] *Set No. 6: From the Side Hill*

           Erie   **17**   (f6180, staff 4, last portion—voice)

016 i   *At Sea* [from] *Set No. 7: Water Colors*

           Consolation   **12-c**   (f6156, m. 2—voice)

           Azmon   **5**   (f6156, m. 6, voice)

016 iii   *The Pond* [from] *Set No. 7: Water Colors*

           David   **13-b,**   or *Hexham*   **28-a,** or *Kathleen Mavourneen*   **112**   (1—horn)

017 i   *The New River* [from] *Set No. 8: Songs Without Voices*

           Tammany   **139**   (f2781, score 1, m. 3—piano)

018 i   *Andante con moto: The Last Reader* [from] *Set No. 9 of Three Pieces*
   Araby's Daughter   **96**   (f2747, m. 6—English horn)

019 ii   *Allegro-Andante: Luck and Work* [from] *Set No. 10 of Three Pieces*
   Nettleton   **42**   (f2770, m. 5—Basset horn)

022   *Emerson Overture for Piano and Orchestra* [incomplete]
   Beethoven, *Symphony No. 5* i 173, or *Missionary Chant*   **37,**   or *Parah*
   48   (f2214, brace 3)

040   *The Pond*
   Kathleen Mavourneen   **112,**   or *David*   **13-b,**   or *Hexham*   **28-a**
   (3—voice or trumpet)

057 ii   Prelude (Allegro) [from] *String Quartet No. 1*
   Beethoven, *Sonata in F Minor for Piano,* Op. 2, no. 1 ii,   **173-a**   (1—violin I)

064   *Decoration Day* for Violin and Piano
   Dies irae   **14-a**   (f0712, m. 4—violin)
   Lambeth   **32**   (f0713, m. 20)
   Yankee Doodle   **92**   (f0714, m. 46—piano)
   Battle Hymn of the Republic   **72**   (0715, m. 60—piano)

065   *From the Steeples and the Mountains*
   Taps   **87**   (f2421, m. 6—trumpets/trombones)

084 i   Largo cantabile: *Hymn* [from] *A Set of Three Short Pieces*
   David   **13-b,**   or *Hexham*   **28-a**, or *Kathleen Mavourneen*   **112**
   (21—solo cello)

087 iii   Largo-Allegro-Largo [from] *Sonata No. 1 for Piano*
   Lebanon   **33**   (69)

088 i   *Emerson* [from] *Sonata No. 2 for Piano: Concord, Mass., 1840–60*
        Crusader's Hymn   **13-a**   (page 3, staff 3, right hand)
        Wagner, Prelude to *Tristan and Isolde* [1],   **189**   (p. 13, staff 4, m. 1)
        Martyn   **35**   (p. 19, score 3, right hand)

088 iv   *Thoreau* [from] *Sonata No. 2 for Piano: Concord, Mass., 1840–60*
        Martyn   **35**   (p. 67, staff 1)

089   *Three-Page Sonata*
        Need   **41**   (37)
        Foeppl, *Cornet Fantasy* on Foley Hall's *Ever of Thee*   **100-a**   (41)

107   *Study No.*   **23**
        Throw Out the Life-Line   **59**   (53)

116   *The Celestial Railroad*
        Throw Out the Life-Line   **59**   (43)
        Long, Long Ago   **119**   (43)
        In the Sweet Bye and Bye   **29**   (f4844, staff 11)

213   *At Sea*
        Bethany   **7**   or *Consolation*   **12-c**   (2—voice)
        Azmon   **5**   (6—voice)
        Missionary Chant   **37**   (8—voice)

235   *Disclosure*
        Olivet   **46**   (2—voice)
        Antioch   **3**   or *Olivet*   **46**   (12—voice)

255   *General William Booth Enters into Heaven*
        Handel, *Hallelujah* [from] *Messiah*   **182-a**   (61—voice)

267   *Hymn*

            David   **13-b,**   or *Hexham*   **28-a,** or *Kathleen Mavourneen* **112**
            (15—voice)

286   *The Last Reader*

            Jesus Loves Me   **30**   or *Watchman*   **61**   (20—voice)

293   *Luck and Work*

            Nettleton   **42**   (5—voice)

332   *Remembrance*

            David   **13-b,**   or *Hexham*   **28-a,** or *Kathleen Mavourneen* **112**
            (1—voice)

372   *The Things Our Fathers Loved*

            Dixie's Land   **76**   (1—voice)

378   *Tom Sails Away*

            Deep River   **14**   (2—voice)

397   *The World's Highway*

            Shining Shore   **54**   (13—voice)

426   *Burlesque Harmonization in C*

            Bingo **148** or *Lebanon*   **33**   (f7444, m. 1—piano)

[11]

Musical Incipits

This table offers a means of identifying any known tune in *The Charles Ives Tunebook*. The following guidelines are used throughout, except where noted.

1. The initial portion of each tune and beginning of the refrain, if one exists, have been transposed to C major, or C minor, as the case may be. Exceptions to this are those examples from Classical music and those newly identified or unidentified tunes, all of which are given in the keys in which one finds them. Letters have been used for the notes of the scale: C = "do"; D = "re"; E = "mi," and so forth.

2. Accidentals are included in the traditional manner.

3. The notes from C, extending upward to B (from middle C to the B above), constitute the normal range for the music; notes falling above or below this range are indicated by one or more horizontal lines drawn above or below, respectively, the letter name(s) involved.

4. The rhythm of each incipit is included.

5. Tunes are arranged alphabetically according to their melodic letter names.

   a. Accidentals are treated as naturals in the alphabetical ordering.

   b. Only the first note in a series of tied notes is counted in determining alphabetical order.

   c. Letter names above or below the normal range are counted as any other letters.

6. Each known tune is identified by main title as determined in chapter 9, *Compositions with Borrowings*.

7. The location, in an Ives composition, of the unidentified tunes, is given.

UNPITCHED

INCIPIT	TUNE
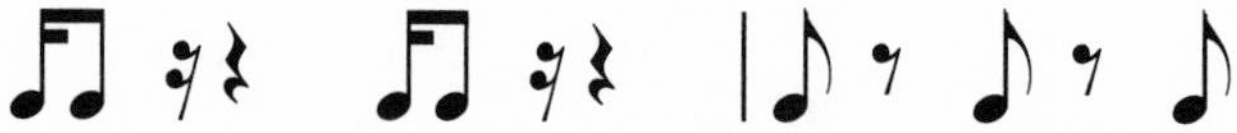	*Street beat* 86-a
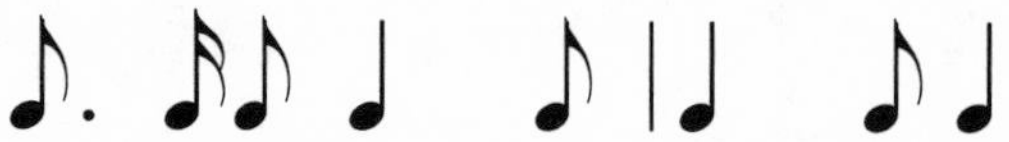	*Brekekekek, ko-ax, ko-ax* 148-a
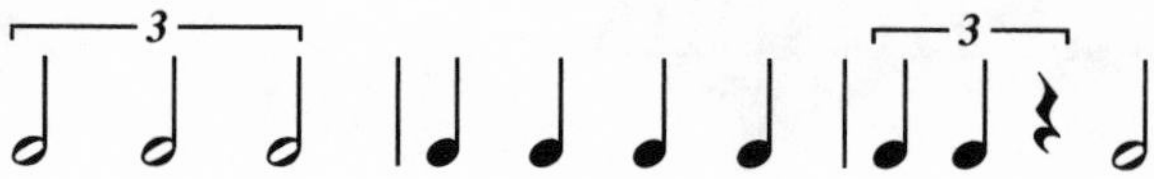	*Yale's Short Cheer* 157-a

PITCHED

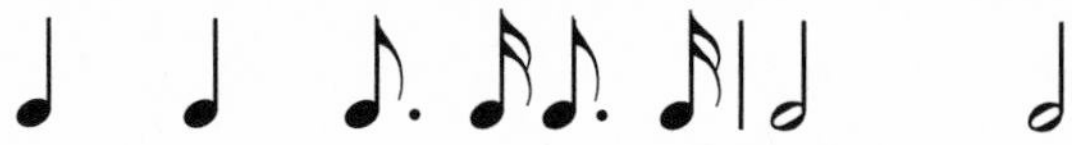

A A $\bar{C}$ B $\bar{C}$ A G E — refrain to *The Beautiful River* 6

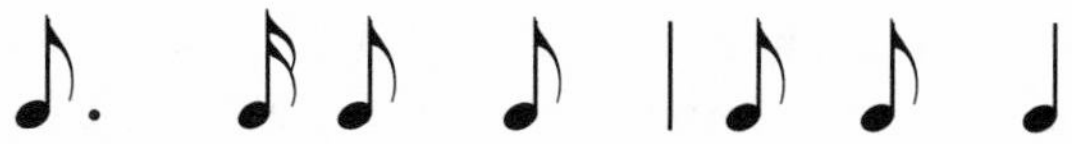

A B A F A B $\bar{C}$ — refrain to *Yankee Doodle* 92

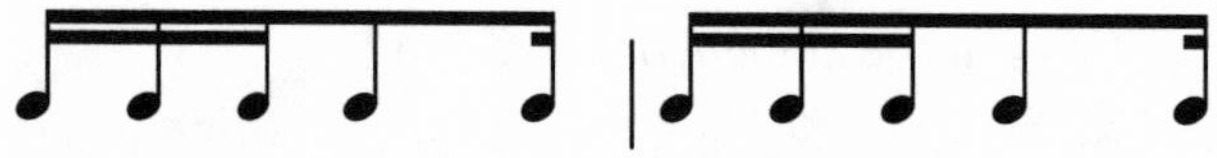

A $\bar{C}$ $\bar{E}$ $\bar{A}$ $\bar{G}$♯ $\bar{A}$ $\bar{E}$ $\bar{C}$ A G♯ — J. S. Bach, *Sinfonia in A Minor* 172

A_   F   E   D♯

Wagner, *Tristan und Isolde: Prelude* [1] 189

A   G♯   A   F♯   E   D   A   D   F♯   A

Brahms, *Symphony No. 2,* first movement, Op. 73, 176

A   G   C   E   C   F   G   F   A

Money Musk 166

A   G   E   E   C   D   C   D

refrain to *Auld Lang Syne* 98

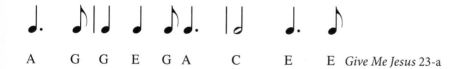

A   G   G   E   G   A   C   E   E

Give Me Jesus 23-a

B♭ A♭   B♭   F   B♭   A♭ F   E♭ C♭   E♭

Debussy, "Golliwog's Cakewalk" 178-a

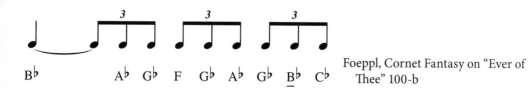

B♭   A♭ G♭   F   G♭ A♭   G♭ B_♭   C♭

Foeppl, Cornet Fantasy on "Ever of Thee" 100-b

B C D D DD G F E

refrain to *Columbia, the Gem of the Ocean* 75

B C̄ D̄ G F B C̄ G Ē

refrain to *Silver Threads Among the Gold* 134

B C̄ D̄ G G A G C̄

refrain to *Old Folks at Home* 129

C B A A G♯ A B C♯ D E F♯ G♯ A F♯ D

Wagner, Prelude to *Tristan und Isolde* [3] 191

C̄♯ B A♯ A G♯ G A B B♯

Debussy, *Prélude à "L'apres-midi d'un faune"* mm. 1–3 178

C̄ B A G A G E D C D

refrain to *Welcome Voice* 63

C̄ B A G E A G E C

refrain to *Massa's in de Cold Ground* 121

C B A G E C D C <u>A</u> *The Girl I Left Behind Me* 102

C B A G F E D C *Antioch* 3

C̄ B A G F E D C E F E E *Garryowen* 163

C C̄ A G A G E C̄ A G E D E C *Pig Town Fling* 167

C C B̲ A̲ G̲ C D E *Old Hundredth* 44

C̄ C̄ B̄ C̄ D̄ C̄ G refrain to *Adeste Fideles* 1

C C B̲ C D D D C *St. Hilda* 51

♩ | ♫ ♫ ♫ ♫ | ♩

C   C C̄ B A G F E D C   *Wild Bells* 65

♪ ♪ ♪ ♪ ♪ ♪ ♪ ♪ | ♪ ♪

C C C C C A G E   C   C   *Harvard Has Blue Stocking Girls* 151

♪ ♪ ♪ ♪ | ♪ ♪ ♪ ♪ | ♪ ♪ ♪ ♪

C C C C C A G E   C C C   *Reuben and Rachel* 131

♪. ♫ ♪ ♪ ♪ ♪ 𝄾 ♪ ♪

C   C C C C   <u>B</u>   C   *Bingo* 148

♩. ♪ ♩ ♩ | ♩ ♩ ♩ ♩

C   C C C   C <u>G</u>   <u>E</u>   <u>G</u>   *Hold the Fort* 152

𝅗𝅥 | 𝅘𝅥 𝅘𝅥 𝅗𝅥 𝅗𝅥 | 𝅝 𝅗𝅥

C   C C C D   <u>B</u>   <u>B</u>   *Parah* 48

♪. ♫♪. ♫♪. ♫♪.♫♪ | ♪. ♫♪. ♫♪.♫♪.♫

C C C CD DD D E EE E F F A A *from refrain to* Push Dem Clouds

                                                       Away 130-b

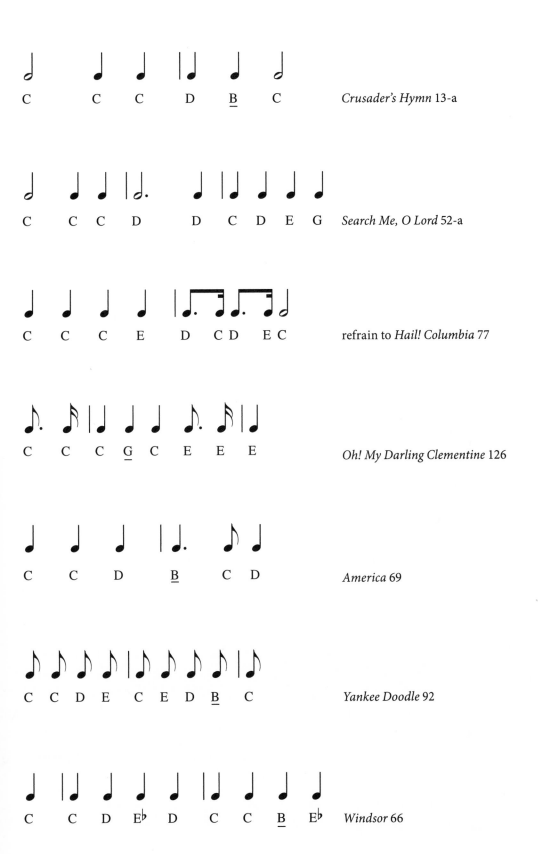

C   C   C   D   <u>B</u>   C   *Crusader's Hymn* 13-a

C   C   C   D   D   C   D   E   G   *Search Me, O Lord* 52-a

C   C   C   E   D   C D   E C   refrain to *Hail! Columbia* 77

C   C   C   <u>G</u>   C   E   E   E   *Oh! My Darling Clementine* 126

C   C   D   <u>B</u>   C   D   *America* 69

C   C   D   E   C   E   D   <u>B</u>   C   *Yankee Doodle* 92

C   C   D   E♭   D   C   C   <u>B</u>   E♭   *Windsor* 66

C   C   D   E   D   E   F   E   D   *Hamburg* 26

C   C   D   E   E   D   C   C   A <u>G</u>   <u>G</u> <u>G</u>   C   *Loch Lomond* 117-a

C   C   D   E   E   F   G   A   G   E   *Long, Long Ago* 119

C   C   E   D   C   <u>G</u>   C   *Hail! Columbia* 77

C   C   E   E   G   G   E   Haydn, *Symphony No. 94* 183

C   C E G   <u>C</u>   A   A <u>C</u> A   G   refrain to *Camptown Races* 100

C   C   <u>G</u>   C   D   <u>G</u>   E   D   E   F   *Adeste Fideles* 1

C D C Bb A Bb A G   Beethoven, *Andante favori* 173-c

C D C C E F G A G G E C   *St. Patrick's Day* 168

C D C F E D C   *Ewing* 20

C D E D C A G E   *Autumn* 4

C D E D C B B A A   *Manoah* 34

C D Eb D C C D Eb G D Eb C   *Streets of Cairo* 137

C D E D C D C A G   *In the Sweet Bye and Bye* 29

C D E D C F A G E   *The Kerry Dance* 165

C D E D♯E C D C♯D <u>B</u> C <u>A</u>   refrain to *On the Banks of the Wabash, Far Away* 130

C D E D E F G   *Watchman* 61

C D E E E D C <u>A</u> <u>B</u> C   *The Battle Cry of Freedom* 71

C D E E E D C D E E E   *Oh, Dem Golden Slippers* 125

C D E E E D C E E E   *White Cockade* 171

C D E E F E D C <u>B</u> <u>A</u> <u>G</u> C <u>G</u>   *Katy Darling* 113

316   **THE CHARLES IVES TUNEBOOK**

C D E   E G   F E D   E F   E   *Woodworth* 67

C   D   E   F F   G   G   E E   *Home! Sweet Home!* 108

C   D E G C B B   A   *Just Before the Battle, Mother* 111

C D E G G A G E C D E E D C D   *Oh! Susanna* 127

C D E G G G G A C   C   *There'll Be No Dark Valley* 58

C D F F F F   F   *Te Deum* 56-a

C   E   C   G   C   *Battell Chimes* 147

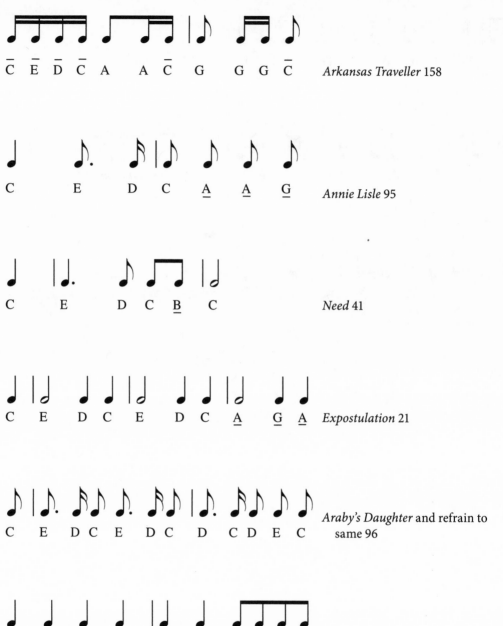

C E D C A A C G G G C   *Arkansas Traveller* 158

C E D C A A G   *Annie Lisle* 95

C E D C B C   *Need* 41

C E D C E D C A G A   *Expostulation* 21

C E D C E D C D C D E C   *Araby's Daughter* and refrain to same 96

C E♭ D F E♭ G♭ F B♭ D♭ C   J. S. Bach, *Sinfonia in F Minor* 172-a

C E♭E♭ C B♭A♭ B♭ C E♭ C B♭   Dvořák, *Symphony No. 9*, second movement 179-b

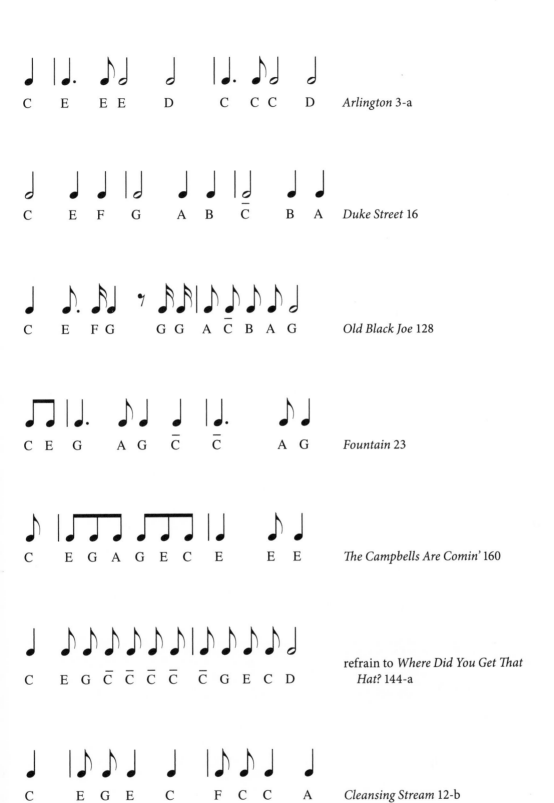

C E E E D C C D   *Arlington 3-a*

C E F G A B C̱ B A   *Duke Street 16*

C E F G G G A C̄ B A G   *Old Black Joe 128*

C E G A G C̄ C̄ A G   *Fountain 23*

C E G A G E C E E E   *The Campbells Are Comin' 160*

C E G C̄ C̄ C̄ C̄ C̄ G E C D   refrain to *Where Did You Get That Hat? 144-a*

C E G E C F C C A   *Cleansing Stream 12-b*

C E G   E D C C   *Welcome Voice* 63

C   E G G A G   E   *Missionary Hymn* 38

C   E G   G C̄   G A   G E   F   *Push Dem Clouds Away* 130-b

C   E G   G   F E   D   D F   *Olivet* 46

C E   G G G G G E C   *De Little Cabins All Am Empty Now* 117

C̄ F̄   Ē D̄ Ē A   D̄   C̄ B♭   J. S. Bach, *Fugue in D Minor* 172-c

C F F F F G A G   E   C   refrain to *That Old Cabin Home upon the Hill* 141

C G C C C D E♭ D E♭ C B♭   *When Johnny Comes Marching Home* 91

C G C G C D E   C   *I've Been Working on the Railroad* 109

C G E G F A G F E G E G F A G F   *Fisher's Hornpipe* 162

D A B A D A B A   Handel, *Hallelujah* [from] *Messiah* 182-a

D B C D G A B C D C B   Handel, *See the Conquering Hero Comes* [from] *Judas Maccabeus* 181

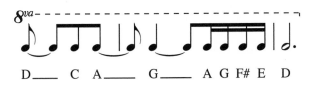

D___ C A___ G___ A G F# E D   J. S. Bach, *Fugue in E Minor* 172-b

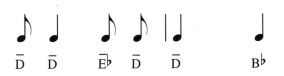

D D E♭ D D   B♭   Beethoven, "Hammerklavier" *Sonata for Piano* 173-b

D   E A D F# A D   E A D F# A   Rossini, Overture to *William Tell* 186

D E   F   F   F   F   F   F   E D   refrain to *De Little Cabins All Am*

Empty Now 117

D E F# G A B C D E D C B A G F# E   Tchaikovsky, *Symphony No. 6,* third

movement 188-a

D F D D F F F   G G G D C   *Git Along Little Dogies* 103

E A A A E A A A F B B B B   *Tammany* 139

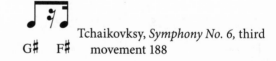

E B B E B   E A   G# F#   Tchaikovksy, *Symphony No. 6,* third

movement 188

E B F# F# F# F# A D# D#   E   Brahms, *Symphony No. 1,* second

movement 175

E C D C | A C G C — *Peter, Peter Pumpkin Eater* 130-a

E C D E C D E C D | B A G — *Alexander* 94

E C | G C — *Goodnight, Ladies* 104

E D C A A G E G C C DE — *Wake Nicodemus!* 144

E D C C | A A — *Bethany* 7

E D C C GE F G AG E G — *Turkey in the Straw* 169

E D C C E G D D — *Nettleton* 42

E   D C   D <u>A</u>   C   C   C C̄   A   *Deep River* 14

E   D C   D   E   <u>G</u>   <u>G</u>   <u>G</u>   *Marching Through Georgia* 79

E   D C E D   C   C̄   A C̄   *Old Folks at Home* 129

E   D   C   <u>G</u>   <u>A</u>   <u>G</u>   *Greenwood* 25

E   D   C   <u>G</u>.   C   E   D   G   *Westminster Chimes* 170

E   D C G   F E C̄   B A G   *Kathleen Mavourneen* 112

E   D.   C G F   E   D   C <u>B</u>   C   *Hexham* 28-a

♪♪♪♩ ♩.   ♩.   ♪♪♪♩ ♩.

E D C G   G   F G A G   *Blessed Assurance* 9

♩   ♩   ♩   ♩   ♩.   ♪ ♫

E̲   D̲♯   D̲   C̲♯   A̲♯   B   F̲♯   G̲♯   Brahms, *Symphony No. 3,* first movement 177-a

♩.   ♪ | ♪ ♪ ♪ ♪ ♪ | ♩ | ♩.

E   D   D C B̲ C F   B̲   *Violets* 143

♩   ♩ ♩ | ♩ ♩ ♩ | ♩   ♩ ♩

E   D E C A̲ G̲   D   C D   *Something for Thee* 55

♩   ♩ ♩ | ♩ ♩ ♩ | ♩   ♩ ♩

E   D E C G̲ A̲   G̲   B̲ D   *Proprior Deo* 49

♩. | ♩ ♩ ♩ | ♩. | ♩. | ♩.

E   D E D C   G̲   C   *Sweet Rosie O'Grady* 138

♪♪♪♪♪♪♪♪♪ | ♩   ♪♩   ♪♪♪

E D♯ E D♯ E D♯ E D♯ E   E C♯   A̲ B̲ C♯   refrain to *Alexander* 94

E D♯E F♯G A♭GA♭ A G♯A B♭A B♭ B

Brahms, *Symphony No. 1,* fourth movement 175-c

E E C D E D C A G

refrain to *Streets of Cairo* 137

E E C F E E D

refrain to *Need* 41

E E D C G

Eventide 19

E E D♯E D♯E D♯E G A A A

Hello! Ma Baby 107

E E D E G G E E D C

There Is a Happy Land 57

E E E C D D D

Martyn 35

E E E   C   D D   E   E   *Dorrnance* 15

E E E   C   D E F   E F A G   *My Old Kentucky Home* 123

E E E   C E G   G   G   E   *Where, O Where* 157

E E E   D C A G   C   refrain to *Tramp, Tramp, Tramp* 89

E E E E   C   D D B   *Missionary Chant* 37

E E E E   D D C E F A   G   *Ever of Thee* 100-a

E E   E E D E F   E   *For He's a Jolly Good Fellow* 101

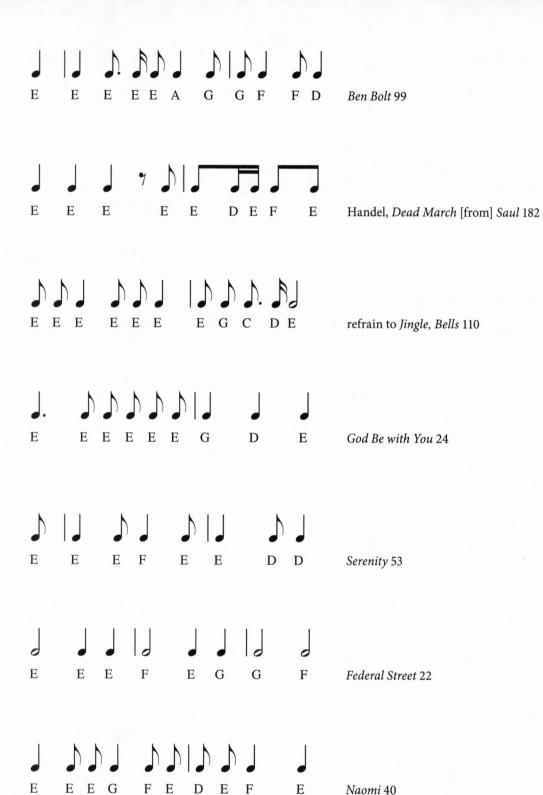

E   E   E   E E A   G   G F   F D   *Ben Bolt* 99

E   E   E   E   E   D E F   E   Handel, *Dead March* [from] *Saul* 182

E E E   E E E   E G C D E   refrain to *Jingle, Bells* 110

E   E E E E E G   D   E   *God Be with You* 24

E   E   E F   E E   D D   *Serenity* 53

E   E E F   E G G   F   *Federal Street* 22

E   E E G   F E D E F   E   *Naomi* 40

E   E F E D C <u>A</u> C   refrain to *Just Before the Battle, Mother* 111

E   E F F   E   E   D C   *Where Is My Wandering Boy?* 64

E   E F G G   A   G   refrain to *Old, Old Story* 45

E   E G <u>A</u> C   D E E E   *Oh, Nobody Knows the Trouble I've Seen* 43

E   F C C C   D E   refrain to *Where Is My Wandering Boy?* 64

E   F E <u>G</u> <u>F</u> D C   <u>E</u>   *Silver Threads Among the Gold* 134

E   F   F♯ G   Ē   ĒĒ D̄♯ Ē   *Liberty Bell March* 78

E F G C̲ B A G C D E   *Christmas* 12

E F G C̄ B A G E G E E C   *The Gods of Egypt Bid Us Hail!* 150-b

E F G C̄ B D̄ C̄ A G   *Lambeth* 32

E F G C̄ D̄ Ē C̄ D̄ ĒD̄ C̄A   *That Old Cabin Home upon the Hill* 141

E F G   C D E   E F E   refrain to *Happy Day* 27

E F G C̄ Ē D̄ C̄ A C̄   refrain to *God Be with You* 24

E F G C F E E D   *Even Me* 18

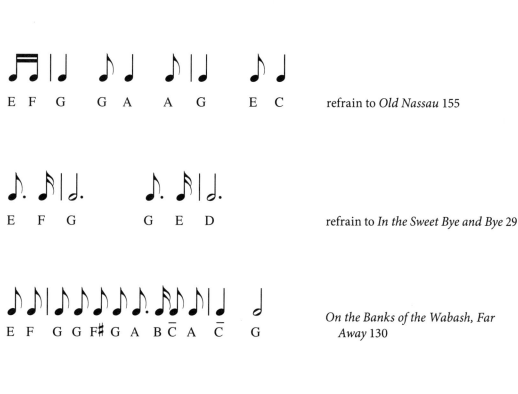

E F G   G A   A G   E C   refrain to *Old Nassau* 155

E F G   G E D   refrain to *In the Sweet Bye and Bye* 29

E F   G G F♯ G A B C̄ A   C̄   G   *On the Banks of the Wabash, Far Away* 130

E   F G G G C̄ G   *Laban* 31

E F G   G G F E A   A G   *Retreat* 50

E G̲ C   E G̲ C   refrain to *Over There* 82

E   G E A   E   G   E   *After the Ball* 93

refrain to *After the Ball* 93

Rock-a-bye Baby 132

refrain to *Shining Shore* 54

refrain to *Marching Through Georgia* 79

refrain to *Give Me Jesus* 23-a

refrain to *Bringing in the Sheaves* 10

refrain to *Turkey in the Straw* 169

E   G   G   G   A   G   E   G

refrain to *There'll Be No Dark Valley* 58

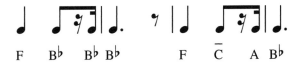

F   B♭   B♭   B♭   F   C̄   A   B♭

Wagner, *Wedding March* [from] *Lohengrin* 191-a

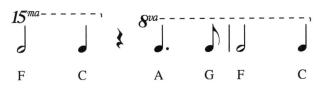

F   C   A   G   F   C

Brahms, *Symphony No. 3*, first movement 177

F̄   D̄   B♭   A   A♭   G   G   F   F   E

Franck, *Symphony in D Minor*, first movement 179-c

F   E♭   D   C   B♭ D C E♭ D F E G   F C F

George Ives, *Fourth Fugue in B-flat* 184

F E D C   D E F A   C̄   C̄ D̄   C̄   C̄ D̄

Tchaikovsky, *Symphony No. 6*, 3rd movement 188-a

F   E   F   D   E   C   D   D

Dies irae 14-a

F E♭ F D♭ F C D♭ B♭

Ethelbert Nevin, *Narcissus* [from] *Water Scenes* 185

F F A A A G G E C D

refrain to *Oh! Susanna* 127

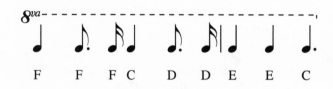

F F F C D D E E C

refrain to *That Old Cabin Home upon the Hill* 141

F# F# G# F# B D̄# D̄# C̄# B

Mercy 36-a

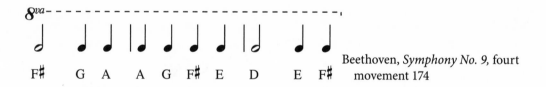

F# G A A G F# E D E F#

Beethoven, *Symphony No. 9,* fourt movement 174

F G A F# G

Wagner, Prelude to *Tristan und Isolde* [2] 190

F̱# G̱ A̱ G̱ A̱ Ḇ C# D Ḇ C#

Tchaikovsky, *Symphony No. 6,* second movement 187

G   A A A   F   G G G   E   refrain to *Cleansing Stream* 12-b

G   A   B C̄ A B   G   refrain to *Ma Blushin' Rosie* 120

G   A B C̄ A C̄   A G   refrain to *Kingdom Coming* 114

G A B C̄ C C G F E G C̄ B C̄   *College Hornpipe* 161

G̲ A C C D E D C D D C A̲   *Loch Lomond* 117-a

G̲   A̲ E   D   C A̲   refrain to *Tammany* 139

G A G A G E F E F E   refrain to *Hello! Ma Baby* 107

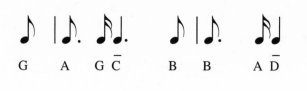

G   A   G C̄   B   B   A D̄   *I've Been Working on the Railroad* 109

G̲   A̲   G̲   C   D E   E   D   C   *More Love to Thee* 39

G   A   G C̄   Ē   Ē   D̄   C̄   *Mercy* 36-a

G   A   G   E   C̄   A   G   *Toplady* 60

G   A   G   E   D   C   C̄   A   *Massa's in de Cold Ground* 121

G   A   G   F   E   F   G   *London Bridge* 118

G   B♭   A   C̄   B̄   D   C♯   E   D   F   D   Brahms, *Symphony No. 1,* fourth movement 175-d

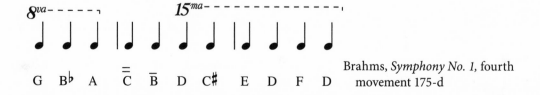

G♯B B G♯B G♯B B G♯B A C C A C   Dvořák, *Symphony No. 9*, first movement 179-a

G C A C B B B   refrain to *My Bonnie Lies Over the Ocean* 122

G C B A G G F E E   *St. Peter* 52

G C B C A G C   Brahms, *Symphony No. 1*, fourth movement 175-b

G C B C C♯ D E D   *Old Nassau* 155

G C B C D C D E F E A   *Grandfather's Clock* 105

G C B C E D C   *Are You the O'Reilly* 97

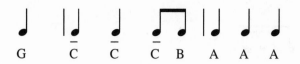

G C̲ C̲ C̲ B A A A   refrain to *The Star Spangled Banner* 86

G̲ C C C B̲ C D   *Lebanon* 33

G̲ C C C C   *Hy-can Nuck A No* 153

G̲ C C C C C E C C C   *Year of Jubilee* 145

G̲ C C C C D E G E   refrain to *Wake Nicodemus!* 144

G̲ C C C D E E E   *Maryland, My Maryland* 81

G̲ C C E D C D   *Auld Lang Syne* 98

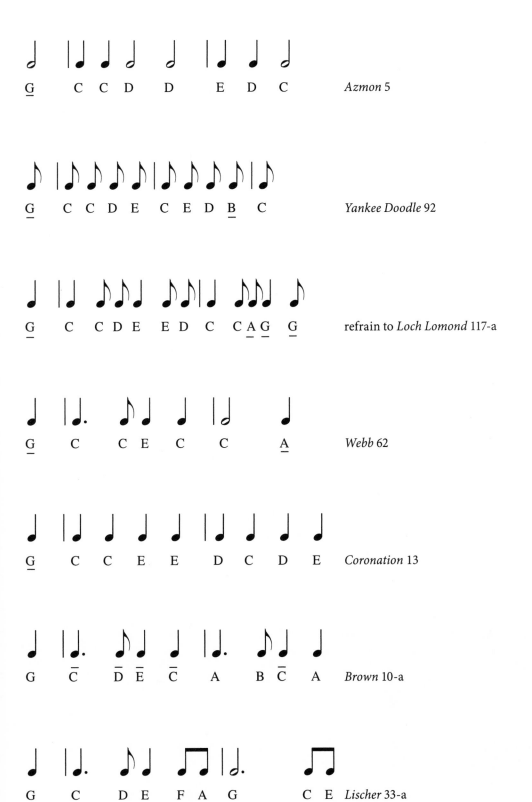

♩ ♩ ♩ | ♩.   ♩ ♩ ♩ | ♩.

G C D E   G C D E   *Happy Day* 27

♩   ♩ | ♩   ♩ ♩ | ♩ ♩ ♩ | ♩ ♩

G C̄ Ē C̄ B A G C̄ G   *Rathbun* 49-a

♪♩ ♪♩ ♪♩ ♪♩ ♪♩ ♪♪♪

G C E C G̲ C E C G̲ C D E D C   *Freshmen in the Park* 150-a

♪ | ♪ ♫♪ ♪ | ♪ ♫ ♪

G   C E C G̲ E C   E C G̲   *Reveille* 83

♩.   ♪♩ ♪ ♪ ♪♪.| ♩.   ♪♩ ♪ ♪ ♪♪.

G   C E D C G̲ A̲   D F E D A̲   refrain to *Oh, Dem Golden Slippers* 125

♪.   ♪♩ | ♩.   ♪ ♪. ♪♩ | ♩

G̲   C E   D E F G   G   *Onward, Upward* 47

♪ | ♪ ♪ ♪ ♪ | ♪   ♪ ♪♪♪♪ | ♪

G   C E E G G Ē Ē D̄ C̄ A G   *Kingdom Coming* 114

G C E G — C E G — refrain to *Year of Jubilee* 145

G C E G — D C#D E D — *Second Regiment Connecticut National Guard March* 84

G C E G G E G C̄ C̄ — *Bright College Years* 149

G C G A A A C A G — *Omega Lambda Chi* 156

G C G C C̄ — refrain to *Little Annie Rooney* 115

G C G C D E D E F G C E D C B — *The British Grenadiers* 73

G C̄ G Ē D C̄ A G E F — *Church Triumphant* 12-a

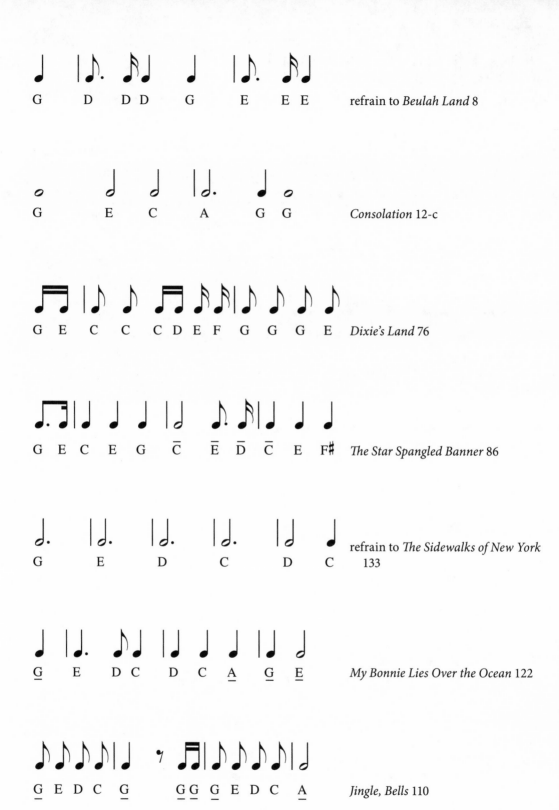

G D D D G E E   refrain to *Beulah Land* 8

G E C A G G   *Consolation* 12-c

G E C C C D E F G G E   *Dixie's Land* 76

G E C E G C̄ Ē D̄ C̄ E F♯   *The Star Spangled Banner* 86

G E D C D C   refrain to *The Sidewalks of New York* 133

G̲ E D C D C A̲ G̲ E̲   *My Bonnie Lies Over the Ocean* 122

G̲ E D C G̲   G̲G̲ G̲ E D C A̲   *Jingle, Bells* 110

G E E D C C B A C G   *Tenting on the Old Camp Ground* 88

G   E E D   E G   C   *Give Me Jesus* 23-a

G E E D E G G   A A C A   A G G   *Jesus Loves Me* 30

G   E   E E   D   C   C C   *Beulah Land* 8

G E   E E D C D E F E   *Throw Out the Life-Line* 59

G   E   E   E   E   F   E   *There's Music in the Air* 142

G E E E E F F F F G G E C D   *Jolly Dogs* 154

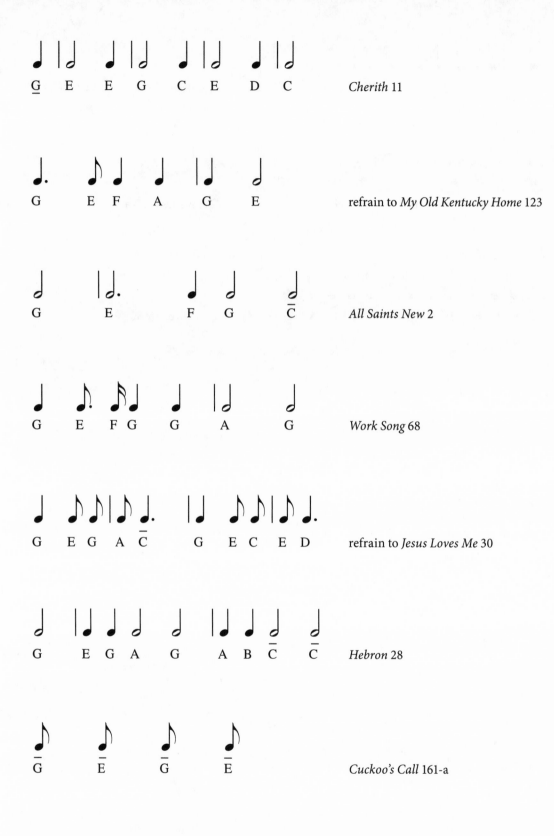

G E E G C E D C — *Cherith* 11

G E F A G E — refrain to *My Old Kentucky Home* 123

G E F G C̄ — *All Saints New* 2

G E F G G A G — *Work Song* 68

G E G A C̄ G E C E D — refrain to *Jesus Loves Me* 30

G E G A G A B C̄ C̄ — *Hebron* 28

G̲ E̲ G̲ E̲ — *Cuckoo's Call* 161-a

G　E G　　G E G　　G G　A C̄ B A G　　　　refrain to *Old Black Joe* 128

G　　E　G　G　　G　F　A　A　　　　*Little Brown Jug* 116

G♭ F E♭ B♭　　C̄♭ B♭ A♭ Ē♭　　D̄ C̄ B♭ Ē♭ D̄♭ C̄♭　　Brahms, *Symphony No. 1*, first movement 175-a

G F　E C C G̲ C　C　E C E G F E　　*Irish Washerwoman* 164

G　　F　　E　G C̄　　D̄ C̄　　C̄　B　　*Tramp, Tramp, Tramp* 89

G　　F　E　G C̄　D̄ Ē　C̄　　refrain to *Battle Hymn of the Republic* 72

G F♯ G　C̄　G E　　E D♯ E　G E C　　refrain to *Ta-ra-ra Boom-de-ay!* 140

G G A B C E G G A B   refrain to *Are You the O'Reilly* 97

G G A G E C A G C E   *Nancy Lee* 123-a

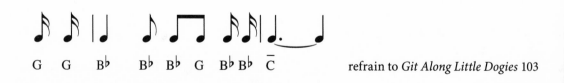

G G A G E C C A   *Erie* 17

G G A G E C E G A G E   *Blow the Man Down* 159

G G A G F♯ G A B C̄ E   *Stop That Knocking at My Door* 136

G G B♭ B♭ B♭ G B♭ B♭ C̄   refrain to *Git Along Little Dogies* 103

G G C C C D E E C D C C B   *The Son of a Gambolier* 135

G G C C C D G F E C   *Columbia, the Gem of the Ocean* 75

G G C C D E C D E   *Shining Shore* 54

G G C E D C A C   refrain to *Dixie's Land* 76

G G C G C E C C C   *Assembly* 70

G G C G C E G C E   *Taps* 87

G G C G G A G G   refrain to *Grandfather's Clock* 105

G G E A G E F G E A   *It's Raining, It's Pouring* 108-a

G G E   C E G E G   E   *Semper Fideles* 85

G G E E G G   D D   *Materna* 36

G G E F E D C C B G A B C   Beethoven, *Sonata for Piano,* Op. 2, no. 1, second movement 173-a

G G E F G A G G E F G   refrain to *The Battle Cry of Freedom* 71

G G E G C C A C B A G E F D   *Valentia* 60-a

G G F♯ G A A B B D C   *Washington Post March* 90

G G F♯ G A G G G F♯ G F   *Riding Down from Bangor* 131-a

G G G   A A A   B B B   A   B   C̄   refrain to *Little Brown Jug* 116

G   G   G   A   A   G   A   B   D̄   *Search Me, O Lord* 52-a

G   G   G   A   G   C̄   C̄   C̄   *Few Days* 150

G G G   A G   E   C̄ C̄ C̄   D̄ C̄   A   *Bringing in the Sheaves* 10

G   G   G A G   E   E   E F E   *Throw Out the Life-Line* 59

G̲ G̲   G̲   C   C   D   D   G   E C   *La Marseillaise* 80

G G G   C̄   G   A A A   G   refrain to *Blessed Assurance* 9

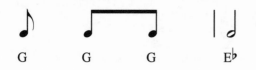

G   G   G   E♭   Beethoven, *Symphony No. 1*, first movement 173

G G G E   D C A G   *Tappan* 56

G   G G E G A G E   *De Camptown Races* 100

G G G F♯ G A G G F♯   *A Band of Brothers in DKE* 146

G G G F♯ G E E E E E D♯ E C C C   *Ta-ra-ra Boom-de-ay!* 140

G G G G B A G F E   refrain to *a Band of Brothers in DKE* 146

G G G G F E G C D   *Battle Hymn of the Republic* 72

G G G G G E G A A

refrain to *Tenting on the Old Camp Ground* 88

G G G G G F E G

refrain to *Has Anybody Here Seen Kelly?* 106

NEWLY IDENTIFIED AND UNIDENTIFIED TUNES

INCIPIT	IN IVES

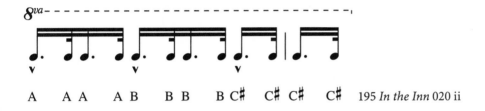

A A A A B B B B C# C# C# C#   195 *In the Inn* 020 ii

A B C# F#   E C# B   C# D#   203 *Symphony No. 4* 004 ii

A C   A G F A   F E E D F D   222 *Down East* 236

A D F# A D F# F#A G F# E F#A G F# E   197 *Washington's Birthday* 005 i

B A♯ B   C B G A   B   G   A E   221 *Old Home Day* 315

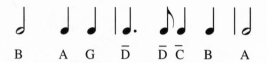

B   A G   D̄   D̄ C̄   B   A   219 *A Set of Three Short Pieces* 84
and *Hymn 267*

B B   A B C̄ D̄   D̄ F A   G A   C̄   198 *Washington's Birthday* 005 i

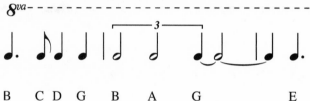

B   C D G   B   A   G   E   200 *Symphony No. 4* 004 ii

B   D̄   B   A G   A   G♯A   B A   212 *String Quartet No. 1* 057 iv

B̲♯D♯G♯   F♯   E G♯A   G♯ F♯ A F♯   E♯ G♯ E♯   213 *String Quartet No. 1* 057 iv

C̄ B♭ A♭ A♭ C̄ D̄♭ C̄ B♭ A♭ B♭   C̄   227 *Orchestral Set No. 3* 009 iii

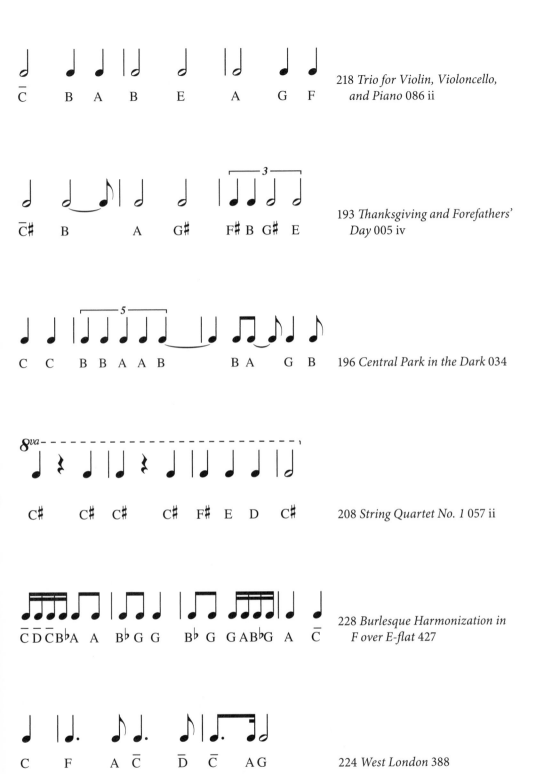

218 *Trio for Violin, Violoncello, and Piano* 086 ii

193 *Thanksgiving and Forefathers' Day* 005 iv

196 *Central Park in the Dark* 034

208 *String Quartet No. 1* 057 ii

228 *Burlesque Harmonization in F over E-flat* 427

224 *West London* 388

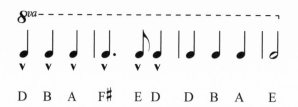

D B A F♯ E D D B A E   207 *String Quartet No. 1* 057 ii

D D F♯ F♯ F♯ A B B B A B A D C♯ D   214 *Trio for Violin, Violoncello, and Piano* 086 ii

D G B B B B C B A G E A A B A   206 *String Quartet No. 1* 057 ii

E♭ D D♭ C A B♭ F G F E♭   192 *Symphony No. 2* 002 ii

E E A B C E D C D D C D E   199 *The Fourth of July* 005 iii

E E A C♯ A E G♯ B A   205 *Symphony No. 4* 004 iv

E F G C̄ B A G E G E E C

206 *Trio for Violin, Violoncello, and Piano* 086 ii

E F G GC̄ GA G E F G GC̄ GA G

194 *In the Inn* 020 ii

F♯ Ā♯ F♯ Ḡ♯ F♯ C♯ A♯ D̄♯ C̄♯ F♯

201 *Symphony No. 4* 004 ii and *The Celestial Railroad* 116

F♯ E F♯ D E

220 *Decoration Day* for Violin and Piano 064

F G A G F C̄

226 *Orchestral Set No. 3* 009 ii

G A B B B B A BA GE F♯

223 *West London* 388

Gb Ab Bb Cb Db Gb Ab Bb Ab Bb Cb Db Eb   Bb   211 *String Quartet No. 1* 057 iii

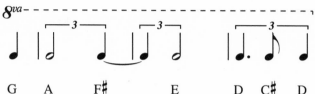

G   A   F#   E   D   C#   D   215 *Trio for Violin, Violoncello,*
                                            and Piano 086 ii

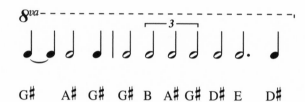

G#   A# G# G# B   A# G# D# E   D#   204 *Symphony No. 4* 004 iv

G   A   G G C E   E   F   E D C   225 *Orchestral Set No. 3* 009 ii

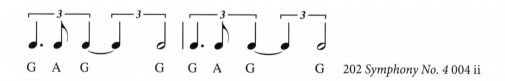

G A G   G   G A   G   G   202 *Symphony No. 4* 004 ii

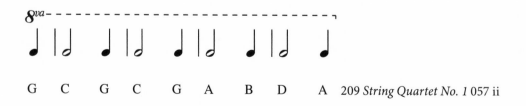

G   C   G   C   G   A   B   D   A   209 *String Quartet No. 1* 057 ii

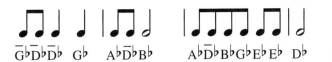

G♭ D♭ D♭   G♭   A♭ D♭ B♭   A♭ D♭ B♭ G♭ E♭ E♭   D♭

210 *String Quartet No. 1* 057 iii

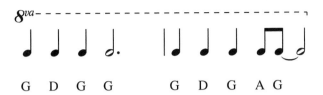

G   D   G   G   G   D   G   A G

217 *Trio for Violin, Violoncello, and Piano* 086 ii

[12]

Editions of Music Used

The author used the following editions of Ives's music and/or the composer's manuscripts to determine the locations of borrowings listed in this *Tunebook*. Specific manuscript page numbers appear in chapter 9, "Compositions with Borrrowings."

001 *Symphony No. 1:* Peer International, 1971
002 *Symphony No. 2:* Peer International, 1951
003 *Symphony No. 3:* Arrow Music Press, 1947
004 *Symphony No. 4:* Associated Music, 1965
005 *A Symphony: New England Holidays*
    i. *Washington's Birthday:* Associated Music, reprint 1974
    ii. *Decoration Day:* Peer International, 1989
    iii. *The Fourth of July:* Associated Music, reprint 1974
    iv. *Thanksgiving and Forefathers' Day:* Peer International, 1991
006 *Universe Symphony:* Ives's manuscripts
007 *Orchestral Set No. 1: Three Places in New England:* Mercury Music, 1976
008 *Orchestral Set No. 2:* Peer, 1999
009 *Orchestral Set No. 3*
    i. David Porter's unpublished performance score and Ives's manuscripts
    ii. *An Afternoon or During Camp Meetin' Week—One Secular Afternoon (In Bethel):* David Porter, *The Third Orchestral Set of Charles Edward Ives (1874–1954).* Master's thesis: California State University, Fullerton: 1979 and Ives's manuscripts
    iii. Ives's manuscripts
010 *Set No. 1:* Ives's manuscripts
011 *Set No. 2:* Ives's manuscripts

012 *Set No. 3:* Ives's manuscripts

013 *Set No. 4: Three Poets and Human Nature:* Ives's manuscripts

014 *Set No. 5: The Other Side of Pioneering, or Side Lights on American Enterprise:* Ives's manuscripts

015 *Set No. 6: From the Side Hill:* Ives's manuscripts

016 *Set No. 7: Water Colors:* Ives's manuscripts

017 *Set No. 8: Songs Without Voices:* Ives's manuscripts

018 *Set No. 9 of Three Pieces:* Ives's manuscripts

019 *Set No. 10 of Three Pieces:* Ives's manuscripts

020 *Set for Theatre Orchestra: New Music* 5, no. 2, Jan. 1932

021 *Alcottt Overture:* Ives's manuscripts

022 *Emerson Overture for Piano and Orchestra:* Ives's manuscripts

023 *Matthew Arnold Overture:* Ives's manuscripts

024 *Overture and March "1776":* Merion Music, 1975

027 *Robert Browning Overture:* Peer International, 1959

028 *Holiday Quickstep:* Merion Music, 1975

029 *March No. 2, with "Son of a Gambolier":* Peer International, 1977

031 *March No. 3, with "My Old Kentucky Home":* Merion Music, 1975

033 *March: The Circus Band:* Peer International, 1969

034 *Central Park in the Dark:* Boelke-Bomart, 1973

036 *"Country Band" March:* Merion Music, 1974

037 *The General Slocum:* Ives's manuscripts

038 *The Gong on the Hook and Ladder or Firemen's Parade on Main Street:* Peer International, 1960

039 *Piece for Small Orchestra and Organ:* Ives's manuscripts

040 *The Pond:* Boelke-Bomart, 1973

042 *Three Ragtime Dances:* Ives's manuscripts

043 *Four Ragtime Dances:* Peer International, 1990

045 *The Rainbow:* Peer International, 1959

046 *Skit for Danbury Fair:* Ives's manuscripts

047 *Take-Off No. 7: Mike Donlin-Johnny Evers:* Ives's manuscripts

049 *Tone Roads et al.:* Peer International, 1949, and Ives's manuscripts

051 *Yale-Princeton Football Game:* Ives's manuscripts

052 *Fantasia on "Jerusalem the Golden":* Associated Music, 1974

053 *March, F and C, with "Omega Lambda Chi":* Associated Music, 1974

054 *March "Intercollegiate," with "Annie Lisle":* Helicon Music, 1973

057 *String Quartet No. 1: From the Salvation Army:* Peer International, 1961

058 *String Quartet No. 2:* Peer International, 1954

059 *Pre-First Sonata for Violin and Piano:* Ives's manuscripts

060 *Sonata No. 1 for Violin and Piano:* Peer International, 1953

061 *Sonata No. 2 for Violin and Piano:* G. Schirmer, 1951

062 *Sonata No. 3 for Violin and Piano:* Merion Music, 1951

063 *Sonata No. 4 for Violin and Piano: Children's Day at the Camp Meeting:* Associated Music, 1942

064 *Decoration Day* for Violin and Piano: Ives's manuscripts

065 *From the Steeples and the Mountains:* Ives's manuscripts

069 *Fugue in Four Keys on "The Shining Shore"*: Ives's manuscripts

070 *The Gong on the Hook and Ladder or Firemen's Parade on Main Street*: Peer International, 1960

080 *Prelude on "Eventide"*: Ives's manuscripts

083 *Scherzo for String Quartet*: Peer International, 1958

084 *A Set of Three Short Pieces*: Peer International, 1966, 1958, 1957

086 *Trio for Violin, Violoncello, and Piano*: Peer International, 1955

087 *Sonata No. 1 for Piano*: Peer International, 1954

088 *Sonata No. 2 for Piano: Concord, Mass., 1840–60*: Associated Music, 1947

089 *Three-Page Sonata*: Mercury Music, 1949

094 *Study No. 6: Andante*: Ives's manuscripts

097 *Study No. 9: The Anti-Abolitionist Riots in the 1830s and 1840s*: Mercury Music, 1949

101 *Study No. 16: Andante cantabile*: Ives's manuscripts

103 *Study No. 19*: Ives's manuscripts

104 *Study No. 20: March*: Merion Music, 1981

105 *Study No. 21: Some Southpaw Pitching*: Mercury Music, 1949

107 *Study No. 23: Allegro*: Merion Music, 1990

109 *March No. 1 for Piano, with "Year of Jubilee"*: Ives's manuscripts

110 *March No. 2 for Piano, with "Son of a Gambolier"*: Ives's manuscripts

111 *March No. 3 for Piano, with "Omega Lambda Chi"*: Ives's manuscripts

112 *March No. 5 for Piano, with "Annie Lisle"*: Ives's manuscripts

113 *March No. 6 for Piano, with "Here's to Good Old Yale"*: Ives's manuscripts

114 *March in G and C for Piano, with "See the Conquering Hero Comes"*: Ives's manuscripts

115 *March for Piano: The Circus Band*: Ives's manuscripts

116 *The Celestial Railroad*: Thomas M. Brodhead unpublished edition

118 *Invention in D*: Ives's manuscripts

122 Set of Five Take-Offs: Peer International, 1991

123 *Four Transcriptions from "Emerson"*: Ives's manuscripts

125 *Waltz-Rondo*: Associated Music, 1978

127 *Drum Corps or Scuffle*: Ives's manuscripts

128 *Three Quarter-Tone Pieces*: Ives's manuscripts

131 *"Adeste Fideles" in an Organ Prelude*: Mercury Music, 1949

137 *Interludes for Hymns*: Ives's manuscripts

139 *Postlude for Thanksgiving Service*: Ives's manuscripts

140 *Variations on "America"*: Mercury Music, 1949

152 *Psalm 90*: Merion Music, 1970

168 *Hymn, Op. 2, no. 1*: Ives's manuscripts

177 *Serenity*: Ives's manuscripts

178 *Turn Ye, Turn Ye*: Mercury Music, 1952

180 *An Election*: Ives's manuscripts

181 *General William Booth Enters into Heaven*: Merion Music, 1964

182 *He Is There!*: Ives's manuscripts

183 *Johnny Poe*: Peer International, 1978

184 *Lincoln, the Great Commoner*: Kalmus reprint of *New Music Orchestra Series* [1932]

186 *The New River*: Peer International, 1971

187 *Sneak Thief:* Ives's manuscripts

188 *They Are There! (A War Song March):* Peer International, 1971

192 *The Bells of Yale:* Ives's manuscripts

193 *The Boys in Blue:* Ives's manuscripts

    Note: The sources for Ives's Songs (Sinclair numbers 205–399) is *Charles Ives 129 Songs,* edited by H. Wiley Hitchcock. Exceptions are Sinclair numbers 243, 318, 335, 357, 440, and 441, where a source title appears following the title of each song, below. An Ives manuscript is the source for Sinclair number 446.

243 *The Ending Year* [in] *Forty Earlier Songs*

318 *On Judges' Walk* [in] *Forty Earlier Songs*

335 *Rock of Ages* [in] *Eleven Songs and Two Harmonizations*

357 *The Song of the Dead* [in] *Forty Earlier Songs*

426 *Burlesque Harmonization in C:* Ives's manuscripts

427 *Burlesque Harmonization in F over E-flat:* Ives's manuscripts

428 *Burlesque Harmonizations of "London Bridge":* Ives's manuscripts

436 *Take-Off on "Surprise Symphony":* Ives's manuscripts

440 *E. Ives: Christmas Carol* [in] *Eleven Songs and Two Harmonizations*

441 *In the Mornin'* [in] *Eleven Songs and Two Harmonizations*

446 *Search Me, O Lord:* Ives's manuscript

447 Two chords, etc. headed "Sun Rise Chord [over East Rock] . . . : Ives's manuscripts

461 Four mm., 2/4 (f0901) [on a manuscript for *Thanksgiving*]: Ives's manuscripts

593 One line on 3 staves: Ives's manuscripts

600 Four mm., 4/4, possibly for *Overture: Nationals:* Ives's manuscripts

632 One line mostly on 2 staves: Ives's manuscripts

NOTES

PREFACE

1. While this is true, it is also true that, before his death, Ives's music was played and written about more often than the "myth" of Ives generally acknowledged. The reader is referred to parts 3 and 4 of *Charles Ives and His World,* edited by J. Peter Burkholder (Princeton, N.J.: Princeton University Press, 1996), for a selected collection of views and reviews of Ives and his music from 1888 through the year after his death. As might be expected, the reviews range from the laudatory: "Master Ives is certainly a musical genius" (p. 275) and "this astonishing artist is one of the pioneers of modern music, a great adventurer in the spiritual world, a poet, a visionary, a sage, and a seer" (p. 317), to bewilderment: "[this reviewer's] memory of it [i.e., the second movement of *Symphony No. 4*] was just simply awful, from beginning to end" (p. 297); "The only impression one gets from playing the work [the *"Concord"* sonata] is that instead of being interpretations of the material and spiritual realms, they are direct delineations of a boiler-shop or the sounds emanating from a conservatory of music when in full blast" (p. 286).

2. If one can point to a single moment when the composer began to emerge from a kind of self-imposed musical anonymity—integrity combined with Yankee privacy and reticence—it is most certainly owing to Gilman's review on January 21, 1939: "[The *"Concord"* sonata] is exceptionally great music—it is, indeed, the greatest music composed by an American, and the most deeply and essentially American in impulse and implication. . . . [John Kirkpatrick's] performance was that of a poet and a master, an unobtrusive minister of genius" (*New York Herald-Tribune,* January 21, 1939, p. 9).

3. The *New York Times* obituary of May 19, 1984, p. 31, described Ives as a "lonely but vital figure in American music to whom public recognition came slowly and almost belatedly," but also remarked on the composer's "widespread recognition in the musical world." Erroneously, the writer added, "Mr. Ives continued to compose until shortly before his death."

4. Some major contributions to the literature are: *Charles E. Ives: Memos,* ed. John Kirkpatrick (New York: W. W. Norton, 1972), hereafter *Memos;* Vivian Perlis, *Charles Ives Remembered* (New Haven, Conn.: Yale University Press, 1974); Frank R. Rossiter, *Charles Ives and His America* (New York: Liveright, 1976); H. Wiley Hitchcock and Vivian Perlis, eds., *An Ives Celebration* (Urbana: University of Illinois Press, 1977); J. Peter Burkholder, *Charles Ives: The Ideas Behind the Music* (New Haven, Conn.: Yale University Press, 1985); Geoffrey Block, *Charles Ives: A Bio-Bibliography* (New York: Greenwood, 1988); Stuart Feder, *Charles Ives, "My Father's Song": A Psychoanalytic Biography* (New Haven, Conn.: Yale University Press, 1992); Lawrence Starr, *A Union of Diversities: Style in the Music of Charles Ives* (New York: Schirmer Books, 1992); J. Peter Burkholder, *All Made of Tunes: Charles Ives and the Uses of Musical Borrowing* (New Haven, Conn.: Yale University Press, 1995); J. Peter Burkholder, ed., *Charles Ives and His World;* Jan Swafford, *Charles Ives: A Life with Music* (New York: W. W. Norton, 1996); Geoffrey Block and J. Peter Burkholder, eds., *Charles Ives and the Classical Tradition* (New Haven, Conn.: Yale University Press, 1996); Philip Lambert, ed., *Ives Studies* (Cambridge, UK: Cambridge University Press, 1997); Philip Lambert, *The Music of Charles Ives* (New Haven, Conn.: Yale University Press, 1997); James B. Sinclair, *A Descriptive Catalogue of the Music of Charles Ives* (New Haven, Conn.: Yale University Press, 1999); *New Grove Dictionary of Music and Musicians* (New York: Oxford University Press, 2003).

5. Quoted phrase from *New York Times* obituary, May 19, 1984, p. 31. One measure of this can be seen in a *New Yorker* cartoon, published a week before Ives's centennial celebration, in which there is no attempt to explain to the reader who Charles Ives is. Four intellectual types are chatting at a cocktail party and one remarks: "And you know who else was heavy? Charles Ives! Charles Ives was very, very heavy." Here "heavy" is being used in its slang sense of being a very important or influential person. Ives had, indeed, become an icon! William Hamilton, *New Yorker,* October 14, 1974.

6. J. Peter Burkholder, ed., *Charles Ives and His World,* 369. Originally in *Disques* (Nov. 1932): 374–76.

7. The musical responses of both composers unfold against locations close to each other. The Hanover Square elevated train station was just south of Wall Street at the junction of Pearl and Stone streets, only blocks away from where the World Trade Center would be built.

8. Kirkpatrick, *Memos*, 92–93.

9. Ibid.

10. David Schiff, "Memory Spaces," *The Atlantic Monthly* (April 2003): 129, 130.

11. Lou Harrison, "On Quotation," *Modern Music* 23 (1946): 166–69; Kurt Stone, "Ives's Fourth Symphony: A Review," *The Musical Quarterly* 52 (Jan. 1966): 1–16; Sydney Robinson Charles, "The Use of Borrowed Material in Ives's Second Symphony," *Music Review* 28 (1967): 102–11; Dennis Marshall, "Charles Ives's Quotations: Manner or Substance?" *Perspectives of New Music* 6 (1968): 45–56; Clayton W. Henderson, "Quotation as a Style Element in the Music of Charles Ives" (Ph.D. diss., Washington University, 1969); Colin Sterne, "The Quotations in Charles Ives's Second Symphony," *Music and Letters* 52 (Jan. 1971): 39–45; Christopher Ballantine, "Charles Ives and the Meaning of Quotation in Music," *The Musical Quarterly* 65 (1979): 167–84; Stuart Feder, "Decoration Day: A Boyhood Memory of Charles Ives," *The Musical Quarterly* 66 (1980): 234–61; J. Peter Burkholder, "The Evolution of Charles Ives's Music: Aesthetics, Quotation, Technique" (Ph.D. diss., University of Chicago, 1983); J. Peter Burkholder, "'Quotation' and Emulation: Charles Ives's Uses of His Models," *The Musical Quarterly* 71 (1985): 1–26; Burkholder, *All Made of Tunes*.

12. Burkholder has calculated that "half the pieces and over two-thirds of the instrumental movements composed after 1902 use borrowed material." *All Made of Tunes*, 417.

13. Part of this is owing to the virtual disappearance of community singing from American life. There is no longer a common core of "old chestnuts" that most Americans are brought up singing. Until World War II, community singing could be found at the beginnings and/or conclusions of public meetings of all sorts, at school assemblies, for national holidays, at impromptu gatherings of families and friends at social events, on long automobile rides; the list could go on and on. With the exception of singing *Happy Birthday, Auld Lang Syne, Take Me Out to the Ball Game,* and *The Star Spangled Banner,* this experience has largely vanished from American society. There is, therefore, not a large body of shared musical experiences to which we can turn. A notable exception to this occurred after the September 11, 2001, attacks when members of Congress and ordinary citizens, as a cathartic act and a show of American solidarity, joined in the repeated impromptu community singing of patriotic songs, *God Bless America* and *My Country, 'Tis of Thee* (*America*) chief among them.

14. Rossiter, *Charles Ives and His America*, 107.

15. Kirkpatrick, *Memos*, 68, note 1.

16. Ives, *Essays Before a Sonata*, 30–31; Ives really means Reeves's *Second Regiment March*.

17. Kirkpatrick, *Memos*, 101–102, note 1.

18. Lou Harrison has compared the compositional techniques of Ives with James Joyce, including the stream-of-consciousness properties of both, in "On Quotation."

19. Kirkpatrick, *Memos*, 97–98.

20. Henry Bellaman's notes for *Symphony No. 4* (based on conversations with Ives), appearing in John Kirkpatrick's preface to the score of that work in *Charles Ives: Symphony No. 4: Performance Score* (New York: Associated Music Publishers, 1965), viii.

21. Charles Ives, *Piano Sonata No. 2 "Concord, Mass., 1840–1860,"* 2nd ed. (New York: Associated Music Publishers); reprint of 1947 Arrow Music Press edition.

22. See Starr, *A Union of Diversities*.

23. Rossiter, *Charles Ives and His America*, 99–100.

24. *TSIAJ* = "This Scherzo Is A Joke."

25. Kirkpatrick, *Memos*, 127.

26. Ibid., 46.

27. John Kirkpatrick remarked that "Ives talked about his father as a personality. He lived, or that side of him lived, almost in a state of Chinese ancestor worship. He talked of his father as if he were still living, as if he were still a member of the household" (Perlis, *Charles Ives Remembered*, 225). Writings that focus particularly on the father-son relationship are Feder, "Decoration Day"; Stuart Feder, "Charles and George Ives: The Veneration of Boyhood," *Annual of Psychoanalysis* 9 (1981): 265–316; Maynard Solomon, "Charles Ives: Some Questions of Veracity," *Journal of the American Musicological Society* 40 (1987): 443–70; Feder, *Charles Ives*.

28. John Kirkpatrick, *Grove Dictionary of Music and Musicians*, p. 503, col. 2, ¶6.

29. Ralph Waldo Emerson, "Quotation and Originality" in *The Portable Emerson*, ed. Mark Van Doren (New York: Viking, 1946), 288.

30. Ibid., 300–301.

31. Following the announcement that Ives had won the Pulitzer Prize in music for 1947, Ethel Beckwith of *The Bridgeport Herald* interviewed Ives at his West Redding, Connecticut, home. When Beckwith explained to the irritated composer that her

words of congratulation were the conventional thing to say, Ives reportedly retorted, "I am not conventional." Beckwith's article is typical of the writings about Ives at the time, dwelling on the person, and giving little space to the music. She writes of the Iveses: "they are Connecticut Yankees 200%. Besides, they look it—Harmony Twichell Ives in her white-haired dignity, the composer, lean, nervous, stubborn and his New England lines strangely blending with those of Tchaikovsky because of his full beard." "His home . . . is lovely in distinctive, though almost pioneer-simple, taste." His wife "leads a Spartan existence because of her uncompromising husband's various caprices." "There are uniformed maids, and an ancient cat, Christophina." "When the Ives [sic] said they don't own a radio, and would not listen to radio music of any kind, your reporter felt the height of un-convention had been reached" (*The Bridgeport Herald*, May 11, 1947). Shortly after Ives's 75th birthday, *Life* magazine carried a W. Eugene Smith photograph of him, with a caption describing the composer as "a fanatically shy, enigmatic man" and described his compositions as "exceedingly difficult to understand and to play" (October 31, 1949).

32. Kirkpatrick, *Memos*, 56: "When I was in college, I used to go down there [Poli's Theatre in New Haven] and 'spell' [the piano player] . . . a little if he wanted to go out for five minutes and get a glass of beer, or a dozen glasses."

33. Felsburg (d. 1909 or 1910) played piano at Sylvester Poli's Bijou Theatre, which was located on Church Street in New Haven. It was part of the theatre chain that E. M. Loewe owned.

34. General John A. Logan of the Grand Army of the Republic declared, in General Order No. 11, that May 30, 1868, would be designated a day for decorating the graves of the fallen Union troops. While this is generally acknowledged to have been the first Decoration Day, a Memorial Day for this same purpose had been observed in several American towns after the end of the Civil War and before 1868. In 1882, Memorial Day became the preferred name for this observance, but we, in Montowese, retained the older name. Ives used both names in referring to this date in May.

ACKNOWLEDGMENTS

1. *A Temporary Mimeographed Catalogue of the Music Manuscripts and Related Materials of Charles Edward Ives, 1874–1954, Given by Mrs. Ives to the Library of the Yale School of Music, September 1955*, compiled by John Kirkpatrick (New Haven,

Conn.: Library of the Yale School of Music, 1960). Hereafter *Catalogue*.

2. Sinclair, *A Descriptive Catalogue of the Music of Charles Ives*.

3. Burkholder, *All Made of Tunes*.

4. Kirkpatrick, *Memos*, 22.

INTRODUCTION

1. Henry Bellaman's notes for *Symphony No. 4* (based on conversations with Ives), appearing in John Kirkpatrick's preface to the score of that work, viii.

2. "Notes on Fourth Violin Sonata," in *Sonata No. 4 for Violin and Piano: "Children's Day at the Camp Meeting"* (New York: Associated Music Publishers, 1942), 21.

3. Burkholder points out that the B-A-C-H motive provides much of the thematic material in the *Three-Page Sonata*. *All Made of Tunes*, p. 240.

4. This organization appeared first in the Kirkpatrick *Catalogue*, 264–66.

5. I have retained the alphabetical listing, by category, which I used in the first edition of the *Tunebook*. Borrowings discovered since the 1990 edition are presented, by category, in their appropriate alphabetical place, together with a suffix. Thus, *Crusader's Hymn*, also known as *St. Elizabeth*, follows *Coronation*, number 13, and is given the entry number 13-a.

6. A valuable help in dating some sources was James J. Fuld's *The Book of World-Famous Music: Classical, Popular and Folk*, rev. and enl. ed. (New York: Crown, 1971).

7. H. Wiley Hitchcock and Stanley Sadie, eds., 4 vols. (London: Macmillan, 1985), 2:509–18.

8. Solomon, "Charles Ives: Some Questions of Veracity." See also J. Peter Burkholder, "Charles Ives and His Fathers: A Response to Maynard Solomon," *Institute for Studies in American Music Newsletter* 18, no. 1 (Nov. 1988): 8–11; Philip Lambert, "Communication," *Journal of the American Musicological Society* 42 (Spring 1989): 204–209; and Gayle Sherwood, "Questions and Veracities: Reassessing the Chronology of Ives's Choral Works," *The Musical Quarterly* 78 (Fall 1994): 429–47.

9. James B. Sinclair and Kenneth Singleton microfilmed all of Ives's manuscripts in 1975–76, and each microfilm page was assigned a print number.

10. An incomplete initial measure is counted as zero (0) and the first complete measure of music is designated one (1). First and second endings are indicated by "a" and "b" respectively. Unbarred pieces, sections, or special circumstances (e.g., the *"Concord"* Sonata) are commented upon at the appropriate time.

11. I thank Vivian Perlis for sharing with me the results of an inventory made by her students of this material.

12. . . . the higher and more important value of this dualism is composed of what may be called reality, quality, spirit, or substance against the lower value of form, quantity, or manner. . . . Substance has something to do with character. Manner has nothing to do with it. The substance of a tune comes from somewhere near the soul, and manner comes from—God knows where.

From Charles Ives, epilogue, *Essays Before a Sonata,* 75, 77.

1. HYMNS

1. Kirkpatrick, *Memos,* 132–33.
2. For discussions of how Ives's experience as an organist informed his compositions, see especially J. Peter Burkholder, "The Organist in Ives," *Journal of the American Musicological Society* 55 (Summer 2002): 255–310, and William Osborne, "Charles Ives the Organist," *The American Organist* 24, no. 7 (1990): 58–64.
3. Hymns feature prominently in all of *Symphony No. 3;* the first, third, and fourth movements of *Symphony No. 4; Decoration Day;* and *Thanksgiving and Forefathers' Day* from *A Symphony: New England Holidays;* all of *Sonata No. 1 for Piano; The Housatonic at Stockbridge* from *Orchestral Set No. 1: Three Places in New England;* all of *String Quartet No. 1: From the Salvation Army;* all of *Sonata No. 3 for Violin and Piano;* and all of *Sonata No. 4 for Violin and Piano: Children's Day at the Camp Meeting.*
4. Kirkpatrick, *Memos,* 57–58. Wilton Merle-Smith (1856–1923) was pastor of Central Presbyterian Church from 1889 to 1920.
5. Ibid., 128.
6. Ibid., 129.
7. Ibid., 128: "Even after giving up the organ position in 1902, I substituted for an occasional Sunday service, . . . and I would always take this opportunity of trying out things that I was working on, things of this character."
8. Ives, *Essays Before a Sonata,* 80. "R.F.O.G." is an Ivesian combination of the organizations Fellow of the Royal College of Organists (F.R.C.O.) and Fellow of the American Guild of Organists (F.A.G.O.).
9. For more on Ives's use of cantus firmus technique, see Burkholder, *All Made of Tunes,* pp. 110–11, 238–40. See also Ann Besser Scott, "Medieval and Renaissance Techniques in the Music of Charles Ives:

Horatio at the Bridge?" *The Musical Quarterly* 78 (Fall 1994): 448–78.

2. PATRIOTIC SONGS AND MILITARY MUSIC

1. George Ives's good reputation, however, would have been sullied by his court-martial and punishment on July 3, 1864. For details, see pp. 41–43 in Feder's *Charles Ives: "My Father's Song."* How many of George's relatives, friends, and neighbors would have been aware of these events is unknown. How much Charles knew of this event in his father's life is uncertain, but he didn't recount it when he constructed the sometimes larger-than-life, heroic figure of his father.
2. Kirkpatrick, *Memos,* p. 84. See also Denise Von Glahn Cooney, "A Sense of Place: Charles Ives and 'Putnam's Camp, Redding, Connecticut'," *American Music* 14, no. 3 (Fall 1996): 276–312.
3. Kirkpatrick, *Memos,* p. 84.
4. Kirkpatrick, *Memos,* p. 42, note 2. Sinclair refers to this figure as "street beat" in *A Descriptive Catalogue,* p. 720; Burkholder calls it a "street beat" or "street cadence" in *All Made of Tunes,* p. 536.
5. Kirkpatrick, *Memos,* p. 42.
6. Ibid.

3. POPULAR SONGS

1. Kirkpatrick, *Memos,* 56.
2. Kirkpatrick, *Memos,* 125.
3. That Ives (and how many other organists?) combined both secular and sacred worlds on occasion is clear from a note that Ned Park, one of his roommates at Poverty Flat, wrote about an experience he had when singing in the choir that Ives conducted at Central Presbyterian church:

> I am sure that various members of the congregation were in a state of continual quandary whether Charlie was committing sacrilegious sins by introducing popular and perhaps ribald melodies into the offertory, etc. I am sure that he was under grave suspicion, but the melodies were so disguised that the suspicious members of the congregation could never be sure enough to take action. I think it is certain that he did interweave them, not from a sense of humor or tantalization, but because that was the way in which his musical mind found a certain satisfaction.

Edwards ("Ned") Park (1877–1969) was a student at the College of Physicians and Surgeons of Columbia

University. Quoted in Kirkpatrick, *Memos*, 263. Poverty Flat, located at 317 West 58th Street in New York City, was a large apartment where Ives and a number of Yale men lived before and after the turn into the twentieth century.

4. Burkholder writes at length about Ives's experience as an organist and the role of improvisation in his music in "The Organist in Ives." See also Osborne, "Charles Ives the Organist."

5. In his preface to *Memos* (p. 11), Kirkpatrick wrote that a severe heart attack shortly after September 1918 "called a halt [to his desire to enter the First World War] and imposed a quiet assessment." Feder argued persuasively that Ives's illness was not a physical one, but a psychological and emotional breakdown (*Charles Ives: "My Father's Song"*). Sherwood wrote convincingly that Ives's symptoms matched those of neurasthenia—"the central explanation for nervous breakdown through the second decade of the century, at least in the United States" ("Charles Ives and 'Our National Malady'," *Journal of the American Musicological Society* 54, no. 3 [Fall 2001]: 578).

6. Kirkpatrick, *Memos*, 105.

7. Thornton was the composer of *When You Were Sweet Sixteen* (1898), a song that enjoyed immense popularity and commercial success.

8. For a discussion about Ives and Foster, see Neely Bruce, "Ives and Nineteenth-Century American Music," in *An Ives Celebration*, ed. Hitchcock and Perlis, 29–43.

9. Kirkpatrick, *Memos*, 56.

10. Ibid.

11. Lyman Denison Brewster (1832–1904), lawyer, judge, and poet was married to Sarah Amelia Ives (1837–1918), Charles's aunt Amelia.

12. Although only anecdotal evidence exists to suggest that ragtime music was introduced to the public at the Columbian Exposition, the anecdotes are sufficiently prevalent to suggest that this was so.

13. Ives, *Essays Before a Sonata*, 94.

14. Kirkpatrick, *Memos*, 53. Mary Smith Parmelee, church singer, widow of Noah Parmelee, and Ives's maternal grandmother. Music example taken from Ives's manuscript.

4. COLLEGE MUSIC

1. John Prentiss Poe, Jr. (Princeton, 1895), was one of six brothers who played football for Princeton in the late 19th and early 20th centuries. He was, among other things, a wanderer in the romantic tradition, an assistant football coach, a mercenary, a raconteur, and a miner. Poe died on September 25, 1915, at the Battle of Loos.

2. This tune is an anthem of the Wolf's Head society, a senior-year secret society to which Ives belonged. As part of the trappings of this society, it was not made available for copying. The music given for tune number 150-b is taken from its citation in measures 178 through 187 of the Scherzo movement of the *Trio*.

5. POPULAR INSTRUMENTAL TUNES

1. *Pig Town Fling*, a tune Ives uses in seven different compositions, is also known as *Warm Stuff* and *Cripple Creek*. Other titles for it undoubtedly exist as well.

2. I've always been a good Jew's harp player . . . , but I don't know exactly how to write for it. . . . [I]n this piece [i.e., *Washington's Birthday*], from a half a dozen to a hundred Jew's harps are necessary—one would hardly be heard. In the old barn dances, about all the men would carry Jew's harps in their vest pockets or in the calf of their boots, and several would stand around on the side of the floor and play the harp more as a drum than as an instrument of tones.

Kirkpatrick, *Memos*, p. 96.

3. From the first edition of *The Charles Ives Tunebook*, p. 153.

4. One is reminded of the ballroom scene in Act II of Mozart's *Don Giovanni*, in which one hears three orchestras playing three different dances simultaneously—minuet, *contre-danse*, and waltz.

5. Kirkpatrick, *Memos*, 97.

6. "Notes" to *Symphony No. 2* (New York: Southern Music Publishing, 1951).

7. Kirkpatrick, *Memos*, 97.

6. CLASSICAL MUSIC

1. Kirkpatrick, *Memos*, 134.

2. Kirkpatrick, *Memos*, 116.

3. Ibid.

4. Ibid.

5. Ibid., 115.

6. In Kirkpatrick, *Memos*, pp. 115–16, Ives wrote: "Parker was a bright man, a good technician, but apparently willing to be limited by what Rheinberger et al and the German tradition had taught him." That Parker was unprepared for Ives's musical experiments and was dismissive in his attitude toward them is understandable, given his own musical

background. The fact that Ives turned to Parker's *Hora novissima* for a model so soon after working with him, gives the lie to Ives's own dismissive stance about his teacher's worth.

7. Kirkpatrick, *Memos,* 30.

8. Ibid.

9. Ibid., 135.

10. Ibid.

11. Ives, *Essays Before a Sonata,* 99.

12. Kirkpatrick, *Memos,* 134.

13. Ives, *Essays Before a Sonata,* 36.

14. Stone, "Ives's Fourth Symphony."

7. NEWLY IDENTIFIED AND UNIDENTIFIED TUNES

1. Peter Burkholder's *All Made of Tunes* is an invaluable source for the identification of borrowings. I thank him for his generosity in sharing with me his "takes" on the identities of "Unknown Tunes" and his suggested emendations to certain tunes, in his letter to me of May 26, 2002. I am not convinced by all of Burkholder's suggestions, but give them here for other readers to consider:

Ives's own invention: 197, 198, 217, 221;

Ives's "doodling" on *Bethany*: 204;

a fraternity tune: 214, 215;

paraphrase of *Bethany*: 222;

paraphrase of *Fountain*: 223, 224.

2. Credit is due the following scholars for identifying particular "Unknown" tunes. I offer my apologies to unknown others who may claim precedence to having done the same. Colin Sterne and Roy V. Magers (192); Lawrence Gushee (194, 195); Arthur Maisel (199); Peter Burkholder (200, 202, 203, 206, 207, 208, 209, 210, 212, 213, 218, 219); Thomas M. Brodhead (201); James B. Sinclair (216); Gianfranco Vinay (220).

SELECTED BIBLIOGRAPHY

BOOKS AND ARTICLES

ASCAP Biographical Dictionary. Compiled for ASCAP by Jacques Cattell Press. 4th ed. New York: R. R. Bowker, 1980.

Badger, R. Reid. *The Great American Fair. The World's Columbian Exposition and American Culture.* Chicago: Nelson Hall, 1979.

Ballantine, Christopher. "Charles Ives and the Meaning of Quotation in Music." *The Musical Quarterly* 65 (1979): 167–84.

Baron, Carol K. "Dating Charles Ives's Music: Facts and Fictions." *Perspectives of New Music* 28 (Winter 1990): 20–56.

———. "George Ives's Essay on Music Theory: An Introduction and Annotated Edition." *American Music* 10, no. 3 (1992): 239–88.

Bellaman, Henry. Notes based on conversations with Ives. In John Kirkpatrick's preface to *Charles Ives: Symphony No. 4: Performance Score.* New York: Associated Music Publishers, 1965.

Block, Geoffrey. *Charles Ives: A Bio-Bibliography.* New York: Greenwood, 1988.

Block, Geoffrey, and J. Peter Burkholder, eds. *Charles Ives and the Classical Tradition.* New Haven, Conn.: Yale University Press, 1996.

Brodhead, Thomas M. "Ives's *Celestial Railroad* and His Fourth Symphony." *American Music* 12 (Winter 1994): 389–424.

Brooks, William. "A Drummer-Boy Looks Back: Percussion in Ives's *Fourth Symphony.*" *Percussive Notes* 22, no. 6 (1984): 4–45.

Bruce, Neely. "Ives and Nineteenth-Century American Music." In *An Ives Celebration,* ed. Hitchcock and Perlis. Urbana: University of Illinois Press, 1977.

Burkholder, J. Peter. *All Made of Tunes: Charles Ives and the Uses of Musical Borrowing.* New Haven, Conn.: Yale University Press, 1995.

———. *Charles Ives: The Ideas Behind the Music.* New Haven, Conn.: Yale University Press, 1985.

———. "Charles Ives and His Fathers: A Response to Maynard Solomon." *Institute for Studies in American Music Newsletter* 18, no. 1 (Nov. 1988): 8–11.

———, ed. *Charles Ives and His World.* Princeton, N.J.: Princeton University Press, 1996.

———. "The Evolution of Charles Ives's Music: Aesthetics, Quotation, Technique." Ph.D. diss., University of Chicago, 1983.

———. "Not Surface, but Center: The Role of Charles Ives's Musical Models." Paper read at annual meeting of the American Musicological Society, Louisville, Ky., October 29, 1984.

———. "The Organist in Ives." *Journal of the American Musicological Society* 55 (Summer 2002): 255–310.

———. "'Quotation' and Emulation: Charles Ives's Uses of His Models." *The Musical Quarterly* 71 (1985): 1–26.

———. "'Quotation' and Paraphrase in Ives's Second Symphony." *19th-Century Music* 11 (Summer 1987).

———. "The uses of existing musical borrowing as a field." *Music Library Association Notes* 50, no. 3 (1994): 851–70.

Burkholder, J. Peter, James B. Sinclair, and Gayle Sherwood. "Charles (Edward) Ives." *New Grove Dictionary of Music and Musicians,* 2nd ed., vol. 12, ed. Stanley Sadie. London: Macmillan, 2001.

Charles, Sydney Robinson. "The Use of Borrowed Material in Ives's Second Symphony." *Music Review* 28 (1967): 102–11.

Claghorn, Charles Eugene. *Biographical Dictionary of American Music.* West Nyack, N.Y.: Parker, 1973.

Cooney, Denise Von Glahn. "New Sources for The 'St. Gaudens' in Boston Common (Colonel Robert Gould Shaw and his Colored Regiment)." *The Musical Quarterly* 81 (1997): 13–50.

———. "Reconciliations: Time, Space, and the American Place in the Music of Charles Ives." Ph.D. diss., University of Washington, 1995.

———. "A Sense of Place: Charles Ives and 'Putnam's Camp, Redding, Connecticut'." *American Music* 14, no. 3 (Fall 1996): 276–312.

Cowell, Henry, and Sidney Cowell. *Charles Ives and His Music*. Paperback ed. with additional material. New York: Oxford University Press, 1969.

Ellinwood, Leonard, and Keyes Porter, eds. *Bio-Bibliographical Index of Musicians in the United States of America Since Colonial Times*. 2nd ed. Washington, 1956; reprint, New York: Da Capo, 1973.

Emerson, Ralph Waldo. "Quotation and Originality." In *The Portable Emerson*, ed. Mark Van Doren. New York: Viking, 1946.

Feder, Stuart. "Charles and George Ives: The Veneration of Boyhood." *Annual of Psychoanalysis* 9 (1981): 265–316.

———. *Charles Ives: "My Father's Song." A Psychoanalytic Biography*. New Haven, Conn.: Yale University Press, 1992.

———. "Decoration Day: A Boyhood Memory of Charles Ives." *The Musical Quarterly* 66 (1980): 234–61.

Forte, Allen. "The Diatonic Looking Glass, or An Ivesian Metamorphosis." *The Musical Quarterly* 76 (1992): 355–82.

Fuld, James J. *The Book of World-Famous Music: Classical, Popular and Folk*. Rev. and enl. ed. New York: Crown, 1971.

Hamm, Charles. *Yesterdays: Popular Song in America*. New York: W. W. Norton, 1979.

Harrison, Lou. "On Quotation." *Modern Music* 23 (1946): 166–69.

Henderson, Clayton W. *The Charles Ives Tunebook*. Bibliographies in American Music, 14. Warren, Mich.: Harmonie Park, 1990.

———. "Quotation as a Style Element in the Music of Charles Ives." Ph.D. diss., Washington University, 1969.

———. "Structural Importance of Borrowed Music in the Works of Charles Ives: A Preliminary Assessment." *Reports of the Eleventh Congress of the International Musicological Congress Held at Copenhagen, 1972*. Ed. Henrik Glahn et al., vol. 1, 437–46.

Hitchcock, H. Wiley. "'A Grand and Glorious Noise!' Charles Ives as Lyricist." *American Music* 15, no. 1 (1997): 26–44.

———. *Ives: A Survey of the Music*. London: Oxford University Press, 1977. Reprint with correc-

tions, Brooklyn: Institute for Studies in American Music, [1985].

———. "Ives's *114* [+15] *Songs* and What He Thought of Them." *Journal of the American Musicological Society* 52 (1999): 97–144.

Hitchcock, H. Wiley, and Vivian Perlis, eds. *An Ives Celebration*. Urbana: University of Illinois Press, 1977.

Hitchcock, H. Wiley, and Stanley Sadie, eds. *The New Grove Dictionary of American Music*. 4 vols. London: Macmillan, 1985, 2: 509–18.

Ives, Charles Edward. *Essays Before a Sonata, and Other Writings*. Ed. Howard Boatwright. New York: W. W. Norton, 1961.

———. *129 Songs*. Ed. H. Wiley Hitchcock. In *Music of the United States of America*, Richard Crawford, editor-in-chief. Middleton, Wisc.: A-R Editions, 2004.

Kirkpatrick, John, ed. *Charles E. Ives: Memos*. New York: W. W. Norton, 1972.

———. "Charles (Edward) Ives." *The New Grove Dictionary of American Music*. Vol. 2. New York: Macmillan, 1986.

———. *Grove Dictionary of Music and Musicians*, p. 503, col. 2, ¶6.

———, compiler. *A Temporary Mimeographed Catalogue of the Music Manuscripts and Related Materials of Charles Edward Ives, 1874–1954, Given by Mrs. Ives to the Library of the Yale School of Music, September 1955*. New Haven, Conn.: Library of the Yale School of Music, 1960.

Lambert, Philip. "Communication." *Journal of the American Musicological Society* 42 (Spring 1989): 204–209.

———, ed. *Ives Studies*. Cambridge, UK: Cambridge University Press, 1997.

———. *The Music of Charles Ives*. New Haven, Conn.: Yale University Press, 1997.

Larson, Eric. *The Devil in the White City*. New York: Crown, 2003.

Lichtenwanger, William. "The Music of 'The Star Spangled Banner'." *College Music Symposium* 18 (Fall 1978): 34–81.

Magers, Roy V. "Aspects of Form in the Symphonies of Charles Ives." Ph.D. diss., Indiana University, 1975.

Maisel, Arthur. "*The Fourth of July* by Charles Ives: Mixed Harmonic Criteria in a Twentieth-Century Classic." *Theory and Practice* 6, no. 1 (Aug. 1981): 3–32.

Marshall, Dennis. "Charles Ives's Quotations: Manner or Substance?" *Perspectives of New Music* 6 (1968): 45–56.

New Grove Dictionary of Music and Musicians. New York: Oxford University Press, 2003.

Osborne, William. "Charles Ives the Organist." The American Organist 24, no. 7 (1990): 58–64.

Perlis, Vivian. Charles Ives Remembered. New Haven, Conn.: Yale University Press, 1974.

Placzek, Adolph K., ed. The Chicago World's Fair of 1893. A Photographic Record with Text by Stanley Appelbaum. Dover Architectural Series. New York: Dover, 1980.

Porter, David Gray. The Third Orchestral Set of Charles Edward Ives (1874–1954). Master's thesis: California State University, Fullerton: 1979.

Rossiter, Frank R. Charles Ives and His America. New York: Liveright, 1976.

Schiff, David. "Memory Spaces." The Atlantic Monthly (April 2003): 129, 130.

Schiff, Judith Ann. "The Greatest College Cheer." Yale Alumni Magazine (May 1998).

———. "Old Yale: The Birth, Near-Demise, and Comeback of 'Bright College Years'." Yale Alumni Magazine (Dec. 1999).

Scott, Ann Besser. "Medieval and Renaissance Techniques in the Music of Charles Ives: Horatio at the Bridge?" The Musical Quarterly 78 (Fall 1994): 448–78.

Sherwood, Gayle. Charles Ives: A Guide to Research. New York: Routledge, 2002.

———. "Charles Ives and 'Our National Malady'." Journal of the American Musicological Society 54, no. 3 (Fall 2001): 555–84.

———. "The Choral Works of Charles Ives: Chronology, Style, and Reception." Ph.D. diss., Yale University, 1995.

———. "Questions and Veracities: Reassessing the Chronology of Ives's Choral Works." The Musical Quarterly 78 (Fall 1994): 429–47.

Shirley, Wayne. "'The Second of July': A Charles Ives Draft Considered as an Independent Work." In A Celebration of American Music: Words and Music in Honor of H. Wiley Hitchcock, ed. Richard Crawford, R. Allen Lott, and Carol J. Oja, 391–404. Ann Arbor: University of Michigan Press, 1990.

Sinclair, James B. A Descriptive Catalogue of the Music of Charles Ives. New Haven, Conn.: Yale University Press, 1999.

Solomon, Maynard. "Charles Ives: Some Questions of Veracity." Journal of the American Musicological Society 40 (1987): 443–70.

Starr, Lawrence. A Union of Diversities: Style in the Music of Charles Ives. New York: Schirmer Books, 1992.

Sterne, Colin. "The Quotations in Charles Ives's Second Symphony." Music and Letters 52 (Jan. 1971): 39–45.

Stone, Kurt. "Ives's Fourth Symphony: A Review." The Musical Quarterly 52 (Jan. 1966): 1–16.

Swafford, Jan. Charles Ives: A Life with Music. New York: W. W. Norton, 1996.

Tick, Judith. "Charles Ives and Gender Ideology." In Musicology and Difference: Gender and Sexuality in Music Scholarship, ed. Ruth A. Solie. Berkeley: University of California Press, 1993.

Tischler, Barbara L. An American Music: The Search for an American Musical Identity. New York: Oxford University Press, 1986.

Vinay, Gianfranco. L'American musicale di Charles Ives. Torino: Giulio Einaudi, 1974.

Wallach, Laurence. "The New England Education of Charles Ives." Ph.D. diss., Columbia University, 1973.

Whitesell, Lloyd. "Reckless Form, Uncertain Audiences: Responding to Ives." American Music 12 (1994): 304–19.

Zuck, Barbara. A History of Musical Americanism. Ann Arbor, Mich.: UMI Research Press, 1980.

HYMNALS, COMPANIONS, MUSIC COLLECTIONS, AND INDICES

Bacon, Leonard Woolsey, compiler. The Church Book. New York: D. Appleton, 1883.

Beattie, John W., et al., eds. and compilers. The Golden Book of Favorite Songs. Chicago: Hall and McCreary, 1923.

———. The New Blue Book of Favorite Songs. Chicago: Hall and McCreary, 1941.

Bedel, Edwin A., compiler. The Church Hymnary. New York: Maynard, Merrill and Co., 1903.

Birchard, Clarence C., et al., eds. and compilers. Twice 55 Community Songs. Evanston, Ill.: Summy-Birchard, 1957.

Boni, Margaret, ed. Songs of the Gilded Age. New York: Golden, 1960.

Caldwell, Samuel Lunt, compiler. The Service of Song. Boston: Gould and Lincoln, 1873.

Christ-Janer, Albert, Charles W. Hughes, and Carleton Sprague Smith, eds. American Hymns Old and New. New York: Columbia University, 1980.

Diehl, Katherine Smith. Hymns and Tunes: An Index. New York: Scarecrow, 1966.

Doane, W. Howard, and E. H. Johnson, eds. The Baptist Hymnal. Philadelphia: American Baptist Publication Society, 1883.

Dykema, Peter W., et al., eds. *Twice 55 Plus Community Songs*. Boston: C. C. Birchard, 1929.

Favorite Songs of the People. Philadelphia: Theodore Presser, 1927.

Fox, Dan, arranger and ed. *Go In and Out the Window*. New York: Henry Holt, 1987.

Frey, Hugo, ed. *America Sings*. New York: Robbins, 1935.

The Friends' Hymnal. New York: Funk and Wagnalls, 1900 and 1908.

Fuller, Richard, et al., eds. *The Baptist Praise Book*. New York: A. S. Barnes, 1872.

Garretson, Ferd. V. D., compiler and arranger. *Carmina Yalensia*. New York: Taintor, 1867.

Goodale, G. Frank, ed. *The New Yale Song Book: A Collection of Songs in Use by the Glee Club and Students of Yale University*. New York: G. Schirmer, 1918.

Gordon, A. J., and Arthur T. Pierson, eds. *The Coronation Hymnal*. Philadelphia: American Baptist Publication Society, 1894.

Harris, George, and William Jewett Tucker, eds. *Hymns of Faith*. Boston: Houghton Mifflin, 1887.

Hitchcock, Roswell D., Zachary Eddy, and Philip Schaff. *Hymns and Songs for Social and Sabbath Worship*. New York: Anson D. F. Randolph, 1875.

The Hymnal 1940 Companion. 3rd rev. ed. New York: The Church Pension Fund, 1951.

Hymns Ancient and Modern New Standard. Norwich: Canterbury, 1983.

Hymns for the Living Age. New York: Century, 1905.

Hymns of Worship and Service. New York: Century, 1905.

Ives, Charles. *Piano Sonata No. 2 "Concord, Mass., 1840–1860,"* 2nd ed. New York: Associated Music Publishers, 1947; reprint of 1947 Arrow Music Press edition.

Kellogg, Frank B., and Thomas G. Shepard. *Yale Songs: A Collection of Songs in Use by the Glee Club and Students of Yale College*. New Haven, Conn.: Kellogg & Shepard, 1882.

Kemp, Robert. *Father Kemp's Old Folks Concert Tunes*. 1st ed. 1860; new ed., Boston: Oliver Ditson, 1934.

Lawrence, Vera Brodsky. *Music for Patriots, Politicians, and Presidents*. New York: Macmillan, 1975.

Liber Usualis. Tournai, Belgium: Desclée and Co., 1952.

Lomax, John A., collector. *Cowboy Songs and Other Frontier Ballads*. New York: Sturgis and Walton, 1910.

Lowry, Robert, and W. Howard Doane, compilers. *Gospel Hymn and Tune Book*. Philadelphia: American Baptist Publication Society, 1879.

Maddy, Joseph E., and W. Otto Miessner, eds. and compilers. *All-American Song Book*. New York: Robbins, 1942.

McCutchan, Robert Guy. *Hymn Tune Names: Their Sources and Significance*. New York: Abingdon, 1957.

The Methodist Hymnal. Nashville: Publishing House of the Methodist Church, South, 1905.

Musician's omnibus complete. Boston: Elias Howe, n.d.

The New Hymnal. New York: H. W. Gray, 1916.

100 Songs of Delta Kappa Epsilon. New York: Council of DKE, 1900–1907.

Robinson, Charles, ed. *Laudes Domini*. New York: Century, 1887.

———. *New Laudes Domini*. New York: Century, 1892.

Rollinson, T. H., arranger. *The Half Dollar Music Series: Favorite Reels, Jigs, and Hornpipes for the Violin with Piano Accompaniment*. Boston: Oliver Ditson, 1907.

Sankey, Ira D., James McGranahan, and George C. Stebbins, eds. *Gospel Hymns Nos. 1 to 6 Complete*. Chicago: Biglow and Main, 1894.

———, compilers. *Sacred Songs No. 1*. New York: Biglow and Main, 1896.

Sankey, Ira D., and George C. Stebbins, eds. *Male Chorus No. 1*. New York: Biglow and Main, 1888.

Smith, Wilson G., ed. *Grand Army War Songs*. Cleveland, Ohio: S. Brainard's, 1884 and 1886.

Sousa, John Philip, ed. *A Book of Instruction for the Field-Trumpet and Drum*. New York: Carl Fischer, 1886.

Spaeth, Sigmund. *Read 'Em and Weep*. New York: Arcod, 1945.

Stebbins, George C., and R. A. Torrey, compilers. *The Greatest Hymns*. Chicago: Tabernacle Publishing, n.d.

Tucker, J. Ireland, and William R. Rousseau, eds. *The Hymnal*. New York: Century, 1894.

Weir, Albert Ernest, ed. *The Book of a Thousand Songs*. New York: Carl Fisher, 1918.

With One Voice. Minneapolis: Augsburg Fortress, 1995.

Worship and Service Hymnal. Chicago: Hope, 1957.

Yale Glees. New Haven, Conn.: Thomas G. Shepard, 1893.

INDEX OF COMPOSERS, ARRANGERS, AUTHORS, AND TRANSLATORS

Biographical data was obtained from a variety of sources, the most helpful of which were the following:

ASCAP Biographical Dictionary, 4th ed.

Claghorn, Charles Eugene, ed. *Biographical Dictionary of American Music,* 1973.

Ellinwood, Leonard, and Keyes Porter, eds. *Bio-Bibliographical Index of Musicians in the United States of America Since Colonial Times,* reprint ed., 1973.

Fuld, James J. *The Book of World-Famous Music: Classical, Popular and Folk,* rev. and enl. ed., 1971.

The Hymnal 1940 Companion.

Slonimsky, Nicolas, ed. *Baker's Biographical Dictionary of Music and Musicians,* 7th ed.

The abbreviations "w" and "m" are used to indicate the author of the words for a tune and the composer of the music.

Adams, Sarah Flower (1804–48)
    w: *Bethany* 7
Adams, Stephen (pseudonym). *See* Michael Maybrick
Alexander, C. P. (1823–95)
    w: *Brown* 10-a
Alford, Henry (1810–71)
    w: *Arlington* 3-a
Aristophanes (ca. 448–380 BC)
    w: *Brekeke kek, koax, koax* 148-a
Arne, Thomas Augustine (1710–78)
    m: *Arlington* 3-a

Bach, Johann Sebastian (1685–1750)
    m: *Sinfonia in A Minor,* BWV 799 172
    m: *Sinfonia in F Minor,* BWV 795 172-a

    m: *Fugue in E Minor,* BWV 855 [from *Well-Tempered Clavier, I*] 172-b
    m: *Fugue in D Minor* [from] *Toccata and Fugue in D Minor,* BWV 538 172-c
Bacon, Leonard (1802–81)
    w: *Duke Street* 16
Barthélémon, Francois-Hippolyte (1741–1808)
    m: *Autumn* 4
Bayly, Thomas Haynes (1797–1839)
    w/m: *Long, Long Ago* 119
Beckett, Thomas à (ca. 1817–ca. 1871). *See* David T. Shaw
Beddome, Benjamin (1717–95)
    w: *David* 13-b
Beethoven, Ludwig van (1770–1827)
    m: *Symphony No. 5,* Op. 67; first movement 173
    m: *Sonata in F Minor for Piano,* Op. 2, No. 1; second movement 173-a
    m: *Sonata for Piano,* Op. 106, first movement ("Hammerklavier") 173-b
    m: *Andante favori in F* 173-c
    m: *Symphony No. 9,* Op. 125, fourth movement 174
Bennett, Sanford Fillmore (1836–98)
    w: *In the Sweet Bye and Bye* 29
Birch, Harry
    w: *Reuben and Rachel* 131
Bishop, Sir Henry Rowley (1786–1855)
    m: *Home! Sweet Home!* 108
Blake, James W. (1862–1935)
    w/m: *The Sidewalks of New York* 133
Bland, James A. (1854–1911)
    w/m: *Oh, Dem Golden Slippers* 125
Bliss, Philip Paul (1838–76)
    m: *Hold the Fort* 152
Bloom, Sol (1870–1949)
    claims m. for *Streets of Cairo* 137. *See also* James Thornton

Durand, H. S. (1861–?)
  w: *Bright College Years=Dear Old Yale* [to *Die Wacht am Rhein*] 149
Dvořák, Antonin (1841–1904)
  Symphony No. 9, Op. 95 ("From the New World"); first movement; measures 115, ff 179-a
  Symphony No. 9, Op. 95 ("From the New World"); first movement; measures 7–18 179-b

Eastburn, R. A. (pseudonym). *See* Joseph Eastburn Winner
Eberwein, Traugott Maximilian (1775–1831)
  m: *Valentia* 60-a
Edwards, Gus (1879–1945)
  m: *Tammany* 139
Elliott, Charlotte (1789–1871)
  w: *Woodworth* 67
Elliott, J. W. (1833–1915)
  m: *Church Triumphant* 12-a
Emerson, Ida
  w: *Hello! Ma Baby* 107
Emmett, Daniel Decatur (1815–1904)
  w/m: *Dixie's Land* 76
English, Thomas Dunn (1819–1902)
  w: *Ben Bolt* 99
Ewing, Alexander (1830–95)
  m: *Ewing* 20

Fane, Julian
  w: *Violets* 143
Farrell, Bob
  m: claimed for *Turkey in the Straw/Zip Coon* 169. *See also* George Washington Dixon
Foepple, Carl
  m: *Cornet Fantasy* on *Ever of Thee* (by Foley Hall 100-a)
Foster, Stephen Collins (1826–64)
  w/m: *De Camptown Races* 100
  w/m: *Massa's in de Cold Ground* 121
  w/m: *My Old Kentucky Home* 123
  w/m: *Old Black Joe* 128
  w/m: *Old Folks at Home* 129
  w/m: *Oh! Susanna* 127
Franck, Cesar (1822–90)
  m: *Symphony in D Minor* 179-c
Fulmer, H. J.
  w/m: *My Bonnie Lies Over the Ocean* 122

Gaunt, Percy (1852–96)
  w/m: *Push dem Clouds Away* 130-b
Gilmore, Patrick Sarsfield (1829–92)
  w/m: *When Johnny Comes Marching Home* 91

Gläser, Carl Gotthelf (1784–1829)
  m: *Azmon* 5. *See also* Lowell Mason
Gooch, William
  m: *Reuben and Rachel* 131
Goodell, Walter
  arranger of m. for *Deep River* 14
Gottschalk, Louis Moreau (1829–69)
  m: *The Last Hope* 180
Greatorex, Henry W. (1813–58)
  adaptation of m. for *Manoah* 34

Hall, Foley
  m: *Ever of Thee* 100-a
Handel, George Frideric (1685–1759)
  m: *Antioch* 3. *See Christmas* 12; *David* 13-b; Lowell Mason
  m: *See the Conquering Hero Comes* [from] *Judas Maccabeus* 181
  m: *Dead March* [from] *Saul,* Act III, Scene 5 182
  m: *Hallelujah* [from] *Messiah* 182-a
Hankey, Katherine (1834–1911)
  w: *Old, Old Story* 45
Harris, Charkes K. (1867–1930)
  w/m: *After the Ball* 93
Harris, William G.
  arranger of m. for *A Band of Brothers in DKE* 146
Hartsough, Lewis (1828–1919)
  w/m: *Welcome Voice* 63
Hastings, Thomas (1787–1872)
  m: *Retreat* 50
  m: *Toplady* 60
Hatton, John (ca. 1710–93)
  m: *Duke Street* 16
Hawks, Annie S. (1835–1918)
  w: first part of *Need* 41
Haydn, Franz Joseph (1732–1809)
  m: *Symphony No. 94,* second movement ("Surprise") 183
Heath, George (1750–1822)
  w: *Laban* 31
Heber, Reginald (1783–1826)
  w: *Missionary Hymn* 38
  w: *All Saints New* 2
Holden, Oliver (1765–1844)
  m: *Coronation* 13
Hopkins, Josiah (1786–1862)
  w/m: *Expostulation* 21
Hopkinson, Joseph (1770–1842)
  w: *Hail! Columbia* 77
How, William Walsham (1823–97)
  w: *St. Hilda* 51
Howard, Joseph E. (1878–1961)
  m: *Hello! Ma Baby* 107

Nevin, Ethelbert (1862–1901)
    m: *Narcissus* [from] *Water Scenes* 185
Nolan, Michael
    w/m: *Little Annie Rooney* 115

Oakeley, Frederick (1802–80)
    translator of w. for *Adeste Fideles* 1
Oliver, Henry Kemble (1800–85)
    m: *Federal Street* 22
Osborne, Louis Shreve
    w/m: *Riding down from Bangor* 156-a

Palmer, Phoebe W. (1807–74)
    w: *Cleansing Stream* 12-b
Palmer, Ray (1808–87)
    w: *Olivet* 46
Parker, Edwin Pond (1836–?)
    arranger of m. *Mercy* 36-a
Payne, John Howard (1791–1852)
    w: *Home! Sweet Home!* 108
Peck, Harlan Page (1837–ca. 1875)
    w: *Old Nassau* 155
Perkins, Theodore Edson (1831–1902)
    m: *Something for Thee* 55
Perronet, Edward (1726–92)
    w: *Coronation* 13
Phelps, Sylvanus Dryden (1816–95)
    w: *Something for Thee* 55
Phile, Philip (1734–93)
    m: *Hail! Columbia* 77
Pierpont, James S. (1822–93)
    w/m: *Jingle, Bells* 110
Prentiss, Elizabeth P. (1818–78)
    w: *More Love to Thee* 39
    w: *Proprior Deo* 49

Randall, James Ryder (1839–1908)
    w: *Maryland, My Maryland* 81
Rankin, Jeremiah E. (1828–1904)
    w: *God Be with You* 24
Reeves, David Willis (1838–1900)
    m: *Second Regiment Connecticut National
        Guard March* 84
Reinagle, Alexander Robert (1799–1877)
    m: *St. Peter* 52
Rexford, Eben Eugene (1848–1916)
    w: *Silver Threads Among the Gold* 134
Robinson, Robert (1735–90)
    w: *Antioch* 3
    w: *Nettleton* 42
Rooney, Pat
    w/m: *Are You the O'Reilly* 97
Root, George Frederick (1820–95)
    w/m: *The Battle Cry of Freedom* 71

    w/m: *Tramp, Tramp, Tramp* 89
    w/m: *Just Before the Battle, Mother* 111
    w/m: *There's Music in the Air* 142
    m: *Shining Shore* 54
Rossini, Gioacchino (1792–1868)
    m: *Overture* [to] *William Tell* 186
Rouget de Lisle, Claude-Joseph (1760–1836)
    w/m: *La Marseillaise* 80

"Sambo"
    w/m: *Year of Jubilee* 145
Sankey, Ira David (1840–1908)
    m: *Onward, Upward* 47
    m: *There'll Be No Dark Valley* 58
Sayers, Henry J. (1854–1932)
    w/m: *Ta-ra-ra Boom-de-ay!* 140
Schneider, Friedrich Johann Christian
    (1786–1853)
    m: *Lischer* 33-a
Scriven, Joseph (1820–86)
    w: *Erie* 17
Shaw, David T. (fl. 1814)
    w/m: *Columbia, the Gem of the Ocean* 75;
        sometimes attributed to Thomas à
        Beckett
Shaw, Knowles (1834–78)
    w: *Bringing in the Sheaves* 10
Smith, Edgar (1857–1938)
    w: *Ma Blushin' Rosie* 120
Smith, John Stafford (1750–1836)
    m: *The Star Spangled Banner* 86
Smith, Samuel Francis (1808–95)
    w: *America* 69
Sousa, John Philip (1854–1932)
    m: *Liberty Bell March* 78
    m: *Semper Fideles* 85
    m: *Washington Post March* 90
Spohr, Ludwig (1784–1859)
    m: *Cherith* 11
Steffe, William (fl. 19th century)
    m: attributed to *Battle Hymn of the
        Republic* 72
Sterling, Andrew B. (1876–1921)
    w: *Alexander* 94
Stites, Edgar P. (1836–1921)
    w: *Beulah Land* 8
Stowe, Harriet Beecher (1812–96)
    w: *Hexham* 28-a
Stowell, Hugh (1799–1865)
    w: *Retreat* 50
Stromberg, John (1853–1902)
    m: *Ma Blushin' Rosie* 120
Sullivan, Arthur Seymour (1842–1900)
    m: *Proprior Deo* 49

INDEX OF FIRST LINES
AND REFRAINS

I'm coming, I'm coming	refrain to *Old Black Joe*	128
I'm lonesome since I cross'd the hill	*The Girl I Left Behind Me*	102
I'm Terrence O'Reilly	*Are You the O'Reilly*	97
If you want to get to Heaven	*Push Dem Clouds Away*	130-b
In a cavern	*Oh, My Darling Clementine*	126
In praise of old Nassau	refrain to *Old Nassau*	155
In the cross of Christ I glory	*Rathbun*	49-a
In the morning when I rise	*Give Me Jesus*	23-a
In the prison cell I sit	*Tramp, Tramp, Tramp*	89
In the sweet bye and bye	refrain to *In the Sweet Bye and Bye*	29
Is that Mister Reilly	*Are You the O'Reilly*	97
I'se got a little baby	*Hello! Ma Baby*	107
I've been working on the railroad	refrain to *I've Been Working on the Railroad*	109
I've reached the land	*Beulah Land*	8
Jerusalem, the golden	*Ewing*	20
Jesus, lover of my soul	*Martyn*	35
Jesus loves me	*Jesus Loves Me*	30
Jingle, bells, jingle, bells	refrain to *Jingle, Bells*	110
Johnnie get your gun	*Over There*	82
Joy to the world	*Antioch*	3
Just as I am	*Woodworth*	67
Just before the battle, Mother	*Just Before the Battle, Mother*	111
Kathleen Mavourneen	*Kathleen Mavourneen*	112
London bridge is falling down	*London Bridge*	118
Look here, Alexander	*Alexander*	94
Lord, I hear of showers	*Even Me*	18
Many are the hearts	refrain to *Tenting on the Old Camp Ground*	88
Michael Kelly with his sweetheart	*Has Anybody Here Seen Kelly?*	106
'Mid pleasures and palaces	*Home! Sweet Home!*	108
Mine eyes have seen the glory	*Battle Hymn of the Republic*	72
More love to Thee	*More Love to Thee*	39
	and *Proprior Deo*	49
My bonnie lies over the ocean	*My Bonnie Lies Over the Ocean*	122
My country, 'tis of thee	*America*	69
My days are gliding swiftly by	*Shining Shore*	54
My faith looks up to Thee	*Olivet*	46
My grandfather's clock	*Grandfather's Clock*	105
My soul, be on thy guard	*Laban*	31
My wife and I	*Little Brown Jug*	116
Nearer, my God, to Thee	*Bethany*	7
Nicodemus, the slave	*Wake, Nicodemus*	144
Ninety years without slumbering	refrain to *Grandfather's Clock*	105
Now from the altar	*Naomi*	40
Now how I came to get this hat	*Where Did You Get That Hat?*	144-a
O Beulah Land	refrain to *Beulah Land*	8
O Columbia, the gem of the ocean	*Columbia, the Gem of the Ocean*	75

INDEX OF TUNES
BY NAME

The tunes are listed alphabetically, with appropriate cross-listings made for those with alternate titles and for those with text. The type of tune is indicated immediately following each main entry (given in small caps) and initial words of text music are given, except for those few hymn tunes for which a definitive text familiar to Ives could not be located.

Text incipits are for the first verse or stanza of the tune, with the following exceptions:

1. When Ives preferred words from a stanza other than the first, the particular text is so indicated.

2. In those instances where Ives borrowed from the melody to the refrain of his source rather than from its verse, the text incipit for the refrain is given.

3. Ives often used melodic fragments from both the verse and refrain of his source; here, double text incipits have been provided.

Abide with me. *See* EVENTIDE 19 (hymn)

ADESTE FIDELES 1 (hymn) "O come, all ye faithful"

AFTER THE BALL 93 (popular) "A little maiden"; refrain = "After the ball is over"

ALEXANDER 94 (popular) "Look here, Alexander"; refrain = "Can't you see the rain and hail"

"All hail the power of Jesus' name." *See* CORONATION 13 (hymn)

ALL SAINTS NEW 2 (hymn) "The Son of God goes forth to war"

"All the world am sad and weary." *See* OLD FOLKS AT HOME 129 (popular)

AMERICA 69 (patriotic) "My country, 'tis of thee"

The Anacreontic Song. *See* THE STAR SPANGLED BANNER 86 (patriotic)

"And when in future years." *See* JOLLY DOGS 154 (college)

ANNIE LISLE 95 (popular) "Down where the waving willows"; refrain = "Wave willows"

ANTIOCH 3 (hymn) "Joy to the world"

ARABY'S DAUGHTER 96 (popular) "How dear to this heart are the scenes of my childhood"; refrain = "The old oaken bucket"

ARE YOU THE O'REILLY 97 (popular) "I'm Terence O'Reilly"; refrain = "Is that Mr. Reilly, can anyone tell?"

ARKANSAS TRAVELLER 158 (instrumental)

ARLINGTON 3-a (hymn) "We walk by faith, and not by sight"

"As I was a-walking one morning for pleasure." *See* GIT ALONG LITTLE DOGIES 103 (popular)

"As I was walking down Paradise Street." *See* BLOW THE MAN DOWN 159 (instrumental)

ASSEMBLY 70 (patriotic)

At the River. *See* THE BEAUTIFUL RIVER 6 (hymn)

AULD LANG SYNE 98 (popular) "Should auld acquaintance be forgot"; refrain = "For auld lang syne, my dear"

AUTUMN 4 (hymn) "For the grandeur of thy nature" = stanza two

"Awake, my soul, stretch ev'ry nerve." *See* CHRISTMAS 12 (hymn)

AZMON 5 (hymn) "O for a thousand tongues"

A BAND OF BROTHERS IN DKE 146 (college) "A band of brothers in DKE, we march along tonight"; refrain = "So merrily sing we all to DKE"

BATTELL CHAPEL CHIMES 147 (college)

THE BATTLE CRY OF FREEDOM 71 (patriotic) "Yes, we'll rally round the flag"; refrain = "The Union forever, hurrah, boys, hurrah!"

BATTLE HYMN OF THE REPUBLIC 72 (patriotic) "Mine eyes have seen the glory of the coming of the Lord"; refrain = "Glory, Glory, Hallelujah!"

The Bear Went Over the Mountain. *See* FOR HE'S A JOLLY GOOD FELLOW 101 (popular)

THE BEAUTIFUL RIVER 6 (hymn) "Shall we gather at the river"; refrain = "Yes, we'll gather at the river"

Beautiful Saviour. *See* CRUSADER'S HYMN 13-a (hymn)

BEN BOLT 99 (popular) "Oh! don't you remember sweet Alice, Ben Bolt"

BETHANY 7 (hymn) "Nearer, my God, to Thee"

BEULAH LAND 8 (hymn) "I've reached the land of corn and wine"; refrain = "O Beulah land"

BINGO 148 (college) "Here's to good old Yale, drink it down"

BLESSED ASSURANCE 9 (hymn) "Blessed assurance, Jesus is mine"

BLOW THE MAN DOWN 159 (instrumental) "As I was walking down Paradise Street"

BREKEKE-KEK, KO-AX, KO-AX 148 (college)

"Bring back, bring back, bring back my bonnie to me." See MY BONNIE LIES OVER THE OCEAN 122 (popular)

Bright College Years. See DEAR OLD YALE 149 (college)

BRINGING IN THE SHEAVES 10 (hymn) "Sowing in the morning"; refrain = "Bringing in the sheaves"

THE BRITISH GRENADIERS 73 (patriotic)

BROWN 10-a; (hymn) "Approach, my soul, the mercy seat"

BUGLE CALL DERIVATIVES 74 (patriotic)

"By yon bonnie banks, And by yon bonnie braes." See LOCH LOMOND 117-a (popular)

Cambridge Quarters. See WESTMINSTER CHIMES 170 (instrumental)

THE CAMPBELLS ARE COMIN' 160 (instrumental) "The Campbells are comin' O-ho, O-ho"

"Can't you see the rain and hail." See ALEXANDER 94 (popular)

CHERITH 11 (hymn) (preferred text unknown)

Chester. See DORRNANCE 15 (hymn)

Children's Corner. See GOLLIWOG'S CAKEWALK 178-a (Debussy) (classical)

China. See JESUS LOVES ME 30 (hymn)

CHRISTMAS 12 (hymn) "Awake, my soul, stretch ev'ry nerve"

CHURCH TRIUMPHANT 12-a (hymn)

Cleansing Fountain. See FOUNTAIN 23 (hymn)

CLEANSING STREAM 12-b; (hymn) "Oh, now I see the cleansing wave!"; refrain = "The cleansing stream I see! I see!"

"The cleansing stream I see! I see!" See CLEANSING STREAM 12-b (hymn)

The College Chorus. See FEW DAYS 150 (college)

COLLEGE HORNPIPE 161 (instrumental)

COLUMBIA, THE GEM OF THE OCEAN 75 (patriotic) "O, Columbia, the gem of the ocean"; refrain = "When borne by the red, white, and blue!"

"Come, brothers, and a song we'll sing, Psi U., Psi U." See FEW DAYS 150 (college)

"Come, thou fount of ev'ry blessing." See NETTLE-TON 42 (hymn)

CONSOLATION 12-c (hymn) "Come, ye disconsolate"

Converse. See ERIE 17 (hymn)

CORNET FANTASY ON "EVER OF THEE" 179-c (Carl Foepple) (classical)

CORONATION 13 (hymn) "All hail the power of Jesus' name"

CUCKOO'S CALL 161-a (instrumental)

Cripple Creek. See PIG TOWN FLING 167 (instrumental)

CRUSADER'S HYMN 13-a (hymn) "Fairest Lord Jesus"

"Darling, I am growing old." See SILVER THREADS AMONG THE GOLD 134 (popular)

"Dar's a colored bud." See MA BLUSHIN' ROSIE 120 (popular)

"Dashing through the snow." See JINGLE, BELLS 110 (popular)

DAVID 13-b (hymn) "Come, Holy Spirit come"

DE CAMPTOWN RACES 100 (popular) "De Camptown ladies sing dis song"; refrain = "Gwine to run all night!"

DE LITTLE CABINS ALL AM EMPTY NOW 117 (popular) "Oh, dis heart ob mine"; refrain = "Oh! I hear the owl ahootin' in the darkness of the night"

"De massa run?" See KINGDOM COMING 114 (popular)

DEAD MARCH [from] SAUL, Act III, Scene 5 (Handel) 182 (classical)

DEAR OLD YALE 149 (college) "Bright college years, with pleasure rife"

DEEP RIVER 14 (hymn) "Deep River, my home is over Jordan"

"Den I wish I was in Dixie." See DIXIE'S LAND 76 (patriotic)

"Den sound de horn." See YEAR OF JUBILEE 145 (popular)

"The despot's heel is on thy shore." See MARYLAND, MY MARYLAND 81 (patriotic)

DIES IRAE 14-a (hymn) Dies irae dies illa

Diligence. See WORK SONG 68 (hymn)

DIXIE'S LAND 76 (patriotic) "I wish I was in de land ob cotton"; refrain = "Den I wish I was in Dixie"

DORRNANCE 15 (hymn) (preferred text unknown)

"Down in front of Casey's." See THE SIDEWALKS OF NEW YORK 133 (popular)

"Down in de cornfield." See MASSA'S IN DE COLD GROUND 121 (popular)

"Down where the waving willows." See ANNIE LISLE 95 (popular)

DUKE STREET 16 (hymn) "O God, beneath Thy guiding hand"

Dundee. See WINDSOR 66 (hymn)

"Eastside, Westside, all around the town." See THE SIDEWALKS OF NEW YORK 133 (popular)

ERIE 17 (hymn) "What a friend we have in Jesus"

Eton. *See* WINDSOR 66 (hymn)

EVEN ME 18 (hymn) "Lord, I hear of showers of blessings"

EVENTIDE 19 (hymn) "Abide with me"

EVER OF THEE 100-a (popular) "Ever of thee I'm fondly dreaming"

"Ev'ry morn I send thee violets." *See* VIOLETS 143 (popular)

EWING 20 (hymn) "Jerusalem, the golden"

EXPOSTULATION 21 (hymn) "Oh turn ye, oh turn ye"

Extinguish Lights. *See* TAPS 87 (patriotic)

Far above Cayuga's waters. *See* ANNIE LISLE 95 (popular)

"Far away in the South among the cotton fields." *See* THAT OLD CABIN HOME UPON THE HILL 141 (popular)

"Farewell, Mother, you may never." *See* JUST BEFORE THE BATTLE, MOTHER 111 (popular)

"Fath'r and I went down to camp." *See* YANKEE DOODLE 92 (patriotic)

FEDERAL STREET 22 (hymn) (preferred text unknown)

FEW DAYS 150 (college) "Come, brothers, and a song we'll sing, Psi U., Psi U."

"Firm, united, let us be." *See* HAIL! COLUMBIA 77 (patriotic)

FISHER'S HORNPIPE 162 (instrumental)

"For auld lang syne, my dear." *See* AULD LANG SYNE 98 (popular)

FOR HE'S A JOLLY GOOD FELLOW 101 (popular) "For he's a jolly good fellow"

"For the grandeur of thy nature." *See* AUTUMN 4 (hymn)

"For we always seem so jolly oh!" *See* JOLLY DOGS 154 (college)

FOUNTAIN 23 (hymn) "There is a fountain filled with blood"

FRESHMEN IN THE PARK 150-a (college); common parody words = "The worms crawl in"

"From ev'ry stormy wind that blows." *See* RETREAT 50 (hymn)

"From Greenland's icy mountains." *See* MISSIONARY HYMN 38 (hymn)

FUGUE IN D MINOR, BWV 538 (J. S. Bach: from *Toccata and Fugue* in D Minor) 172-c (classical)

FUGUE IN E MINOR, BWV 855 (J. S. Bach: *Well-Tempered Clavier I*) 172-b (classical)

FUGUE NO. 4 IN B FLAT (George Ives) 184 (classical)

Ganges. *See* WHERE, O WHERE 157 (college)

GARRYOWEN 163 (instrumental)

THE GIRL I LEFT BEHIND ME 102 (popular) "I'm lonesome since I cross'd the hill"

GIT ALONG LITTLE DOGIES 103 (popular) "As I was a-walking one morning for pleasure"; refrain = "Whoopee ti yi yo, git along little dogies"

"Give me a home in the dear old South." *See* THAT OLD CABIN HOME UPON THE HILL 141 (popular)

GIVE ME JESUS 23-a (hymn) "In the morning when I rise"

"Glory! Glory Hallelujah." *See* BATTLE HYMN OF THE REPUBLIC 72 (patriotic)

Glory, Hallelujah. *See* BATTLE HYMN OF THE REPUBLIC 72 (patriotic)

GOD BE WITH YOU 24 (hymn) "God be with you till we meet again"; refrain = "Till we meet"

THE GODS OF EGYPT BID US HAIL! 150-b (college) (formerly Unknown Tune 216) "The Gods of Egypt Bid Us Hail!"

GOLLIWOG'S CAKEWALK 178-a; (Debussy); (classical) [from] *Children's Corner*

"Gone are the days when my heart was young and gay." *See* OLD BLACK JOE 128 (popular)

GOODNIGHT, LADIES 104 (popular) "Goodnight, ladies!"

"The 'Good Time' Coming." *See* WAKE NICODEMUS 144 (popular)

GRANDFATHER'S CLOCK 105 (popular) "My grandfather's clock was too large for the shelf"; refrain = "Ninety years, without slumbering"

GREENWOOD 25 (hymn) (preferred text unknown)

"Gwine to run all night!" *See* DE CAMPTOWN RACES 100 (popular)

"Ha! Ha! Ha! 'tis you and me." *See* LITTLE BROWN JUG 116 (popular)

HAIL! COLUMBIA 77 (patriotic) "Hail, Columbia, happy land"; refrain = "Firm, united, let us be"

Hallelujah. *See* NETTLETON 42 (hymn)

HALLELUJAH 182-a (classical) (from Handel's *Messiah*)

HAMBURG 26 (hymn) "When I survey the wondrous cross"

HAPPY DAY 27 (hymn) "O happy day that fixed my choice"

HARVARD HAS BLUE STOCKING GIRLS 151 (college) "Harvard has blue stocking girls, Yale has blue stocking men"

HAS ANYBODY HERE SEEN KELLY? 106 (popular) refrain = "Has anybody here seen Kelly?"

HEBRON 28 (hymn) "Whither, oh, whither should I fly"

HELLO! MA BABY 107 (popular) refrain = "Hello! ma baby, hello! ma honey"

"Here's to good old Yale." *See* BINGO 148 (college)

HEXHAM 28-a (hymn) "Still, still with Thee"

"Hiawatha was an Indian." *See* TAMMANY 139 (popular)

Lauriger Horatius. *See* MARYLAND, MY MARYLAND 81 (patriotic)

LEBANON 33 (hymn) "I was a wand'ring sheep"

LIBERTY BELL MARCH 78 (patriotic)

LISCHER 33-a (hymn)

LITTLE ANNIE ROONEY 115 (popular) "A winning way"; refrain = "She's my sweetheart! I'm her beau!"

LITTLE BROWN JUG 116 (popular) "My wife and I live all alone"; refrain = "Ha! Ha! Ha! 'tis you and me"

"A little maiden." *See* AFTER THE BALL 93 (popular)

LOCH LOMOND 117-a (popular) "By yon bonnie banks, And by yon bonnie braes"; refrain = "Oh! ye'll take the high road, and I'll take the low road"

LONDON BRIDGE 118 (popular) "London bridge is falling down"

"London bridge is falling down." *See* LONDON BRIDGE 118 (popular)

LONG, LONG AGO 119 (popular) "Tell me the tales"

"Look here, Alexander, I was only fooling." *See* ALEXANDER 94 (popular)

"Lord, I hear of showers of blessings." *See* EVEN ME 18 (hymn)

MA BLUSHIN' ROSIE 120 (popular) "Dar's a colored bud"; refrain = "Rosie, you are ma posie"

Malbrook. *See* FOR HE'S A JOLLY GOOD FELLOW 101 (popular)

MANOAH 34 (hymn) (preferred text unknown)

"Many are the hearts that are weary tonight." *See* TENTING ON THE OLD CAMP GROUND 88 (patriotic)

MARCHING THROUGH GEORGIA 79 (patriotic) "Bring the good old bugle, boys!"; refrain = "Hurrah! Hurrah! we bring the Jubilee!"

LA MARSEILLAISE 80 (patriotic) "Ye sons of France, awake to glory"

MARTYN 35 (hymn) "Jesus, lover of my soul"

MARYLAND, MY MARYLAND 81 (patriotic) "The despot's heel is on thy shore"

MASSA'S IN DE COLD GROUND 121 (popular) "Round de meadows am a-ringing"; refrain = "Down in de cornfield"

MATERNA 36 (hymn) "O mother dear, Jerusalem"

MERCY 36-a (hymn) "Softly now the light of day." *See also* THE LAST HOPE 180

Messiah (Handel). *See* HALLELUJAH 182-a (classical)

"'Mid pleasures and palaces." *See* HOME! SWEET HOME! 108 (popular)

"Mine eyes have seen the glory." *See* BATTLE HYMN OF THE REPUBLIC 72 (patriotic)

MISSIONARY CHANT 37 (hymn) "Ye Christian heralds, go, proclaim"

MISSIONARY HYMN 38 (hymn) "From Greenland's icy mountains"

MONEY MUSK 166 (instrumental)

MORE LOVE TO THEE 39 (hymn) "More love to Thee, O Christ!" *See also* PROPRIOR DEO 49

MY BONNIE LIES OVER THE OCEAN 122 (popular) "My bonnie lies over the ocean"; refrain = "Bring back, bring back, bring back my bonnie to me"

"My country, 'tis of thee." *See* AMERICA 69 (patriotic)

"My days are gliding swiftly by." *See* SHINING SHORE 54 (hymn)

"My faith looks up to thee." *See* OLIVET 46 (hymn)

"My grandfather's clock." *See* GRANDFATHER'S CLOCK 105 (popular)

MY OLD KENTUCKY HOME 123 (popular) "The sun shines bright in the old Kentucky home"; refrain = "Weep no more, my lady"

"My soul, be on thy guard." *See* LABAN 31 (hymn)

"My wife and I live all alone." *See* LITTLE BROWN JUG 116 (popular)

NANCY LEE 123-a (popular) "Of all the wives as e'er you know"

NAOMI 40 (hymn) "Now from the altar of my heart"

NARCISSUS (Ethelbert Nevin) 185 (classical)

"Nearer, my God, to Thee." *See* BETHANY 7 (hymn)

NEED 41 (hymn) "I need Thee ev'ry hour"

NETTLETON 42 (hymn) "Come, thou fount of ev'ry blessing"

"Nicodemus, the slave, was of African birth." *See* WAKE NICODEMUS 144 (popular)

"Ninety years, without slumbering." *See* GRANDFATHER'S CLOCK 105 (popular)

"Nobody knows de trouble I've seen." *See* OH, NOBODY KNOWS DE TROUBLE I'VE SEEN 43 (hymn)

"Now from the altar of my heart." *See* NAOMI 40 (hymn)

"Now how I came to get this hat." *See* WHERE DID YOU GET THAT HAT? 144-a (popular)

"O beautiful, for spacious skies." *See* MATERNA 36 (hymn)

"O Beulah Land." *See* BEULAH LAND 8 (hymn)

"O Christmas Tree." *See* MARYLAND, MY MARYLAND 81 (patriotic)

"O Columbia, the gem of the ocean." *See* COLUMBIA, THE GEM OF THE OCEAN 75 (patriotic)

"O come, all ye faithful." *See* ADESTE FIDELES 1 (hymn)

"O come, let us adore him." *See* ADESTE FIDELES 1 (hymn)

"O for a thousand tongues." *See* AZMON 5 (hymn)

"O God, beneath Thy guiding hand." *See* DUKE STREET 16 (hymn)

"O happy day." *See* HAPPY DAY 27 (hymn)

"O Jesus, Thou art standing." *See* ST. HILDA 51 (hymn)

"O mother dear, Jerusalem." *See* MATERNA 36 (hymn)

"Oh say! Can you see." *See* THE STAR SPANGLED BANNER 86 (patriotic)

"O Tannenbaum." *See* MARYLAND, MY MARYLAND 81 (patriotic)

"O the days of the Kerry dancing." *See* THE KERRY DANCE 165 (instrumental)

"O tod, wie bitter." *See* VIER ERNSTE GESÄNGE 177-b (Brahms) (classical)

"O where is my boy tonight?" *See* WHERE IS MY WANDERING BOY? 64 (hymn)

OH, DEM GOLDEN SLIPPERS 125 (popular) "Oh my golden slippers am laid away"; refrain = "Oh, dem golden slippers"

"Oh, dis heart ob mine." *See* DE LITTLE CABINS ALL AM EMPTY NOW 117 (popular)

"Oh! don't you remember sweet Alice." *See* BEN BOLT 99 (popular)

"Oh! give me a home in the dear old South." *See* THAT OLD CABIN HOME UPON THE HILL 141 (popular)

"Oh! I hear the owl ahootin' in the darkness of the night." *See* DE LITTLE CABINS ALL AM EMPTY NOW 117 (popular)

"Oh, I was born in Mobile town." *See* I'VE BEEN WORKING ON THE RAILROAD 109 (popular)

OH, MY DARLING CLEMENTINE 126 (popular) "In a cavern, in a canyon"; refrain = "Oh my darling, Oh my darling, Oh my darling Clementine"

"Oh my golden slippers am laid away." *See* OH, DEM GOLDEN SLIPPERS 125 (popular)

OH, NOBODY KNOWS THE TROUBLE I'VE SEEN 43 (hymn) "Oh, nobody knows de trouble I've seen"

"Oh, now I see the cleansing wave!" *See* CLEANSING STREAM 12-b (hymn)

"Oh say, does that Star-spangled." *See* THE STAR SPANGLED BANNER 86 (patriotic)

OH! SUSANNA 127 (popular) "I came from Alabama wid my banjo on my knee"; refrain = "Oh! Susanna, Oh! don't you cry for me"

"Oh, the moonlight's fair tonight along the Wabash." *See* ON THE BANKS OF THE WABASH, FAR AWAY 130 (popular)

"Oh, they tell me thou art dead, Katy darling." *See* KATY DARLING 113 (popular)

"Oh, turn ye, oh, turn ye." *See* EXPOSTULATION 21 (hymn)

"Oh! ye'll take the high road, and I'll take the low road." *See* LOCH LOMOND 117-a (popular)

OLD BLACK JOE 128 (popular) "Gone are the days when my heart was young and gay"; refrain = "I'm coming, I'm coming, for my head is bending low"

OLD FOLKS AT HOME 129 (popular) "Way down upon de Swanee Ribber"; refrain = "All de world am sad and weary"

OLD HUNDREDTH 44 (hymn) (preferred text unknown)

OLD NASSAU 155 (college) "Tune every harp and every voice!"

"The old oaken bucket." *See* ARABY'S DAUGHTER 96 (popular)

The Old Oaken Bucket. *See* ARABY'S DAUGHTER 96 (popular)

OLD, OLD STORY 45 (hymn) "Tell me the old, old story"

Old Zip Coon. *See* TURKEY IN THE STRAW 169 (instrumental)

OLIVET 46 (hymn) "My faith looks up to thee"

OMEGA LAMBDA CHI 156 (college)

ON THE BANKS OF THE WABASH, FAR AWAY 130 (popular) "Round my Indiana homestead wave the cornfield"; refrain = "Oh, the moonlight's fair tonight along the Wabash"

ONWARD, UPWARD 47 (hymn) "Onward! upward! Christian soldier"

OVER THERE 82 (patriotic) "Johnnie get your gun"; refrain = "Over there, over there"

OVERTURE [TO] WILLIAM TELL (Rossini) 186 (classical)

PARAH 48 (hymn) (preferred text unknown)

"People of the living God." *See* LAMBETH 32 (hymn)

"Peter, Peter, pumpkin eater." *See* PETER, PETER, PUMPKIN EATER 130-a (popular)

PETER, PETER, PUMPKIN EATER 130-a (popular) "Peter, Peter, pumpkin eater"

Phi Marching Song. *See* A BAND OF BROTHERS IN DKE 146 (college)

PIG TOWN FLING 167 (instrumental)

The Poor Little Country Maid. *See* STREETS OF CAIRO 137 (popular)

Portuguese Hymn. *See* ADESTE FIDELES 1 (hymn)

PRÉLUDE À "L'APRES-MIDI D'UN FAUNE" (Debussy) 178 (classical)

The President's March. *See* HAIL! COLUMBIA 77 (patriotic)

PROPRIOR DEO 49 (hymn) "More love to Thee." *See* also MORE LOVE TO THEE 39

Psi U., Psi U. *See* FEW DAYS 150 (college)

PUSH DEM CLOUDS AWAY 130-b (popular) "If you want to git to heaven on de nickel-plated road";

refrain = "Just push! Don't shove! Just push dem clouds away!"

RATHBUN 49-a (hymn) ("In the cross of Christ I glory")

The Red, White, and Blue. *See* COLUMBIA, THE GEM OF THE OCEAN 75 (patriotic)

Renar. *See* JESUS LOVES ME 30 (hymn)

RETREAT 50 (hymn) "From ev'ry stormy wind that blows"

REUBEN AND RACHEL 131 (popular) "Reuben, I have long been thinking"

"Reuben, I have long been thinking." *See* REUBEN AND RACHEL 131 (popular)

REVEILLE 83 (patriotic)

RIDING DOWN FROM BANGOR 131-a (popular) "Riding down from Bangor, On an eastbound train"

"Ring out, wild bells." *See* WILD BELLS 65 (hymn)

ROCK-A-BYE BABY 132 (popular) "Rock-a-bye, baby, on the tree top"

"Rock of ages, cleft for me." *See* TOPLADY 60 (hymn)

"Rosie, you are my posie." *See* MA BLUSHIN' ROSIE 120 (popular)

"Round de meadows am a-ringing." *See* MASSA'S IN DE COLD GROUND 121 (popular)

"Round my Indiana homestead wave the cornfield." *See* ON THE BANKS OF THE WABASH, FAR AWAY 130 (popular)

Sailor's hornpipe. *See* COLLEGE HORNPIPE 161 (instrumental)

St. Edith. *See* ST. HILDA 51 (hymn)

St. Elizabeth. *See* CRUSADER'S HYMN 13-a (hymn)

ST. HILDA 51 (hymn) "O Jesus, Thou art standing"

SAINT PATRICK'S DAY 168 (instrumental)

ST. PETER 52 (hymn) (preferred text unknown)

"Saviour, Thy dying love." *See* SOMETHING FOR THEE 55 (hymn)

"Say, darkeys, hab you seen de massa." *See* KINGDOM COMING 114 (popular)

SEARCH ME, O LORD 52-a (hymn)

SECOND REGIMENT CONNECTICUT NATIONAL GUARD MARCH 84 (patriotic)

SEMPER FIDELES 85 (patriotic)

SERENITY 53 (hymn) (preferred text unknown)

"Shall we gather at the river." *See* THE BEAUTIFUL RIVER 6 (hymn)

"She's my sweetheart! I'm her beau!" *See* LITTLE ANNIE ROONEY 115 (popular)

SHINING SHORE 54 (hymn) "My days are gliding swiftly by"

"Should auld acquaintance be forgot." *See* AULD LANG SYNE 98 (popular)

THE SIDEWALKS OF NEW YORK 133 (popular) "Down in front of Casey's"; refrain = "Eastside, Westside, all around the town"

SILVER THREADS AMONG THE GOLD 134 (popular) "Darling, I am growing old"

SINFONIA IN A MINOR, BWV 799 172 (J. S. Bach) (classical)

SINFONIA IN F MINOR, BWV 795 172-a (J. S. Bach) (classical)

Siroe. *See* CHRISTMAS 12 (hymn)

"A smart and stylish girl you see." *See* TA-RA-RA BOOM-DE-AY! 140 (popular)

"So merrily sing we all." *See* A BAND OF BROTHERS IN DKE 146 (college)

"Some talk of Alexander." *See* THE BRITISH GRENADIERS 73 (patriotic)

SOMETHING FOR THEE 55 (hymn) "Saviour, Thy dying love"

THE SON OF A GAMBOLIER 135 (popular) "I'm a rambling wretch of poverty"

"The Son of God goes forth to war." *See* ALL SAINTS NEW 2 (hymn)

SONATA IN B FLAT FOR PIANO, Op. 106, first movement) ("Hammerklavier") 173-b (Beethoven) (classical)

SONATA IN F MINOR FOR PIANO, Op. 2, No. 1, second movement 173-a (Beethoven) (classical)

"Sowing in the morning." *See* BRINGING IN THE SHEAVES 10 (hymn)

"Stand up, stand up for Jesus." *See* WEBB 62 (hymn)

THE STAR SPANGLED BANNER 86 (patriotic) "Oh say! Can you see"; refrain = "Oh, say, does that Star-spangled"

STOP THAT KNOCKING AT MY DOOR 136 (popular) "I once did lub a colored gal"

STREET BEAT 86-a (patriotic)

STREETS OF CAIRO 137 (popular) "I will sing you a song"; refrain = "She never saw the streets"

"The sun shines bright in the old Kentucky home." *See* MY OLD KENTUCKY HOME 123 (popular)

SWEET ROSIE O' GRADY 138 (popular)

"A sweet tuxedo girl you see." *See* TA-RA-RA BOOM-DE-AY! 140 (popular)

SYMPHONY No. 1, Op. 68, first movement (Brahms) 175-a (classical)

SYMPHONY No. 1, Op. 68, fourth movement, measures 12–14 (Brahms) 175-b (classical)

SYMPHONY No. 1, Op. 68, fourth movement, measures 273–78 (Brahms) 175-c (classical)

SYMPHONY No. 1, Op. 68, fourth movement, measures 385–88 (Brahms) 175-d (classical)

"Way down upon de Swanee Ribber." *See OLD FOLKS AT HOME* 129 (popular)

"We won't go home until morning!" *See FOR HE'S A JOLLY GOOD FELLOW* 101 (popular)

WEBB 62 (hymn) "Stand up, stand up for Jesus"

WEDDING MARCH [from] LOHENGRIN (Wagner) 191-a (classical)

"Weep no more, my lady." *See MY OLD KENTUCKY HOME* 123 (popular)

WELCOME VOICE 63 (hymn) "I hear Thy welcome voice"; refrain = "I am coming, Lord! Coming now to Thee!"

"We're tenting tonight on the old camp ground." *See TENTING ON THE OLD CAMP GROUND* 88 (patriotic)

WESTMINSTER CHIMES 170 (instrumental)

Westminster Quarters. *See WESTMINSTER CHIMES* 170 (instrumental)

"What a friend we have in Jesus." *See ERIE* 17 (hymn)

"When borne by the red, white, and blue!" *See COLUMBIA, THE GEM OF THE OCEAN* 75 (patriotic)

"When I survey the wondrous cross." *See HAMBURG* 26 (hymn)

WHEN JOHNNY COMES MARCHING HOME 91 (patriotic) "When Johnny comes marching home again"

"Where are the Hebrew children?" *See WHERE, O WHERE* 157 (college)

WHERE DID YOU GET THAT HAT? 144-a (popular) "If I go to the opera house in the opera season"; refrain = "Where did you get that hat?"

"Where did you get that hat?" *See WHERE DID YOU GET THAT HAT?* 144-a (popular)

WHERE IS MY WANDERING BOY? 64 (hymn)

WHERE, O WHERE 157 (college)

"Where, O where is pretty little Susie?" *See WHERE, O WHERE* 157 (college)

THE WHITE COCKADE 171 (instrumental)

"Whither, oh, whither should I fly." *See HEBRON* 28 (hymn)

"Whoopee ti yi yo." *See GIT ALONG LITTLE DOGIES* 103 (popular)

WILD BELLS 65 (hymn) "Ring out, wild bells, to the wild, wild sky"

WINDSOR 66 (hymn) "That awful day will surely come"

"A winning way." *See LITTLE ANNIE ROONEY* 115 (popular)

Wolf's Head Anthem. *See GODS OF EGYPT BID US HAIL!* 150-b (college)

WOODWORTH 67 (hymn) "Just as I am, without one plea"

"Work, for the night is coming." *See WORK SONG* 68 (hymn)

WORK SONG 68 (hymn)

"The worms crawl in, the worms crawl out." *See FRESHMEN IN THE PARK* 150-a (college)

YALE'S SHORT CHEER 157-a (college)

YANKEE DOODLE 92 (patriotic) "Fath'r and I went down to camp"; refrain = "Yankee Doodle keep it up"

"Ye Christian heralds, go, proclaim." *See MISSIONARY CHANT* 37 (hymn)

"Ye sons of France, awake to glory!" *See LA MARSEILLAISE* 80 (patriotic)

YEAR OF JUBILEE 145 (popular) "I come up Norf, on a little bender"; refrain = "Den sound de horn"

"Yes, Jesus loves me." *See JESUS LOVES ME* 30 (hymn)

"Yes, we'll gather at the river." *See THE BEAUTIFUL RIVER* 6 (hymn)

"Yes, we'll rally round the flag, boys." *See THE BATTLE CRY OF FREEDOM* 71 (patriotic)

Zip Coon. *See TURKEY IN THE STRAW* 169 (instrumental)

A music historian and pianist, Clayton W. Henderson is Professor Emeritus of Music at Saint Mary's College in Notre Dame, Indiana. He has written articles on Charles Ives, on American blackface minstrelsy, and is author of *On the Banks of the Wabash: The Life and Music of Paul Dresser*. He is currently writing a biography of Emma Wixom Nevada, a prominent American opera singer of the late nineteenth century.